Using Web 2.0 Tools in the K-12 Classroom

Beverley E. Crane

Neal-Schuman Publishers, Inc.

New York   London

Don't miss the companion Web site that accompanies this book available at:
www.neal-schuman.com/webclassroom

Published by Neal-Schuman Publishers, Inc.
100 William St., Suite 2004
New York, NY 10038

Printed and bound in the United States of America.

The paper used in this publication meets the minimum requirements of American National Standard for Information Sciences-Permanence of Paper for Printed Library Materials, ANSI Z39.48-1992.

Library of Congress Cataloging-in-Publication Data

Crane, Beverley E.
    Using Web 2.0 tools in the K–12 classroom / Beverley E. Crane.
        p. cm.
    Includes bibliographical references and index.
    ISBN 978-1-55570-653-1 (alk. paper)
    1. Teaching—Computer network resources. 2. Internet in education. 3. Education, Elementary—Curricula. 4. Education, Secondary—Curricula. I. Title.

LB1044.87.C74 2009
371.33'44678—dc22

                                                                2008046167

Dedication

For my family, with love—
My parents who stressed the importance of education;
My husband who instilled the need for education
in our sons Michael, Mark, Kenneth, and Scott;
and, as fathers, our sons who continue to emphasize the value of education
with our grandchildren.

Table of Contents

Chapter 3. Experiencing History Through Podcasts   39

Chapter 4. Creating Literature Wikis in the Classroom   61

Chapter 7. Enhancing English Language Learning with Web 2.0 Tools   131

List of Figures
and Tables

FIGURES

TABLES

content areas, how the tool integrates into the curriculum, as well as advantages for using it in the classroom. Part 2, "Getting Started," provides examples of a Web 2.0 tool and illustrates step by step how to begin using the tool. Part 3, "Practical Applications," includes practical unit-plan models in different content areas at both the elementary and secondary levels. The unit explains how the technology combines with broad-based examples in core content areas—language arts, social studies, and science. Educators can use the plans as they are presented or modify them to meet the individual needs of students and curricula. Two sets of exercises in each chapter offer opportunities for readers to practice what they have just learned, become familiar with Web 2.0 tools, and reflect on the content of the chapter. Each chapter also contains a glossary of new terms and a list of Web sites that will be useful for the topic under discussion. Appendix A includes a list by chapter of all URLs contained in the book. Appendix B describes the accompanying Web site.

In addition to its focus on a different Web 2.0 tool, each chapter also incorporates a different subject area, topic, and age level. Chapter 2, "Blogging in the Language Arts," for example, illustrates blogging in secondary English. The topic of contemporary issues is ideal for an I-Search paper, and the unit plan emphasizes the science topic of "stem cell research." Chapter 3, "Experiencing History Through Podcasts," lets upper elementary or middle school students explore in groups the current hot topic of "immigration" through research and creating a podcast. Taking the topic a step further, they analyze the concept of the "American Dream." Chapter 4, "Creating Literature Wikis in the Classroom," explores the novel *The Great Gatsby*, taught to secondary English students. The unit lets students collaborate easily using wiki technology. Chapter 5, "Digital Storytelling: Cross-Curricular Connections," enables middle school students to focus on their preferred learning style as they create stories and incorporate video and audio into a digital story. Chapter 6, "Google in the Classroom—More Than Just Research," goes beyond using Google for research and introduces a suite of other tools for collaborating, blogging, exploring the earth, and much more. The unit for this chapter uses the popular WebQuest to explore Cuba, the island that has been isolated for over 20 years. Chapter 7, "Enhancing English Language Learning with Web 2.0 Tools," lets non-native English speakers collaborate on culture with students in other countries. Finally, Chapter 8, "Social Bookmarking and Putting It All Together," introduces a new tool and culminates with a science unit on the environment, which combines several Web 2.0 tools discussed throughout the book.

In addition to this printed book, *Using Web 2.0 in the K–12 Classroom* features a companion Web site: www.neal-schuman.com/webclassroom. The Web site provides curriculum examples from pioneering educators around the world, as well as exercises and lessons in subject areas and grade levels not highlighted in the book. A "What's New" section will keep readers up to date with interesting technologies and ones where space in the book prevented covering them. A link on the Web site provides access to Bev's Edublog so readers can share tips on technologies and innovative lesson ideas. Web site notations in each chapter indicate places where the Web site might provide additional information.

Using Web 2.0 Tools in the K–12 Classroom is intended to encourage educators to learn more about and try Web 2.0 tools that many of their students are already using outside the classroom. The explanatory material, step-by-step explanations, examples and model units should prompt teachers and library media specialists to try these new technologies, and the accompanying Web site will continue to expand their knowledge and skills. All educators seek to motivate students to learn the content we are teaching, to think critically while learning, and to communicate on broad levels both inside and outside the classroom. Students are already using Web 2.0 tools discussed in this book in their daily lives. We must take advantage of their knowledge and skill to make learning that much more exciting and meaningful for them. A successful experience using Web 2.0 tools in the classroom can make all the difference!

Acknowledgments

This book is the result of the time and effort of teachers, library media specialists, and IT educators who spent hours learning about Web 2.0 technology and, more important, integrating it into content area lessons and libraries so that motivated students may learn the skills they will need for tasks and jobs in the twenty-first century. Thanks to the educators who appear in my book for permission to use illustrations of their excellent ideas that appear on their Web sites.

Special thanks to Sandy Wood, my editor at Neal-Schuman, who provided valuable suggestions on content and organization of the book. Thanks also to Paul Seeman, whose help with Bev's Web site has added a further dimension to *Using Web 2.0 in the K–12 Classroom*.

A New Information Revolution

It is not the strongest of the species that survives, nor the most intelligent that survives. It is the one that is the most adaptable to change.

—Charles Darwin

The illiterate of the 21st century will not be those who cannot read and write, but those who cannot learn, unlearn, and relearn.

—Alvin Toffler, futurist, in *Rethinking the Future* (Gibson, 1999)

PART 1: IDEAS AND INSIGHTS

Picture this: In one corner of Ms. Crane's classroom, one group discusses conserving water, a topic they plan to present at the Earth Day Fair. They have surfed the Internet and bookmarked on their Diigo page about seven sites, including YouTube, blogs, and research sites. In the middle of the room another group is brainstorming possible ideas for recycling that their group can undertake. The scribe for the group is taking notes on their wiki so that the rest of the group can add comments and corrections. Another group has Ms. Crane's eye as they squabble over who is playing which part in their podcast. Two students are studiously writing the script for the podcast on global warming. The most vocal group is creating their paper grocery bags to distribute to the local stores in town. These students are painting their grocery bags with recycling phrases and pictures while the other part of the group is writing a script for a VoiceThread to send to their partner class in Australia. Finally, off to the left three students are working on their Google Docs spreadsheet itemizing the litter they collected for their pollution project. The other half of the group is reviewing Google Maps to identify the areas where they collected the most litter to help eliminate pollution. Busy, busy, busy. While all of this activity is going on, Ms. Crane is circulating throughout the classroom, making comments and suggestions, answering student questions and facilitating the process of learning in a Web 2.0 classroom.

Web 2.0 programs are rapidly becoming tools of choice for a growing body of classroom educators, who are discovering that these tools provide compelling teaching and learning opportunities. Web 1.0, or the Web that most of us have been fairly familiar with for some years now, has largely been a *one-way* medium: The information flowed in one direction—we searched the web for the wealth of information on it. Web 1.0 actually worked just like our approach to teaching where educators dispensed the knowledge to groups of students who assimilated what we had to say. However, in 2004 a group of new web tools began to appear. These tools made it easy for non-tech persons to add content to the web. Educators with no programming skills were suddenly publishing their own journals, photographs, videos, podcasts, wikis, slideshows, and more. The web became a two-way street. Everyday people were now creating the content. By 2007, a second generation of the Web had taken over—Web 2.0.

Also known as the Read Write Web, the new Web is a breeding ground for creative and engaging educational endeavors. Web 2.0 is a two-way medium, representing the next phase in using the Internet. With Web 2.0 almost anyone can become a publisher or a "content producer." In Web 2.0 the creation of material or information on the Web is as much a part of the experience as the finding or reading of data had been in Web 1.0.

The Web is no longer just a place to search for resources. It's a place to find people, to exchange ideas, and to demonstrate creativity before an audience. The Internet has become not only a great curriculum resource but also a great learning resource. Students are now creating online content, collaborating with other students around the world, and showcasing their work to a global audience. Web 2.0 facilitates networking. It provides authentic learning experiences for students, and it encourages global awareness, creativity, innovation, critical thinking, and collaboration. The knowledge our students gain from engaging with Web 2.0 technologies fosters communication and information literacy skills that are required in the twenty-first century.

Trends for the Twenty-First Century

As you read about some of the new Web 2.0 tools in the rest of this book, you will begin to see trends appearing that differ from how students have been taught in the past. As you read further, you will notice how these trends are already becoming part of some classrooms.

- **Trend #1: A New Publishing Revolution.** The Internet is becoming a platform for unparalleled creativity, and educators and students are creating the new content of the Web. The Web that we've known for some years has really been a one-way medium, where we read and received as passive participants. The new Web, or Web 2.0, is a two-way medium, based on contribution, creation, and collaboration—often requiring only access to the Web and a browser. Blogs, wikis, podcasts, video/photo-sharing, social networking, and any of the hundreds of software services are changing how, and why, content is created.
- **Trend #2: A Tidal Wave of Information.** The publishing revolution is having an impact on the volume of content available to us that is hard to even comprehend. There are over 100,000 blogs created daily, and MySpace alone has over 375,000 new users every day who are creating content. The amount of information presents a challenge as we decide to what information we should give our time and attention.
- **Trend #3: Everything Is Becoming Participative.** Amazon.com is a good example of how the participative Web works. Book readers write reviews of books that are a significant factor in readers' decisions to purchase a book. Moreover, Amazon takes the information of its users and by tracking their behavior provides data suggesting other books that readers might like to read.

> ➤ *The Web site that accompanies this book (www.neal-schuman.com/webclassroom) will allow readers to participate with Web 2.0 as they read about it in this book.*

- **Trend #4: The New Consumers.** The new consumer combines "producer" and "consumer." New consumers not only acquire knowledge but also contribute to the production of that knowledge.
- **Trend #5: The Age of the Collaborator.** We are most definitely in a new age; the age of the collaborator is here. The era of trusted authority (e.g., *Newsweek*, for instance) is changing to an era of transparent and collaborative scholarship (e.g., Wikipedia). The expert is giving way to the collaborator.

> ➤ *Join Bev's blog at http://bevcrane.blogspot.com/ to collaborate with other educators on topics of interest.*

- **Trend #6: An Explosion of Innovation.** The combination of an increased ability to work on specialized topics by gathering teams from around the globe and the diversity of those collaborators should bring an incredible amount of innovation.
- **Trend #7: Social Learning Gains Headway.** We move from thinking of knowledge as an "answer" that we transfer from teacher to student to a social view of learning. The model now is students as contributors.
- **Trend #8: Social Networking.** Students today are using social networking on Facebook and YouTube, among others, on a weekly, if not daily, basis. Schools have still not caught up. Some educators are promoting social networking, if merely to communicate with their colleagues. These leaders are now introducing Web 2.0 into the classroom to their students. (Hargadon, 2008)

Objectives of This Chapter

Chapter 1 provides an introduction to Web 2.0 tools on the Internet, as well as teaching strategies, both of which are illustrated in the chapters that follow. After reading Chapter 1, educators will be able to:

- identify the importance of Web 2.0 tools for K-12 students;
- describe teaching strategies necessary for twenty-first-century learning;
- state how Web 2.0 tools enhance twenty-first-century teaching strategies; and
- formulate the framework of an Internet unit incorporating Web 2.0 tools.

Glossary

Acceptable Use Policy (AUP): A written agreement, signed by students, their parents, and teachers, outlining the terms and conditions of Internet use.

blog: A Web site usually maintained by an individual with regular entries of commentary, descriptions of events, or other material such as graphics or video.

Creative Commons: A nonprofit organization devoted to expanding the range of creative works available for others to legally build upon and share.

Google Tools: Tools released or acquired by Google that include all major desktop, mobile, and online products.

podcast: A series of digital media files that are distributed over the Internet using RSS feeds for playback on MP3 players and computers.

RSS: A family of Web-feed formats used to publish frequently updated content such as blogs, news headlines, and podcasts in a standardized format.

social bookmarking: A method for Internet users to store, organize, search, and manage bookmarks of Web pages on the Internet.

VoiceThread: An online media album that can hold essentially any type of media (images, documents, and videos) and allows people to make comments.

wiki: A collection of Web pages designed to enable anyone who accesses them to contribute or modify content.

Becoming an Information-Literate Person in the Twenty-First Century

In 1987, the American Association of School Librarians (AASL) and the Association for Education Communication and Technology (AECT) joined together to redesign the role of the library media specialist in K–12 education. The result of this endeavor was *Information Power: Guidelines for School Library Programs*, which provided a philosophical basis for developing library media programs that would meet the needs of students. The premise of *Information Power* was that teachers, principals, and library media specialists would form partnerships and "plan together to design and implement a program that best matched the instructional needs of the school" (1988: Chapter 7:1). The mission as stated in *Information Power* emphasized the following objectives:

- to provide intellectual and physical access to information;
- to provide learning experiences that encourage users to become discriminating consumers and skilled creators of information;
- to provide leadership, instruction, and consulting assistance in the use of instructional and information technology;
- to provide resources and activities that contribute to lifelong learning;
- to provide a facility that functions as the information center of the school; and
- to provide resources and learning activities.

These objectives were aligned with national curriculum standards and state framework goals and formed the basis for how the library and educators operated in K–12 education. They are still relevant today.

Today, the Internet has moved from users "receiving" information to users "creating information," thus the "read-write" Web. In a Web 2.0 world, instead of merely reading a newsletter, for example, you might begin to publish one of your own. If you're frustrated by the way your current software compiles data, Web 2.0 services can make it easier to display the data in a different way. Web 2.0 allows groups of people to work on a document or spreadsheet simultaneously while in the background a computer keeps track of who made what changes where and when.

In general, the key characteristics of Web 2.0 are the following:

- Web-based applications can be accessed from anywhere.
- Simple applications solve specific problems.
- Value lies in content, not the software used to display content.
- Data can be readily shared.
- Distribution is bottom-up, not top-down.
- Students and educators can access and use tools on their own.
- Social tools encourage people to create, collaborate, edit, categorize, exchange, and promote information.
- Network effects are encouraged; the more people who contribute, the better the content gets.

PART 2: GETTING STARTED—TEACHING STRATEGIES AND WEB 2.0 TOOLS

"Today's graduates need to be critical thinkers, problem solvers, and effective communicators who are proficient in both core subjects and new, twenty-first-century content and skills," according to "Results that Matter: 21st Century Skills and High School Reform" (2006), a report issued by the Partnership for 21st Century Skills. These new skills include learning and thinking skills, information- and communications-technology literacy skills, and life skills. Students of today enter an increasingly global world in which technology plays a vital role. They must be good communicators, as well as great collaborators. The new work environment requires responsibility and self-management, as well as interpersonal and project-management skills that demand teamwork and leadership.

Web 2.0 Tools

Tim O'Reilly (2005), who helped coin the phrase "Web 2.0," offers his definition: "Web 1.0 was about connecting computers and making technology more efficient for computers. Web 2.0 is about connecting people and making technology more efficient for people." Web 2.0 creates new ways for large groups of people to collaborate and exchange information while reducing the importance of the computer itself as an information-delivery platform. As long as the applications and the data reside online, a variety of devices can function as information terminals whether they are smart phones, music players, or computers. Web 2.0 not only makes all this possible, it also makes it inexpensive and easy to deploy.

Philosophically, Web 2.0 is all about simplicity. It does not matter which computer you use or where it is. Web 2.0 tools encourage free exchange of information and ideas between different tools and groups of users. Lastly, because it encourages large-scale collaboration, Web 2.0 facilitates new forms of problem solving that can provide educators with valuable ideas and insights.

Web 2.0 Tools Covered in This Book

Any number of Web 2.0 tools are available on the Internet today. It would be impossible to mention them all in this book, let alone cover them in detail. I have chosen representative tools from different categories: tools for collaborating, ones for saving online pages, others to permit subscriptions to Web sites, map tools, presentation tools, and tools to aid learners no matter if they are audio or visual learners or those whose first language is not English. Each chapter focuses on one type of tool; for example, in Chapter 2 you will learn about blogs. You will discover what the technology is, benefits to using it in the classroom, and examples showing how teachers and librarians are already using blogs. In order to get you started, several examples are illustrated, showing how the tool is being used in the classroom. Finally, you will view a sample, detailed unit plan in a specific subject area and grade level to use as a model so that you can create your own lessons with your own students using this technology.

Covered in this book are blogs; podcasts; wikis; video for digital storytelling; Google Tools, including Google Maps, Google Earth, Google Docs and more; VoiceThread; and social book-marking. Each chapter begins with a glossary that defines new vocabulary with which you may not be familiar.

Teaching and Learning Strategies

Although Web 2.0 tools energize and motivate students, teaching and learning strategies are equally or more important. Each of the teaching and learning strategies described next will be incorporated into unit plans in the following chapters.

Critical Thinking Defined

In my book *Teaching with the Internet*, which described tools for Web 1.0, I defined critical thinking based on Bloom's taxonomy (1956). Now with new tools available, a digital revised taxonomy has been formulated and discussed on many educational blogs. Led by a former student of Bloom's, Lorin Anderson (2001) assembled cognitive psychologists, curriculum theorists, instructional researchers, and testing and assessment specialists to see if they could change the taxonomy to make it more relevant for the twenty-first century. The new taxonomy focuses the stages of development on verbs instead of nouns, and revises the higher order thinking skills. See Figure 1-1.

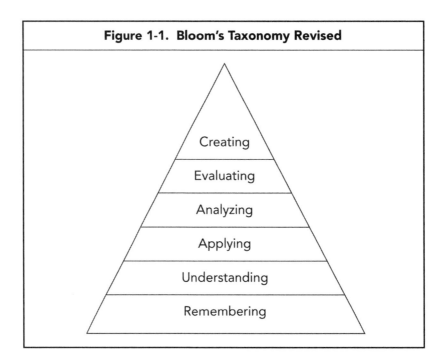

Figure 1-1. Bloom's Taxonomy Revised

Creating

Evaluating

Analyzing

Applying

Understanding

Remembering

Collaborative/Cooperative Learning

Research by Johnson et al. (1984) and Slavin (1995) indicates that lessons structured around cooperative learning result in improvements both in the achievement of students and in the quality of their interpersonal relationships. These studies have shown that cooperative learning can foster:

- higher intrinsic motivation;
- a more positive attitude toward instruction and instructors;
- the development of leadership abilities;
- a sense of teamwork;
- improved self-esteem;
- greater acceptance of differences; and
- decreased dependence on the teacher.

These researchers set up a structure with specified components for implementing cooperative learning in classrooms. The components include the following:

- *Group heterogeneity* results in more critical thinking and greater perspectives when discussing material. This type of group pulls in varied genders, races, cultural and language differences, problematic behaviors, and past academic achievement.
- *Positive group interdependence* is the feeling among group members that no one is successful unless everyone in the group succeeds, for example, task interdependence, in which each student's task is necessary to complete the project.
- *Individual accountability* usually ensures that each student contributes to the group. Students must know in advance what they will be responsible for attaining, and teachers must be able to monitor what each student has contributed and the level of mastery of required skills.
- *Group processing* requires that teachers and students discuss and evaluate the functioning of the groups.

Making sure that these components are part of each cooperative-learning project helps insure the success of the activity. Through collaboration children acquire social skills, experience different viewpoints, and learn how to work together with people who are the same and with those different from themselves. For example, working with students from another country can instill in students a real excitement for school, thus motivating them to work on their projects.

Project-Based Learning

Project-based learning is a dynamic approach to teaching in which students explore real-world problems and challenges, simultaneously developing cross-curricular skills while working in small collaborative groups. Because project learning is filled with active and engaged learning, it inspires students to obtain a deeper knowledge of the subjects they are studying. Research (Thomas, 2000) also indicates that students are more likely to retain the knowledge gained through this approach far more readily than through traditional textbook-centered learning. In addition, students develop confidence and self-direction as they move through both team-based and independent work.

Projects are an important part of the elementary curriculum because they offer children the chance to ask questions that guide an investigation and make decisions about the activities to be undertaken. Activities may include drawing, writing, reading, recording observations, and interviewing others. Dramatic activities can help children express new understanding and new vocabulary. Project work provides a context for applying skills the students have learned in the more formal parts of the curriculum and lends itself to group cooperation. It also supports children's natural impulses to investigate things around them. Even at the secondary level, project work can be a conduit for students to explore topics, resolve conflicts, share responsibility for carrying out tasks, and make suggestions—all skills necessary for living and working in society.

Project-based instruction can be divided into three phases:

1. Phase 1 is devoted to selecting and refining the topic to be investigated. At least some of the children should have knowledge of the topic, and it should allow for integrating a range of subjects, such as science, language arts, and social studies.
2. Phase 2 focuses on fieldwork, which is the direct investigation of objects, sites or events. Sources of information can be primary such as field trips or secondary such as information acquired from research. As a result of the information obtained from these sources, students can make observations from which they can draw conclusions.
3. Phase 3 contains culminating and debriefing events that include preparing and presenting reports of results.

Inquiry-Based Learning with Essential Questions

As all educators know, an effective questioning strategy by teachers is required to promote thinking by students. Essentially, these questions should: (1) direct the course of student research and require that students spend time pondering the meaning and importance of information; (2) engage students in real-life applied problem solving; and (3) usually lend themselves well to multidisciplinary investigations. As such, essential questions are powerful, directive, and commit students to the process of critical thinking through inquiry. Ultimately, the answer to an essential question will require that students craft a response that involves knowledge construction. This new knowledge building occurs through the integration of discrete pieces of information obtained during the research process. Answers to essential questions are a direct measure of student understanding.

There is no "right" or "wrong" answer to an essential question as long as the answer is based on the data gathered and can be reasonably justified. Before students proceed very far, they list suppositions, pose hypotheses, and make predictions—many of which will be revised as they gather information. This thought process helps to provide a basis for construction of meaning. In order to solve the problem or propose an answer to an "essential question," students need to ask themselves, "What do I need to know about that topic in order to solve this problem?" The questions that they come up with must be answered before they can solve the "problem" or "essential question." Subsidiary questions give students a direction and the data that they will need in order to come up with an answer to the "essential question."

Teaching approaches that are inquiry-based, constructivist, project-based, or student-centered foster essential questioning. While varying in specifics, these approaches all emphasize the importance of students exploring ideas, conducting "hands-on" investigations, engaging in projects on topics they choose, working collaboratively, discussing their ideas, and gaining conceptual understanding. In general, these approaches view knowledge as something individuals construct for themselves through action, reflection, and discussion; not as something that can be simply transmitted from teachers or books to students. Thus, educators need to organize courses not around answers but around questions and problems to which "content" represents answers.

Other Issues

Other issues besides content need to be addressed when Web 2.0 tools are included in the curriculum. Two of the main issues to be addressed are copyright and safety issues.

Copyright: Creative Commons

A new way of looking at copyright has also unfolded with the advent of Web 2.0. Wikipedia, a user-produced encyclopedia, describes Creative Commons as a nonprofit organization devoted to expanding the range of creative works available for others to legally build upon and share. The organization has released several copyright licenses known as Creative Commons licenses. These licenses, depending on the one chosen, restrict only certain rights (or none) of the work instead of traditional copyright, which is more restrictive.

The project, founded by Lawrence Lessig, provides several free licenses that copyright owners can use when releasing their works on the Web. Much more information about Creative Commons is available on the Wikipedia Web site (http://en.wikipedia.org/wiki/Creative_Commons_licenses).

Acceptable Use Policies (AUPs)

Those educators who are using Web 1.0 tools have had to be cognizant of student safety and appropriate use on the Internet of Web 1.0 tools. Educators also need to make sure that students are protected when using Web 2.0 tools. Several educators have created sample acceptable use policies that can serve as models for new educators who incorporate Web 2.0 tools into their curriculum. The following sites contain AUPs useful as models:

1. http://docs.google.com/View?docid=dfqjmd6d_24dfbht8d4. This AUP begins with personal responsibility.
2. www.doe.virginia.gov/VDOE/Technology/AUP/home.shtml. This is a very comprehensive AUP from the Virginia Department of Education–Technology Division, including components, samples from other schools, and templates.
3. http://del.icio.us/techsavvygirl/acceptable_use?setbundleview=show. This site lists a number of AUPs for Web 2.0 tools in general and more specifically for tools such as blogging and social networking.
4. http://k12wiki.wikispaces.com/Social+Networking+Acceptable+Use. This AUP is for social networking, including wikis, and contains a code of ethics.

PART 3: PRACTICAL APPLICATIONS

The term "unit" is one that is often used rather loosely. An instructional unit can comprise anything from a few days of concentrated study to a whole course. Units range from a five-day writing workshop to a yearlong study of Mexico. A teacher may have several units going at the same time. For example, a social studies teacher can be exploring a map-study unit while studying Latin America. In one week a language arts class may work on a writing unit on Fridays and a drama unit on Monday through Thursday.

The Unit Plan

In this book, model units contain the teacher's preplanning of the unit; the body of the lessons, including how the topic fits into national standards, goals, and objectives; a series of activities to meet the objectives, before, during and after the unit; and evaluation of the unit.

The teaching of any unit depends on the needs, interests, and abilities of the students for whom it has been designed. Building a unit should be based on the teacher's assessment of what a class can and cannot do. Educators will get the most out of the practical models in this book by envisioning their own curriculum and students and how the models in each chapter can be adapted with their own content to fit their particular students. The units contain activities for individualized instruction, as well as small or whole-group learning. This allows teachers to adapt those plans that fit their own teaching styles or to experiment with another type of unit in their own classrooms.

When creating Internet units incorporating Web 2.0 tools, we will follow steps similar to building most instructional units. Each unit is based on content, not on technology. The technology tool that is the focus of each unit is included to enhance instruction, whether it is in social studies, science, language arts or second-language learning. The following steps serve as a model for the subject-specific units in subsequent chapters.

Step 1: Applying Framework Standards—What Should Be Taught?

What areas should we include in our plans in a subject area and at a specific grade level? We begin by looking at national standards and the frameworks for teaching established by content-area curriculum development committees at state and national levels. Each state has its own guidelines and has outlined content and skills for students to achieve at each grade level. California framework standards, for example, require that history and social science courses beginning in kindergarten work toward "improving students' competency in the knowledge of history, geography, and citizenship, as well as their understanding of issues such as diversity, criticism, conflict, and interdependence" (California State Department of Education, 1988). The framework also stresses specific themes and attributes like communication, reasoning, personal development or civic responsibility. This material helps schools focus on broad goals as they create their own programs of study, and it provides core content and skills to form the basis of teachers' units and lesson plans.

Some concepts and skills cross all subject areas. In California, framework standards from language arts, social sciences, and science emphasize achieving the following goals:

- Students will work collaboratively. Studies have shown that students profit immeasurably from environments that encourage shared learning. Since most businesses today emphasize the team approach to completing projects, working cooperatively is a skill students need to attain before they finish school. Web 2.0 tools present an especially good environment for collaboration, one in which students work together creating presentations, sharing information with other students around the world, and more. These types of projects require learning teamwork and shared responsibility.

- Students will become aware that communication takes many forms. For example, writing is a means of clarifying thinking and is a process that embodies several stages, including prewriting, drafting, receiving responses, revising, editing, and postwriting activities. Using information gathered from a variety of sources, including Internet sites such as blogs, wikis, and students worldwide to name a few, enables students to practice their writing on meaningful, far-reaching topics. Oral responses to questions, analysis of information, and synthesis of data from various types of sources help students to acquire and use higher-order thinking skills in all subject areas. Students no longer are bound by the walls of their classrooms.
- Teachers and library media specialists will encourage and assist students to use all technological resources. Students must see how Web 2.0 tools enhance learning and prepare them for responsibilities in the twenty-first century.

Another set of framework standards has been created by the International Society of Technology in Education (ISTE) called *National Educational Technology Standards for Students: The Next Generation* (2007). These standards incorporate (1) creativity and innovation; (2) collaboration and communication; (3) research and information fluency; (4) critical thinking, problem solving, and decision making; (5) digital citizenship; and (6) technology operations and concepts. These standards should also be integrated into a unit plan using Web 2.0 tools.

The Internet provides a rich variety of media through which to learn; thus, teachers can adapt their instruction and accommodate different learning styles by providing stimuli for visual, auditory, and kinesthetic learners.

Step 2: Designing Unit Goals and Creating Specific Lesson Objectives

Because broad content and skills are often described for teachers by national standards, state frameworks or by local or school curriculum committees, general goals for instruction can be "givens" or fixed parts of the curriculum. However, teachers can create units that incorporate these mandated goals within their own list of unit goals and objectives.

An objective is a statement of what the learner will have attained once the learning experience has been successfully completed. Objectives define where the teacher is going with instruction, and they communicate these expectations to the students. They also act as a guide for selecting instructional strategies, learning activities, and evaluation techniques.

Objectives can be stated in a number of ways:

- As a list of skills or processes the student will master
- As a list of course activities that the student will read, talk about, or write about
- As a description of products—for example, creating a podcast
- As a list of activities that the student will be able to perform at the end of the unit

Step 3: Deciding on Materials and Resources

Good materials enhance and reinforce good instruction. They can help a lesson have a stronger impact and improve learner motivation. Thus, teachers need to select the media—whether it is a blog, wiki, podcast, Google maps, or other resources—so that the tools reinforce the lessons they plan to teach. In your Web 2.0 notebook, it is a good idea to keep a separate page for different subjects and types of tools. For each subject enter the topic you plan to teach, annotated URLs that fit the topic, learning strategies you will use, and tools that will reinforce the learning.

Step 4: Planning the Instruction

After creating the goals and objectives and gathering the materials, we must plan the instruction, as well as any Web 2.0 tools we plan to use. We must choose a sequence of materials and activities that meet the unit objectives and provide an interesting mix of activities to accommodate small group instruction, peer learning, different learning styles, individual work, projects, and a variety of technological tools.

Step 5: Preparing for Teacher and Student-Based Assessment

No matter what we teach, it is important to evaluate how well students are progressing to make sure that they are learning what we assume they are. Research (Thomas, 2000) could not be clearer that increasing formative assessment is the key to improvement on tests of all kinds, including traditional ones. And, more "authentic" and comprehensive forms of assessment provide not only significant gains on conventional tests but also more useful feedback because the tasks are more realistic.

What do I mean by "authentic assessment"? It is simply performances and product requirements that are faithful to real-world demands, opportunities, and constraints. Students are tested on their ability to "do" the subject in context, to transfer their learning effectively. Students improve and are engaged when they receive feedback and opportunities to work on realistic tasks requiring transfer at the heart of learning goals and real-world demands.

Assessment can take many forms:

- *Monitoring by observation.* Process and lab skills or small group projects can be monitored by observing students while they are engaged in activities.
- *Monitoring by student evaluations.* Students should be given opportunities to review and discuss cooperatively each other's assignments and projects.
- *Monitoring by examination.* A prepared list of questions tests students for understanding and application of the main ideas in the unit.
- *Monitoring by problem solving.* Exercises to test concepts taught in the unit require students to apply concepts they have learned.

Some specific assessment strategies to consider are:

- *Interviews.* Student/teacher dialogues in person or using Web 2.0 tools like blogs or wikis can determine the approaches used in problem solving and students' views of what was learned.
- *Anecdotal records.* Teachers keep anecdotal records of the class and record student questions and behaviors. Blogs, wikis, and Google Notebook automatically keep track of students' work. Often the fact that all work is on one Web site makes evaluating less cumbersome.
- *Learning logs.* Students' comments using Web 2.0 tools reflect their thoughts and ideas about their learning.
- *Pictures/illustrations.* Students draw pictures, for example, using VoiceThreads, illustrating their thoughts regarding a particular concept.
- *Class notebooks.* Google Notebook helps students keep records of their daily experiences and activities.
- *Active participation.* Teachers rate student involvement in active participation tasks and cooperative exercises. Rubrics make a good tool for this type of evaluation.
- *Role-play.* Students are asked to role-play parts of a process, for example, creating a podcast about concepts they have learned and sharing those concepts with other classes.
- *Student-taught lessons.* Students plan, research, and create a product that they share with another class. They might use a podcast, VoiceThread, digital story or other Web 2.0 tool to create the product.
- *Self-assessment.* Students rate their own progress and support their feelings.
- *Product.* Students are asked to create a product that demonstrates their knowledge of a content area. Many of the Web 2.0 tools covered in this book are useful to assess content area knowledge.

- *Peer assessment.* Other students in a cooperative group rate the performance of the group's members.

These assessment techniques provide unique ways of evaluating student progress and assessing the lessons teachers create at the same time. Many of the strategies will be used as assessment in the units in subsequent chapters.

Summary

Effective schools' literature shows that when teachers work together to build a coherent learning experience for students in all grades and within and across subject areas—one that is guided by common curriculum goals and expectations—they are able to improve student achievement (Lee, Bryk, and Smith, 1993). Effective instruction includes curricular goals and coherent learning experiences. The five steps just discussed form the basis for any good unit plan in any subject area. While teachers may emphasize one section more than another in their planning, each area is important to the learning process.

Table 1-1. General URLs	
URL	**Description**
www.edutopia.org/mary-scroggs-elementary-school	Video about Mary Scroggs Elementary School learning with technology
www.21centuryconnections.com/node/128	Article about twenty-first-century learning—Intro to digital video
http://blogsearch.google.com/	Google Blog Search
http://images.google.com/	Google Image Search
www.del.icio.us.com	A social bookmarking site
www,technorati.com	An Internet search engine for searching blogs
www.youtube.com	A video-sharing Web site where users can upload, view, and share video clips

CONCLUSION

This book is all about Web 2.0 and the student. There is a whole other aspect to Web 2.0 and that is how educators can use these tools to further their own development, communicate with other teachers and librarians, and have others listen to their personal voices. However, that is for another book! In *Using Web 2.0 Tools in the K–12 Classroom*, we are interested in ways Web 2.0 tools can enhance the curriculum and improve student learning.

➣ *Use the accompanying Web site (www.neal-schuman.com/webclassroom) to expand your knowledge of Web 2.0 tools as you read about them in the chapters that follow.*

This is an exciting time to be an educator. Explore these new tools and include them in your toolbox of teaching strategies. After all, when Rip Van Winkle awakens, we want him to march into our schools and see that he is, indeed, in a new, different educational environment.

REFERENCES AND FURTHER READING

American Association of School Librarians and Association for Educational Communications and Technology. 1988. *Information Power: Guidelines for School Library Media Programs.* Chicago: American Association of School Librarians, and Washington, DC: Association for Educational Communications and Technology.

Anderson, L. W., and Krathwohl, D. R., eds. 2001. *A Taxonomy for Learning, Teaching and Assessing: A Revision of Bloom's Taxonomy of EducationalObjectives: Complete Edition.* New York: Longman.

Bloom, Benjamin S., ed. 1956. *Taxonomy of Educational Objectives Handbook 1: Cognitive Domains.* New York: David McKay.

California State Department of Education. 1988. *History-Social Science Framework for California Public Schools, Kindergarten Through Grade Twelve.* Sacramento: California State Department of Education.

From Now On, 6, no. 1 (September 1996). Available: www.fno.org/sept96/questions.html (accessed October 1, 2008).

Gibson, Rowan, ed., with a foreword by Alvin Toffler and Heidi Toffler. 1999. *Rethinking the Future.* London: Nicholas Brealey.

Hargadon, Steve. 2008. "Web 2.0 Is the Future of Education." (March 5). Available: www.techlearning.com/blog/2008/03/web_20_is_the_future_of_educat_1.php (accessed October 1, 2008).

International Society for Technology in Education. 2007. *National Educational Technology Standards for Students: The Next Generation.*

Johnson, David W., Roger T. Johnson, Edythe J. Holubec, and Patricia A. Roy. 1984. *Circles of Learning: Cooperation in the Classroom.* Alexandria, VA: Association for Supervision and Curriculum Development.

Krathwohl, David R. "A Revision of Bloom's Taxonomy: An Overview—Benjamin S. Bloom, University of Chicago." *Theory Into Practice.* (Autumn 2002). FindArticles.com. 05 May. 2008. Available: http://findarticles.com/p/articles/mi_m0NQM/is_4_41/ai_94872707 (accessed October 1, 2008).

Lee, Valerie E., Anthony S. Bryk, and Julia B. Smith. 1993. "The Organization of Effective Secondary Schools." In *Review of Research in Education*, vol. 19. edited by Linda Darling-Hammond. Washington, DC: American Educational Research Association, pp. 171–267.

McKenzie, Jamie. 2001. "From Trivial Pursuit to Essential Questions." *The Educational Technology Journal*, 10, no. 5 (February). Available: www.fno.org/feb01/pl.html (accessed October 1, 2008).

Newmann, Fred M., Anthony S. Bryk, and Jenny K. Nagaoka. 2001. "Authentic Intellectual Work and Standardized Tests: Conflict or Coexistence?" Consortium on Chicago School Research, University of Chicago.

O'Reilly, Tim. 2005. "What is Web 2.0?". (September 9). Available: www.oreillynet.com/pub/a/oreilly/tim/news/2005/09/30/what-is-web-20.html (accessed October 1, 2008).

"Results that Matter: The Partnership for 21st Century Skills and High School Reform." Partnership for 21st Century Skills. (March 2006). Available: www.21stcenturyskills.org/index.php?Itemid=114&id=204&option=com_content&task=view (accessed October 1, 2008).

Slavin, Robert. 1995. *Cooperative Learning: Theory, Research, and Practice.* Needham Heights, MA: Allyn and Bacon.

Thomas, J. W. 2000. "A Review of Research on Project-Based Learning." Available: www.autodesk.com/foundation (accessed July 11, 2008).

CHAPTER 2

Blogging in the Language Arts

PART 1: IDEAS AND INSIGHTS

There has been a shift from a World Wide Web that is "read only" to a Web that is being described as the "Read Write Web" or Web 2.0. The Web is evolving to become more of an area for social and idea networking. The Web surfer negotiates the connections within a social or idea network, exchanges bits of content, creates something new, and then begins the cycle again. Two Web 2.0 tools—blogs and RSS feeds—work together as part of this new Web phenomenon. Blogs or Weblogs provide a communication space that teachers can utilize with students whenever there is a curriculum need whether it is to develop writing, share ideas, or reflect on work being undertaken in the classroom.

But, how can blogging help your students improve their writing? Some comments from teachers currently using this technology in their classrooms illustrate why this is an important new motivational tool for English/language arts.

> "Even when they're out sick, students work on their blogs." (Carol Barsotti)
>
> "I've got 6th graders coming in during their lunch and after school to add articles to their blog and to respond to their classmates' articles." (Al Gonzales)
>
> "My students are floored when, as they say, 'some random person from Texas commented on my blog!' The students are getting real world experience with writing." (Brian McLaughlin)
>
> "Why would my students want to write on paper for their teacher to see, when they could write on their blog for the whole world to see?" (Kathy Cassidy)
>
> "In fifteen years of teaching, I have never seen anything come along even close to motivating students to write like blogging does." (Mark Ahlness)

These comments from educators give us a peek into the power of blogging that we will illustrate in this chapter.

Objectives of This Chapter

This chapter is designed to be used by English/language arts educators and library media specialists at both the elementary and secondary levels. By the end of the chapter, educators will be able to:

- state advantages of using Web 2.0 tools in the language arts classroom;
- describe a blog, identify characteristics and uses of educational and English/language arts blogs;
- set up a blog and RSS feeds, as well as understand the necessary dos and don'ts of blogging; and
- build an English/language arts writing unit that includes blogging.

An English/language arts curriculum has the responsibility to teach students to listen well, speak effectively, read and think critically, and write clearly and with purpose for a specific audience. To accomplish these tasks, we, as English/language arts educators, expose students to literature and require them to discuss and create meaning from texts they read. We also provide opportunities for students to speak in small groups and to the whole class. We create assignments that require students to write about their thoughts and experiences, and we ask them to work together and share ideas. Some of the new Web 2.0 tools lend themselves to use in English/language arts. We'll look at one—blogging—in this chapter.

> ➤ *Bev's Web site at www.neal-schuman.com/ webclassroom provides examples of blogs in other subject areas.*

Glossary

Review these new words in order to understand better the concepts that appear in this chapter.

aggregator: *See* RSS READER.

Atom: A format similar to RSS; like RSS, the files may also be called feeds or channels.

blog (web+log): A Web site powered by software that simplifies publishing, organizing, and syndicating Web content, usually maintained by individuals, groups of individuals or institutions, containing regular entries of commentary, descriptions of events, or other material such as graphics or video. Entries are commonly displayed in reverse chronological order. Many blogs have RSS feeds.

blogger: One who contributes to a blog.

blogging: Creating and maintaining a Weblog.

blogsphere: The collective term encompassing all Weblogs or blogs as a comunity or social network.

edublog: A blog written by someone with an interest in education.

folksonomy: The collaborative but unsophisticated way in which information is being categorized on the Web or socially constructed taxonomies within Internet communities.

I-Search: An inquiry-based approach to teaching the research process.

keyword tags: Help other people using a site to quickly find information that interests them.

RSS: A family of Web feed formats used to publish frequently updated content such as blogs, news headlines, and podcasts in a standardized format (RSS = Really Simple Syndication = Rich Site Summary).

RSS buttons (XML, RSS): A subscribe button to an RSS feed on a Web site.

RSS file or **RSS feed** or **RSS channel:** Contains a list of *items* or *entries*, each of which is identified by a link. Each item can have any amount of other data associated with it as well.

RSS reader or **news reader** or **RSS aggregator:** A program that keeps a list of your chosen feeds, checks those feeds regularly, and displays their contents for you in a readable format.

tagging: The process of assigning meaning to a piece of information via tags.

tag: A keyword or term associated with or assigned to a piece of information (e.g., a picture, article, or video clip), thus describing the item and enabling keyword-based classification of information.

Technorati: A Weblog search site that allows you to find new Weblogs, and thus new feeds to subscribe to.

Introduction

We have come a long way from ten years ago when the number of educators using the Internet to support English studies was not even included in the top ten curriculum areas ("National Survey of Internet Usage," 1997). Many language arts educators are now using the Internet in their classroom assignments for such tasks as researching a term project, learning more about authors of fiction, poetry, nonfiction, and drama, and communicating with other schoolchildren around the world to increase their writing skills. As educators, it is also our goal to provide opportunities for students to speak in small groups and to the whole class about their experiences in literature and about the research they have conducted. Library media and computer specialists often provide advice and support to classroom teachers. However, new technologies are available daily and it takes time, effort, and knowledge for educators to keep up with them all. Although we have begun to introduce technology into a limited number of assignments, we still have a long way to go.

This chapter explores ways to integrate Web 2.0 tools—Weblogs or blogs, a shortened form of Weblogs, and RSS feeds—into English and language arts content instruction. In a 2006 report, statistics compiled by Pew International and American Life Project (Lenhart and Fox, 2006) showed that about 67 percent of all Americans—135 million people—used the Internet. Approximately 31 million of those Internet users, or 23 percent, said they had read someone else's blog; and about 12.2 million, or 9 percent, had created one. That's a lot of bloggers, and their numbers have continued to grow over the past few years.

Part 1 of this chapter provides an introduction to blogging and examples of how teachers are using blogs in English/language arts. Part 2 suggests how to get started, including the technology and rules for using blogs and RSS feeds. In Part 3, a sample unit plan illustrates the use of blogs as part of a writing project at the secondary level.

What Are Blogs?

Weblogging, a term first used by Jorn Barger in December 1997, is a popular and fast-growing application. A Weblog or blog is someone's personal dated "log" frequently updated with new information about a particular subject or range of subjects. Creating and maintaining a Weblog is called "blogging." If you have a Weblog, or contribute to a Weblog, you are a "blogger." Bloggers may form "online communities."

Not surprisingly, people have slightly different opinions about what exactly constitutes a Weblog, but there is a general acceptance that the format in which content is published matters, as well as the style in which the content is created. Additionally, Weblogs are usually defined by what they generally are, rather than trying to provide a specific definition.

According to an article entitled "Blogging to Teach Reading" (2007), blogging is about reading first, especially about reading what is of interest to you, your culture, or your community. It is also about your ideas. It is about engaging with the content and with the authors of what you have read—reflecting, criticizing, questioning, and reacting. If a student has nothing to blog about, it is not because he or she has nothing to write about or has a boring life. It is because the student has not yet stretched out to the larger world, has not yet learned to engage meaningfully in a community. For blogging in education to be a success, this first must be embraced and encouraged.

Another definition indicates that Weblogs are Web sites that are easily created and updated by those with even a minimum of technology knowledge. You don't have to know complicated codes because blog publishing is now almost as easy as sending e-mail. You just log-in to your blog site from any Internet connection, enter the content in a typical Internet form, press a button, and your Weblog is updated. Blogs can display not only text but pictures, video, audio, and even store other files to link to like Microsoft PowerPoint presentations or Microsoft Excel spreadsheets. To sum up, a Weblog is a dynamic, flexible tool that is easy to use whether you're creating with it or simply viewing the results.

Characteristics of Blogs

A list of common characteristics of Weblogs may help you understand the concept. Weblogs:

- present content (called posts) generally in reverse chronological order with the most recent entry listed first;
- are usually informal and generally personal;
- are updated regularly; and
- don't usually involve professional editors in the process (that is, someone who is getting paid explicitly to review the content).

Beyond that, format, style, and content vary greatly. Some people post long essays, some just write short posts. Some talk about their work, others about their personal lives and others only talk about politics or sports. There are numerous Weblogs that are ways for small groups to share information efficiently within their schools' networks or to create a place to store projects. Some people post links they find interesting or humorous. Some add commentary to a post. Others only comment on Weblog entries written by others. Many blogs talk about technology. Some Weblogs have a huge number of readers; others only a few dozen. Some are so personal that they are read only by the person who writes them. A few public Weblogs are anonymous; however, most identify the author of the blog. Some are updated many times a day, others once a day, others a few times a week.

Blogs allow people to "share" in unique ways. Instead of simply using the Internet for reading information or to "look something up" on the Web, blogs let people write, react, and share on the Internet. Bloggers, like any writers, need to know their audience. Successful bloggers aim their writing at that target audience.

Blog Components

Review Figures 2-1 and 2-2 for the following components of a blog:

- *Post Date*—date and time the post was published
- *Title*—main title of the post

Figure 2-1. Components of a Blog

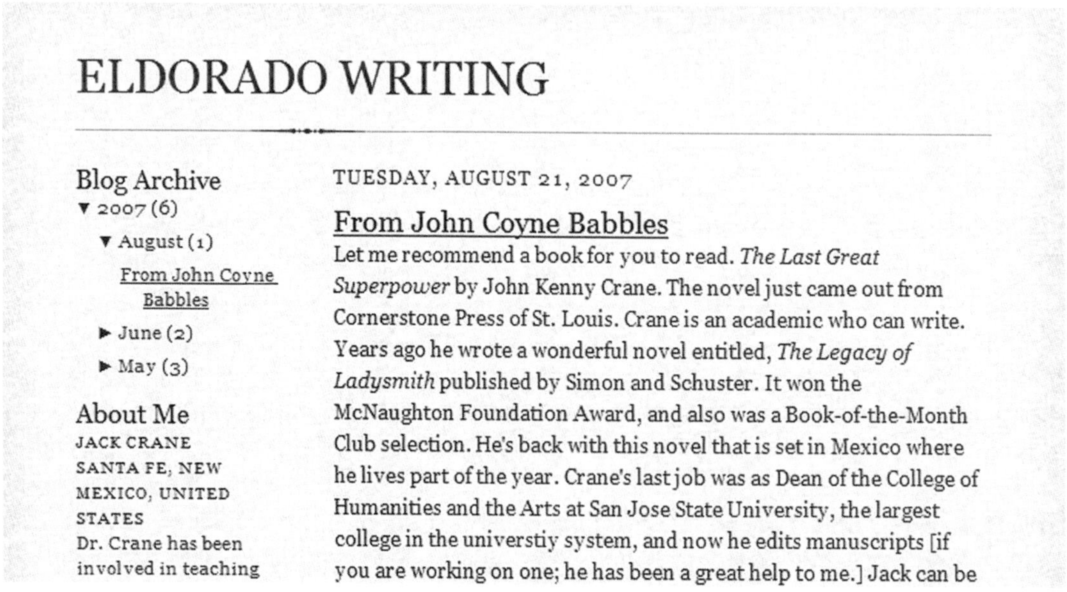

ELDORADO WRITING

Blog Archive
▼ 2007 (6)
 ▼ August (1)
   From John Coyne
   Babbles
 ► June (2)
 ► May (3)

About Me
JACK CRANE
SANTA FE, NEW
MEXICO, UNITED
STATES
Dr. Crane has been
involved in teaching

TUESDAY, AUGUST 21, 2007

From John Coyne Babbles

Let me recommend a book for you to read. *The Last Great Superpower* by John Kenny Crane. The novel just came out from Cornerstone Press of St. Louis. Crane is an academic who can write. Years ago he wrote a wonderful novel entitled, *The Legacy of Ladysmith* published by Simon and Schuster. It won the McNaughton Foundation Award, and also was a Book-of-the-Month Club selection. He's back with this novel that is set in Mexico where he lives part of the year. Crane's last job was as Dean of the College of Humanities and the Arts at San Jose State University, the largest college in the universtiy system, and now he edits manuscripts [if you are working on one; he has been a great help to me.] Jack can be

- *Body*—main content of the post
- *Link*—the URL of the full, individual article
- *Comments*—comments added by readers
- *Tags or Labels*—category the post is labeled with (can be one or more)
- *Footer*—usually at the bottom of the post, often shows post date and time, author, tags, and stats such as number of comments

Blogs usually include links to Web sites, other blogs, news articles, or even pictures. Some blogs have the capability of showing pictures as part of the blog itself.

Blog writers often "tag" their entries with keywords. According to Wikipedia (2008), a "tag" is defined as "a (relevant) keyword or term associated with or assigned to a piece of information (e.g., a picture, article, or video clip), thus describing the item and enabling keyword-based classification of information." Tags have become an important tool for educators to find blog posts, photos, and videos that are related. A tag is like a subject or category. Another word used for tagging is folksonomy—an Internet-based information retrieval methodology consisting of collaboratively generated, open-ended labels that categorize content. The process of tagging is intended to make a body of information increasingly easier to search, discover, and navigate over time. Users who originate the tags and those that are the primary users of them now have a shared vocabulary that makes searching easier. For example, the sample blog entry shown in Figure 2-2 has the "tag" or "label" *writing tip*.

Thus, in summary, blogs offer a blogger the ability to archive content that is posted by date. The commenting feature of blogs allows for immediate feedback by those reading a post. The content posted to a blog includes text, images, files, audio, and video. Publishing posts to an intranet or the

Figure 2-2. Tagging

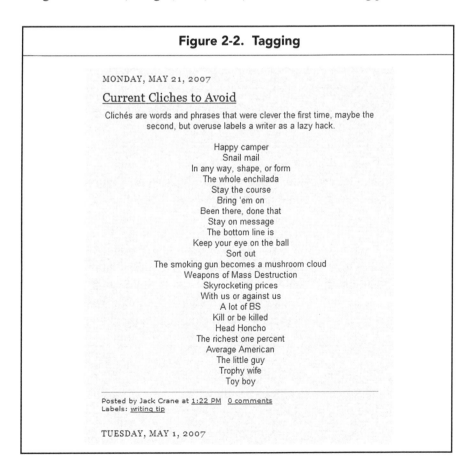

Internet can by done quickly and easily. Blogs are so simple to create and edit that they are ideal for the classroom teacher or school librarian.

Implications for Education

Blogs can be used in many aspects of education. For example, clubs and activities, sports teams, and parent groups use Weblogs to post scores, meeting minutes, and links to relevant issues and topics. Weblogs are also used by teachers to contact parents or for dialogue with other teachers and administrators. Blogs can contain notes to parents about classroom activities, meals, and vacations; a letter from the principal; a newsletter for parents by parents; and photo galleries of school events.

Many librarians have realized their power in communicating information about resources, starting conversations about books and literacy, and providing book recommendations. Blogs enable teachers to initiate online conversations with their students, prompting thoughtful comments about current events, science experiments, field trips, books or math problems. Many teachers use blogs to display course notes, showcase student work, distribute assignments, archive handouts, post homework assignments, and answer questions virtually.

Why Use Blogs in the Classroom?

Why consider blogging for the classroom? Here's why. Easy to use, fun, empowering and inexpensive, blogs can be created and maintained by a technology novice. They offer a wide range of advantages in teaching and learning in the classroom. For example, blogs can:

1. Create a learning community, open 24/7, which is a place different from the traditional classroom.
2. Provide an authentic audience for student writing, including peers, parents, and a potential worldwide audience, while promoting a cross-curricular connection with social studies lessons.
3. Allow for feedback from the networked students, teachers, and other interested persons. Learning in a class blog setting is now a social activity.
4. Support differentiation. The blog can give some of the more verbally reserved students a forum for their thoughts.
5. Encourage reading. To make a meaningful comment, or to choose their favorite post, students first need to read what's out there.
6. Encourage and teach research skills prompting students to extend their research beyond the assigned work.

Blogs are, above all, about expression. Blogs and the Web in general allow students to look at many viewpoints easily, cross-reference them or look for second, third, and fourth opinions. Peter Grunwald (2006) of Bethesda, Maryland, who has studied the ways young people use Web tools, says, "Kids are looking for opportunities for self-expression and to find their own identities. More and more students are becoming producers of information rather than passive consumers of it." Teachers have been devising ways to treat learners as producers rather than products for a long while. The blog will help.

Examples of Blogs in the Library and Classroom

With the explosion of sites such as MySpace (www.myspace.com), many students are blogging outside of school hours. Educators should be aware of the rising popularity of blogs and use it to their advantage. Librarians and teachers from different subject areas can collaborate to educate students about using blogs in their classrooms. This partnership will increase students' and teachers' awareness of the library and its usefulness, as well as helping teachers to find examples of how to incorporate this technology into the classroom. For example, blogs on the Web site of the Magnolia Elementary School in Joppa, Maryland, highlight fifth-grade writers, kindergarteners' artwork, and facts about Maryland history from fourth graders. The Buckman Arts Magnet Elementary School in Portland, Oregon, has a number of community-building blogs, such as the Book Nook, a collection of teacher recommendations, books of the week, and descriptions of new acquisitions.

Several specific examples illustrate the use of blogs in both elementary and secondary English/language arts classrooms.

Example 1: Blogs in Literature

One advantage of using blogs is the commenting capabilities that many of the blogging software packages have. This technique allows for easy peer review of student writing and makes bringing in experts or mentors from outside the classroom easy. Example 1 comes from a Modern American Literature class that was reading Sue Monk Kidd's book *The Secret Life of Bees* (http://weblogs.hcrhs.k12.nj.us/beesbook). The teacher used a Weblog to continue discussion of the book outside of class. She had her students write questions about the characters and plot of the book and then contacted the author who wrote a 2,300-word response to students' questions. See Figure 2-3.

Figure 2-3. *The Secret Life of Bees*

The Secret Life of Bees

Welcome to the Discussion!

So, what did you think? Leave your feedback here.

Home

About

Schedule

Discussion
Recent Discussion
Create New Topic

Departments
Artistic Interp.
Chap. Summaries
Characters
Class Discussions
Historical Events
Links
Miscellany

Chapter 14 Highlights

Chapet 14 starts off with Lily's mind on her mother. She tries and tries not to think about her mother but it seems that the more she tries not to, the more she does. The next day she finally feels like eating and goes inside only to find that there is no food ready to eat for once. Rosaleen tells Lily that she is going to register to vote again in her new dress that June had gone shopping for with Rosaleen. They ask Lily to come but she declines. Then Lily decides to call Zach and he asks her if she has to go back to Sylvan. She says T suppose so. Once Rosaleen gopt back she called all the sisters and tells them all that she has registered to vote and who she is voting for. That night Lily goes on a cleaning frenzy and cleans the entire Honey House until it is spotless. She takes all her mothers things and the mouse bones tied together with a ribbon and puts them all on the shelf by the fan. Lily wakes the next morning to find August wanting to show her something with the bees. They go look at a hive that is missing a queen and talk about for a while. Eventually they both go inside. Lily is sitting by herself when there is a knock on the door. Lily doesnt think anything of it because she thinks it is August's friend that is bringing the new queen for the hive. When no one answers the door on the third knock she goes and opens the door. To her suprise it is T-Ray. At first she asks him to come in and acts like it is a casual visit. Eventually he flips out on her, slaps her and grabs her all in his mindset that it is actually Deborah Fontanel Owens and not Lily. Eventually her snaps out of it when Lily screams Daddy. Soon Rosaleen and August almost walk in but Lily waves them off as August goes to call the Daughters of Mary to come. Once they get there, they all stand there with Lily and T-Ray realizes he cant win. He walks out the door and gets into his truck. Lily runs outside and asks T-Ray for the last time if she actually was the one who killed her mother. He says yes. Life returns good again as Lily becomes good friends with another white girl and goes to a school where Zach also goes. The book ends on a good note. - goto
Posted by Garrett K on 3/3/03; 2:15:45 PM from the Chapter Summaries dept.

Discuss (1 response)

In fact, the project was so successful that the teacher created another Weblog for the students' parents who were interested in reading the book. About a dozen parents held their own discussions on the book (http://weblogs.hcrhs.k12.nj.us/beesparents).

Example 2: Blogs in Writing

Example 2 shows how a teacher uses blogs as part of her students' writing assignments. This teacher requires that all assignments be turned in via blogs. She has found that the conversational nature of blog writing encourages students to think and write more in depth than traditional formal essays or short-answer assignments. Another advantage of receiving assignments in blog format is that both she and her students can subscribe so that students can see one another's work.

The blog assignments are designed to train students to think critically and to post informed, well-considered opinions. One classroom activity, for instance, had students read the blogged entries of others and write persuasive reactions—one in agreement, another in disagreement—and post these writings as comments to their classmates' blogs. According to the teacher, students initially struggled with the task, but they eventually learned the goal was not necessarily to find an idea with which they personally disagreed but to find another side to an idea and write persuasively from that perspective. For a genetics assignment, students assumed a range of positions—some that discouraged work in genetic manipulation based on security, cost, and ethics, and others that supported it based on the potential cure for disease, life extension, and increased food production. In response to these blogged assignments, the teacher also posted assessments in the form of comments.

Other ideas for English/language arts classes include:

- using blogs for real-world writing experiences (e.g., stem cell research, violence against animals);
- prolonging discussions outside the classroom;
- communicating questions and answers with guest speakers;
- providing teacher feedback to students quickly, as well as students to each other;
- tracking student writing development;
- using peer networks to develop students' own knowledge; and
- updating new information such as homework and assignments.

> ➤ *For examples of blogs in other subject areas, see Bev's Web site at www.neal-schuman.com/webclassroom.*

Teacher Exercises: Now You Try It . . .

Review the following blogs to see how you might incorporate one of these ideas into your English/language arts class. Choose one that coincides with the age level you teach.

- Ms. Howard's class writing blog, Yukon, Takhini Elementary (http://dl1.yukoncollege.yk.ca/takpilotblog/).
- Mr. Tubb's sixth-grade homework and student blogs (http://jtubbs.21publish.com/).
- Wyoming Middle School, Rooms 208 and 209 poetry blog (http://bobsprankle.com/writingblog/) – Mr. S and Mr. I student poetry.

> ➤ *Examples in different subject areas and at various age levels provide options for educators who do not teach language arts.*

As Will Richardson (2004), supervisor of instructional technology at Hunterdon Central Regional High School in Flemington, New Jersey, and known as one of the leading proponents of blogging in education, says, "Blogging as a genre of writing may have great value in terms of developing all sorts of critical thinking skills, writing skills and information literacy among other things. We teach exposition and research and some other types of analytical writing already, I know. Blogging, however, offers students a chance to a) reflect on what they are writing and thinking as they write and think it, b) carry on writing about a topic over a sustained period of time, maybe a lifetime, and c) engage readers and audience in a sustained conversation that then leads to further writing and thinking." Blogging is a part of students' lives. It is now up to librarians and teachers to make it a part of their education.

PART 2: GETTING STARTED

There are many questions to contemplate as you think about setting up a blog for your classroom or library. One of the first considerations is your "audience." Is the blog going to be public so that others may view and comment to it? Is it private, just for yourself? Is it only for a specific class, for other teachers, for parents?

Considerations Before Setting Up a Blog

We'll look at some things to consider before setting up a blog in a moment.

Step 1: Choose a Service

One thing you need to decide is what blogging service to use for your Weblogs. There are many blogging hosts available and more being offered daily. Several used by educators are listed here.

- **Blogmeister**, created by David Warlick with teachers and students in mind, is a good tool at the elementary level. It is offered free for classrooms, provides total teacher approval and is usually not blocked by schools. Approximately 3,500 schools are using Blogmeister. The Landmark Project (http://landmark-project.com) provides this free space for teachers as part of their mission to "redefine literacy for the 21st Century." To set up an account, the first person from your school must obtain a password. You can review how to get your password and sign up for the service at www.classblogmeister.com/.
- Another free blog site is **Edublogs**, a site created by teachers for teachers. A sign up page for teachers and students is accessible from the Home page at http://edublogs.org, along with ways to use your blog with students and how to use your blog to communicate with other educators.
- **Blogger** (www.blogger.com), a free blogging service, has safety controls like anti-spam and comment moderation, which lets the teacher view all comments before they appear on the classroom blog. This feature gives the teacher a chance to approve or reject them as desired.

You will want to check these Web sites and others to determine which host you want to use for your blog. *Note:* See a full range of features at www.teachersfirst.com/content/blog/tools3.cfm.

> ➤ *Go to Bev's Educational Blog at http://bevcrane.blogspot.com to participate in a blog before signing up.*

Step 2: Select an Aggregator

There are thousands of educational blogs alone. How does one keep track of all the information you are interested in? A second piece of equipment to help in your blogging is called an aggregator or

RSS Reader. An *aggregator* enables you to read RSS content. (More on RSS in a moment.) Readers periodically check for new items in the RSS feeds you have selected on a time schedule that you have chosen. So, instead of looking for the news, it comes directly to you, saving you time and effort.

Basically, an aggregator is a piece of software designed to subscribe to sites through syndication and automatically download updates from Web sites and blogs. If the aggregator is running on your computer or other device, once you have the content you can either read it in "offline" mode or if the aggregator is Web-based, it will require connectivity to the Internet at all times.

There are two main categories of aggregators: "Web page style" and "e-mail style." "Web page style" aggregators present new entries they have received as a Web page, in reverse chronological order, so the result looks very much like a Weblog put together by the software. "E-mail style" aggregators generally display new posts as messages, also in reverse chronological order, so that you can click and view on a separate area of the screen.

Two other popular aggregators online are Bloglines (www.bloglines.com), an online service for searching, subscribing, creating and sharing news feeds, blogs and rich Web content and Google Reader (www.google.com/reader), free with a gmail (e-mail) account (see Figure 2-4).

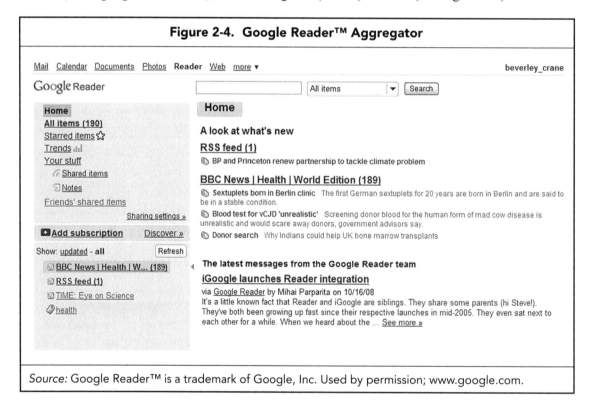

Figure 2-4. Google Reader™ Aggregator

Source: Google Reader™ is a trademark of Google, Inc. Used by permission; www.google.com.

RSS Feeds

RSS and Atom feeds are becoming a standard for sharing data between different Web applications. RSS is an acronym that stands for Rich Site Summary (version 1.0), although it is often alternatively defined as Really Simple Syndication (version 2.0). A Web feed is a way for Web sites to continuously "feed" you announcements of their latest content, with links to each new item (see Figure 2-5). To instantly learn what's new on a site, just check its feed. **RSS**, **Atom enabled**, **XML** and ⧉ are symbols used to identify that a feed is available on a particular Web site. RSS delivers information through podcasts, blogs, social networks, search agents, and peer-produced content and the venues are increasing every day.

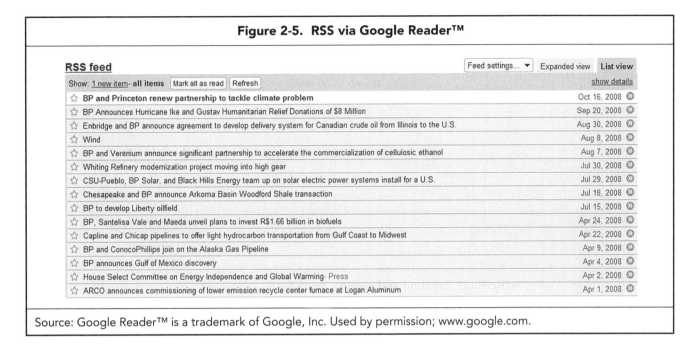

Figure 2-5. RSS via Google Reader™

Source: Google Reader™ is a trademark of Google, Inc. Used by permission; www.google.com.

Which is best for you depends on how you use RSS and how urgent you consider the messages to be. If you're only checking your RSS feeds once a day, then an online reader is just fine. However, if you check feeds constantly, then it is better to have the RSS software on your desktop. A complete list of feed readers is available from RSS Compendium at http://allrss.com/rssreaders.html.

➤ *For more about RSS feeds and how to set one up, check Bev's Web site at www.neal-schuman .com/webclassroom.*

Step 3: Set Up Your Blog

In many cases, the teacher sets up a blog account and then adds student accounts, which reside under the teacher's account. Teachers can decide whether student blogs will be public or private; they can also review student posts or comments on posts and leave online feedback for students to improve their writing. Thus, students' blog articles are published in a controlled environment that is hidden from public view. A video tutorial on Edublogs at www.edublogs.org illustrates how to use a blog, create one and more.

The following example from www.blogger.com will show you how to set up a typical blog.

- *Step 1:* Select "create an account." Enter a user name and password and your e-mail address (Figure 2-6).
- *Step 2:* Name your blog (e.g., Bev's Educational Blog) and enter a URL address as in Figure 2-7 (e.g., bevcrane@blogspot.com).
- *Step 3:* Choose a template for your blog. There are many on the site from which to select (Figure 2-8).
- *Step 4:* Your blog is created—it's that easy. Now you can begin to post entries to the blog (Figure 2-9).

Blogging Guidelines

If you're going to have a blog at your school, you should set up in advance some very clear guidelines for your blog and students. Rules should be created, reviewed at the school site, and signed by both students in a blogging project and their parents.

Figure 2-6. Create an Account

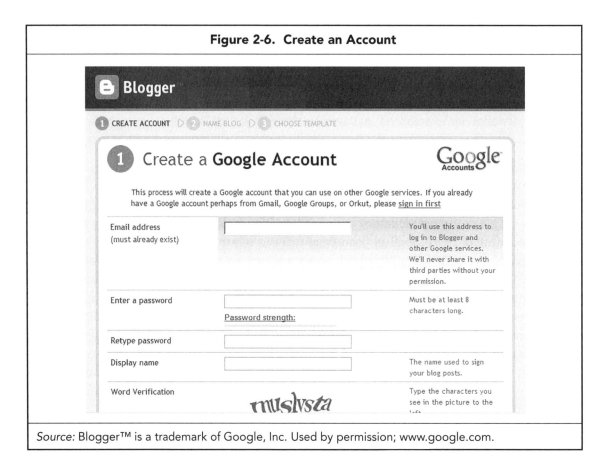

Source: Blogger™ is a trademark of Google, Inc. Used by permission; www.google.com.

Figure 2-7. Name the Blog

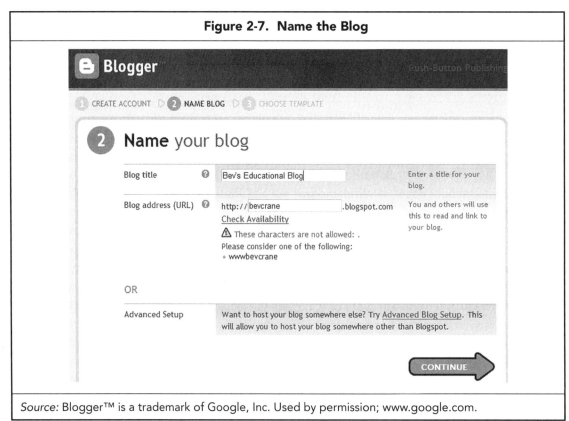

Source: Blogger™ is a trademark of Google, Inc. Used by permission; www.google.com.

Figure 2-8. Choose a Template

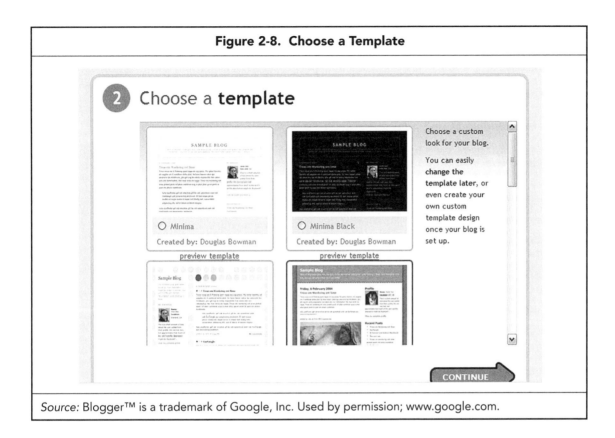

Source: Blogger™ is a trademark of Google, Inc. Used by permission; www.google.com.

Figure 2-9. Start Your Posts

Source: Blogger™ is a trademark of Google, Inc. Used by permission; www.google.com.

As part of your preparation for blogging, here are some guidelines:

- The principal is aware of the blog.
- Parents provide permission for students to participate in the blog.
- All posting and commenting is monitored and approved by the teacher.
- Access to read posts and comments is by password only (shared with students and parents).
- Privacy is maintained; for example, no student names, rather initials or pseudonyms, no student profiles online, no recognizable student images.
- Students must read and sign a blog user agreement.

- Students must sign a district's Acceptable Use Policy (AUP), if available, and recognize it is applicable even when they use the blog from home.
- Consequences for misuse of the blog are spelled out in advance and administered through the school's student disciplinary system.
- The blog is hosted on a reputable, established Web site.
- The district Internet filtering does not block the chosen blogging tool.

Figure 2-10 illustrates a sample contract that you can modify. Other sample blog agreements can be found at:

- www.budtheteacher.com/wiki/index.php?title=Blogging_Rules—A blogging guide created by a Colorado teacher for his students
- http://classblogmeister.com/bloggers_contract.doc—A blogging pledge created by Blog-meister blogging service as a sample
- www.teachersfirst.com/content/blog/Sample%20Blogger%20Agreement.doc—A sample blogger agreement that you may edit to fit your circumstances

---

Figure 2-10. Blogging Contract

Purpose of the blog:

_____
_____
_____

Safety:

_____
_____
_____

Terms & Conditions:

_____
_____
_____

Consequences:

_____
_____
_____

Signatures:

I agree to the terms and conditions of the class blog for (name of class here) for the (add dates) school year. I permit my student to participate in the blogging project.

_____
Student signature   Date

_____
Parent signature   Date

Parent membership

I wish to be a registered member of the class blog. Please add me to the list:

_____

Rules for Writing Your Blog

It is important to set guidelines for students who are going to use the blog. Here are some rules to consider as you plan the blogging experience.

1. If you want to write your opinion on a topic, make sure you're not going to be offensive as you write it.
2. Always make sure you check over your post for spelling errors, grammar errors, and your use of words. Paste your post in a word processor and run spell check or download a spell checker for your browser.
3. Never disrespect someone else in your blog, whether it's a person, an organization, or just a general idea. You don't want someone making an inappropriate remark about something that is important to you; don't do it to someone else.
4. Don't write about other people without permission; if you can't get their permission, use first names only. Never share someone else's last name.
5. Watch your language! This is part of your school community. Language that is inappropriate in school is also inappropriate in your blog.
6. Make sure things you write about are factual. Don't be posting about things that aren't true. Link to your sources.
7. Keep the blog education-oriented. That means that you probably shouldn't discuss your plans for the weekend, the last dance, etc. (Adapted from http://patterson.edublogs.org/all-about-blogs/)

Once you have the blog set up, your next and most important consideration is how you will use it in the classroom to enhance student learning. Part 3 provides an illustration to show you how.

PART 3: PRACTICAL APPLICATIONS

Teachers have known for a long time that students develop better communication skills when they are authentically communicating. A number of educators are helping their students develop their writing skills by having them publish their work as blogs and then invite comments from other students in the class or students worldwide.

Unit Plan for Secondary English/Language Arts

A unit plan will illustrate using a blog or Weblog in writing assignments in the English/language arts classroom. This unit, for the secondary level, emphasizes writing across the curriculum because the writing topics focus on important issues in today's society. Students have the choice of selecting a topic about science, such as stem cell research, history, such as a political debate or heroes, or another curriculum area.

➤ URLs in different subject areas are available on Bev's Web site (www.neal-schuman.com/webclassroom) so educators can see models of this unit using other topics.

The unit is designed to make students think critically about both sides of a controversial issue and experience a variety of speaking and listening activities that integrate with reading and writing. Students will work individually, in small groups based on their topic, and with a partner to respond specifically to their writing. They will also use the Internet for research about their issue, place their writing on a blog and comment on other students' writing using the blog.

For our purposes we will be using an *edublog*, a blog written by someone with an interest in education. Examples of edublogs might include blogs written by or for teachers or librarians, blogs maintained for the purpose of classroom instruction or blogs written about educational policy.

I-Search Project

The Web gives teachers access to an enormous wealth of models for student writing. Ken Macrorie (1988) introduced the concept of the I-Search paper, which sees the research paper as "hunting stories" for which students seek answers to questions that interest them. The I-Search paper can differ from the traditional research paper in several ways. Often the topic for the paper is chosen by the student, although it must be something the student "needs" to know, not just a casual interest. In essence, the papers are stories of how and what students are discovering about topics. In this unit on a contemporary issue, the I-Search paper format is a natural vehicle to incorporate an Internet research component, as well as a blog to demonstrate the writing.

The topic for this I-Search paper—stem cell research—is a controversial subject that has been in the news frequently. This topic is broad enough to give students freedom to choose subtopics they are interested in and conduct research from various points of view.

A blog allows students to experience the writing as a public document rather than just a piece of paper that has been set before them. By making responses and revisions to posts publicly available to other students, the Weblog format enables the teacher to encourage the revision process. Because the teacher's response to a student's post is available to others, the teacher needs to make appropriate comments that encourage revision without criticizing the student or making the person uncomfortable. Furthermore, by publishing student writing, including drafts and revisions, on the Web, the class can make its writing process available to parents and community members at the discretion of the students. Moreover, the ease of creating hyperlinks on a blog provides students with an opportunity to point out sites that might be helpful to other students or information they would like class members to respond to.

Step 1: Apply Framework Standards—What Should Be Taught?

This unit supports the California framework standard of providing a challenging curriculum for all students studying English/language arts.

Content Standards

Secondary frameworks in English contain the following standards relevant to the assignment:

- The research will illustrate interdisciplinary connections.
- Students will use analysis and evaluation—critical-thinking skills—as they research their topic.
- The activities using the Internet will help develop students' research skills—to find answers to curriculum-related questions.
- Students will enhance their reading and writing skills, write for an authentic audience, and be able to communicate globally using blogs.

Performance-based assessment will be used to measure whether students can use the Internet to (1) find specific required information, (2) analyze and evaluate the information they research, (3) communicate that information to others, and (4) respond in a thoughtful way to student writing.

NETS Standards

In addition to curriculum content standards, the *National Educational Technology Standards for Students* (NETS) (2007) at http://cnets.iste.org/students/s_stands.html includes the following technology standards appropriate for this unit. Students will:

- Demonstrate creative thinking, construct knowledge, and develop innovative products and processes using technology, including:

- using digital media and environments to communicate and work collaboratively, even at a distance, to support individual learning and contribute to the learning of others;
- interacting, collaborating, and publishing with peers, experts or others employing a variety of digital environments and media;
- locating, organizing, analyzing, evaluating, synthesizing, and ethically using information from a variety of sources and media;
- evaluating and selecting information sources and digital tools based on the appropriateness to specific tasks; and
- processing data and reporting results.
- Practice digital citizenship by advocating and practicing safe, legal, and responsible use of information and technology.

As a result of engaging in the activities in this unit and working together using blogging, students will become information literate in using the Internet and Web 2.0 tools in the English/language arts classroom.

Step 2: Identify General Goals and Specific Objectives
The goals and main objectives for this unit are based on national standards for English, the California English Language Arts Framework and current NETS technology standards. After completing this unit, students should be prepared to do topical research, present opinions supported by research, question Internet content based on bias and collaborate and provide helpful responses to their peers on contemporary issues using the latest technology.

Goals
When searching for information for their I-Search project, students will:

- use search engines to find information about a current issue, specifically stem cell research;
- analyze and evaluate what they read, thus building critical thinking skills;
- use Web 2.0 tools, specifically blogging and RSS feeds, to improve reading, writing, and collaborating skills to become more information literate.

Objectives
More specifically, as part of each goal, students will:

- choose and link to appropriate Web sites to research information about stem cell research;
- identify bias and opinion in the information they find that is not based on fact;
- define blogs, identify their uses in English/language arts;
- create and use blogs to write and comment on a contemporary issue; and
- improve reading and writing skills using blogs.

Step 3: Gather Materials
Numerous Web sites provide information on contemporary issues like animal rights, abortion, stem cell research, immigration, and more. Sites are also available where educators and educational organizations help in teaching writing and illustrate writing projects. Some of the resources listed in Table 2-1 will be used in the activities in this unit for the example stem cell research.

Step 4: Introduce the Unit
This research unit on a contemporary issue introduces students to both sides of an issue from Web sites containing opinion only to factually based sites. Each search students complete will require that they employ increasingly higher levels of critical thinking from merely finding information, to

| Table 2-1. Sample URLs for Stem Cell Research Project ||
URL	Description
www.npr.org/takingissue/takingissue_stemcell .html	Arguing the ethics of stem cell research, an NPR site with pros and cons on the issue
www.npr.org/templates/story/story.php?storyId=14556298	Finding less controversial stem cell information
www.npr.org/templates/story/story.php?storyId=13961314	Stem cell research could rebuild heart tissue
www.npr.org/templates/story/story.php?storyId=11279411	Political point of view on stem cell research (Bush side)
www.npr.org/templates/story/story.php?storyId=5252449	Key moments in the stem cell debate
www.npr.org/templates/story/story.php?storyId=9533577	Q&A about the science behind the stem cell debate-exploding the myths
http://usliberals.about.com/od/stemcellresearch/Stem_Cell_Research_Basics_Issues_Advocacy_Positions.htm	Pros and cons of embryonic stem cell research
www.whitehouse.gov/news/releases/2001/08/20010809-2.html	Bush speech on stem cell research issue
http://archives.cnn.com/2001/HEALTH/07/17/stem.cell.hearing/	Political con side of embryonic research
www.biotechnologyonline.gov.au/human/sctypes.cfm	Types of stem cells
www.biotechnologyonline.gov.au/human/usessc.cfm	Potential uses of stem cells
www.biotechnologyonline.gov.au/human/ethicssc.cfm	Ethics of stem cell research; Australian student worksheet
www.bmj.com/cgi/content/full/ 332/7546/866?ijkey=B56vvkOcFrlPcPz&keytype=ref	Regulation of the collection and use of fetal stem cells

analyzing it for currency and concrete support, to synthesizing information from numerous sources and evaluating their own and other students' writing on the blogs through their comments. Students will work alone and in groups to gather the information and in pairs to critique each other's writing. Although students will brainstorm different issues and each group will ultimately select their own issue, we will follow the example of stem cell research through the activities.

The Product
The product for this unit will be divided into the following parts. Students will post information they find for their I-Search project on the classroom blog using the following format:

- *Part 1:* What do I want to know (statement of the problem)? The first posts will contain what they know, assume they know, or what they imagine about the topic they have chosen. This information will be posted during the introduction to the unit.
- *Part 2:* How do I find the information (procedures followed)? Here they must test the previous assumptions by researching the topic. They will use different forms of media from books and magazines to Internet Web site sources and blogs to authorities or agencies, to interviews, where possible. All sources must be documented as they proceed. Since the search process is written in the first person in narrative format, it is ideal for the informality of blog writing.

Students can record the steps they took to gather their data. They will also include important links to sites they visited containing valuable information about the topic. These activities will be conducted during the unit.

- *Part 3:* What did I learn (summary of findings)? When the research is completed, students should compare what they found out with what they assumed they knew before starting the research (Part 1). These blog posts will be completed just before follow-up to the unit.
- *Part 4:* What will I do with this information (conclusion)? Students must offer some personal comments and draw conclusions as part of the follow-up to the unit. In their last series of posts, they must also select an audience (e.g., their congressman) to try to persuade the person or group to a particular point of view.

Posts will be completed regularly with each student providing at least three (3) posts related to each question and at least three to five comments for each post from others' points of view.

The Process
As part of the process students from each team will be responsible for research and comments in each part of the I-Search project. Teachers will comment on student writing and their approaches to the issue. Students must respond to their classmates' posts. They will also answer any other comments, for example, those posted by parents or classes worldwide.

Step 5: Create Sample Activities

Activities to Begin the Unit
At the beginning of the unit, students must assess their prior knowledge about researching on the Internet and blogging. Information in Parts 1 and 2 of this chapter will provide background information.

As an introduction to this unit, students in each team of four will:

- Review and define vocabulary that will be used during the unit—for example, I-Search, blogging, Weblogs and more. See the glossary at the beginning of this chapter.
- Discuss what they know about several contemporary issues (e.g., animal rights, stem cell research, censorship and tolerance, immigration) and have students post their opinions on each issue on the blog.
- Create one post about what else they want to know about a particular issue. This will provide a brainstormed list with a series of questions the team wants to research.
- Select, based on the blog posts, an issue of common interest to the group to research.
- Select a team leader and divide the work so that each team member will find answers to certain questions.

Note: Depending on how the blog is set up, each team can do Parts 1 and 2 of the I-Search process on their own "team" blog and then start posts to the class blog.

Activities to Use During the Unit
Teams are now ready to start the research process. Each team member must gather a list of Web sites and/or blogs and other resources that represent both sides of the issue for the entire group to discuss. The list of sites for the stem cell topic in Table 2-1 provides a sample of resources. As students are working on their assignments, teachers should check on social skills of team members and for individual accountability. When teams complete their work, they will explain how their group reached a conclusion or made a decision. These spot checks and assurances help keep all

members working cooperatively and effectively together. Teachers may want teams to divide the following tasks among their members so each student is responsible for specific learning outcomes. Student progress reports are also a good idea to encourage individual accountability. See Figure 2-11.

During the unit, students will:

- Research part of the issue based on the questions that arose from the first series of posts and comments in Part 1, for example, What is the issue? Why is it a problem? Why can't different sides agree on a course of action? What are the ethical aspects? What are political ramifications? How may these issues affect presidential, congressional, and local elections? What are the benefits of this research? What groups may be represented in the controversy? Each team

---

Figure 2-11. Student Progress Report

Name: _____ Date: _____

Progress Report Number: _____

Tasks accomplished this week:

A. Stem Cell Research
1. _____
2. _____
3. _____
4. _____
5. _____

Problems encountered this week and ways I resolved them.
1. _____
2. _____

Successes I had this week.
1. _____
2. _____

The most exciting thing I learned/did this week.
_____
_____

Questions I have for my teacher this week.
_____
_____

Status of my progress:

_____ My team is progressing on schedule and we will be ready to turn our assignments in on time.

_____ My team needs more time because _____
_____

I am having trouble completing my part of the assignment because _____
_____
_____

member selects questions to answer and becomes the expert to inform other team members about the answers to these questions.

- Interview local groups, read newspaper articles, check the library to include other sources in their blog posts.
- Make sure each team member posts at least one or more entries a day.

Activities to Be Used as Follow-Up to the Unit

As follow-up to the unit, students should answer I-Search questions Parts 3 and 4. They should also reflect on using blogs in the English/language arts assignments. To complete these activities, students will:

- compare/contrast entries posted by each group after research on the issue with those that were placed on the blog when the unit was introduced;
- write posts that persuade their audience to some point of view based on their issue. For example, what can students do about this issue? As a worldwide issue, can they find other schools that might also be interested in commenting on or suggesting ways to resolve the issue?
- correspond with some person or organization that the team may be able to influence to make a difference on the issue;
- comment on how using a blog made or did not make a difference in the project. Did they enjoy the activity—why or why not?
- write posts about what they felt were important facts they learned about each issue;
- review entries different from those on the topic they researched, select two issues and write how they are similar and different; and
- complete a checklist about using a blog in English/language arts.

Step 6: Evaluate What Was Learned

It is important to evaluate both student work (the product) and students' working (the process). For this unit evaluation will be based on:

- Assessment of the blog entries posted by each group. For example, comments were thoughtful, encouraging more research or stretching thinking; team members contributed required number of posts; and posts exhibited standard American English. Evaluation will also take into account (a) content (the information was thorough and accurate) and (b) process (students were able to use the Internet for research and blogs for collaboration), (c) ability to differentiate fact from fiction, and (d) support their views with valid information. See Figure 2-12.
- Student self-evaluation of Internet research and blogging skills.
- Thoroughness with which students responded as peer evaluators.

Summary

This unit considered important contemporary issues where information about them is more easily found online or by interviews or listening to news on television and radio than in textbooks. To complete the assignments, students had to collaborate verbally, read critically, express their opinions using support in writing and evaluate others' opinions and writings using a blog format. This unit provides a bridge for English/language arts teachers to collaborate across curriculum areas to science, health, and social studies. Researching issues of importance in students' everyday lives makes practicing reading and writing more meaningful. Using Web 2.0 tools that students already use outside of school enables students to see how school and their everyday lives coincide and makes what they learn in school seem more authentic.

Figure 2-12. Research Evaluation Checklist

1. **Is it clear who has written the information?**

   Who is the author? Is it an organization or an individual person? Is there a way to contact them?

2. **Are the aims of the site clear?**

   What are the aims of the site? What is it for? Who is it for?

3. **Does the site achieve its aims?**

   Does the site do what it says it will?

4. **Is the site relevant to me?**

   List five things to find out from the site.
   1. _____
   2. _____
   3. _____
   4. _____
   5. _____

5. **Can the information be checked?**

   Is the author qualified to write the site? Has anyone else said the same things anywhere else? Is there any way of checking this out? If the information is new, is there any proof?

6. **When was the site produced?**

   Is it up to date? Can you check to see if the information is up to date and not just the site?

7. **Is the information biased in any way?**

   Has the site got a particular reason for wanting you to think in a particular way? Is it a balanced view or does it only give one opinion?

8. **Does the site tell you about choices open to you?**

   Does the site give you advice? Does it tell you about other ideas?

Teacher Exercises: Now You Try It . . .

To prepare your integrated plans using the Internet and RSS for research and blogs for communication, complete the following exercises:

1. Start your students out blogging by providing sample posts to which they must respond. This tests the concept before you create a complete unit.
2. Select one of the issues illustrated in the sample unit and research the sites listed in the unit as if you were a student in the class. This will allow you to experience the same activities, frustrations and skill-building as your students. You will also be able to identify where you might need to teach a specific skill or offer students additional help before you teach a unit containing Internet research and blogging.
3. Select a topic where you think a blog would be useful. Write a unit plan including the components in this unit.
4. Do one of the following:
   - Sign up for a blog at one of the sites listed in Part 2.
   - Post comments to a blog on a topic of interest to you.

Table 2-2. General URLs on Blogging	
URL	**Description**
http://millersenglish10.blogspot.com/	English teacher blog
www.copyblogger.com/embrace-brevity/	Tips for writing blogs
www.geocities.com/vance_stevens/papers/evonline 2002/week5.htm	Lots of blog examples
http://learnerblogs.org/	Free blogging service
http://librarygoddess.blogspot.com	A high school librarian who reviews books written for, or appropriate for, teens.
http://ewleditorials.blogspot.com/	Students write editorials on classic novels
www.weeklyreader.com/readandwriting/	Official blog of Read and Write Magazine Online
http://opencontent.org//docs/begin_blog.html	Beginner's guide to blogs
http://mywebspace.quinnipiac.edu/PHastings/ what.html	Blogging across the curriculum
www.alistapart.com/stories/writebetter/	Rules for writing good blog posts

> ➤ *For more exercises related to blogs and RSS, go to Bev's Web site at www.neal-schuman.com/webclassroom.*

CONCLUSION

Blogging offers several writing incentives with its emphasis on content, the possibility of speedy feedback, the option of working with both words and images, and the ability to link one post to another. Because students know they're going to have an audience, they often produce higher quality work for their blogs than students who write only for the teacher.

REFERENCES AND FURTHER READING

"Blogging to Teach Reading." (January 20, 2007). Available: http://weblogg-ed.com/2007/blogging-to-teach-reading/ (accessed October 1, 2008).

California State Department of Education. 1987. *English—Language Arts Framework for California Public Schools: Kindergarten Through Grade Twelve*. Sacramento: California State Department of Education.

Grunwald, Peter. "Stats on Kids and New Media." FETC 2006 presentation on March 23, 2006. Available: www.speedofcreativity.org/2006/03/23/stats-on-kids-and-new-media/ (accessed: March 18, 2008).

Irwin, Tanya. "Study: Kids Are Master Multitaskers On TV, Web, Mobile." *Online Media Daily*. (March 10, 2008). Available: http://publications.mediapost.com/index.cfm?fuseaction=Articles.showArticle&artaid= 78118 (accessed October 1, 2008).

Lenhart, Amanda, and Susannah Fox. "A Blogger Portrait." *Pew Internet & American Life Project Report*, The Pew Research Center. (July 19, 2006). Available: http://pewresearch.org/pubs/236/a-blogger-portrait (accessed October 1, 2008).

Macrorie, Ken. 1988. *The I-Search Paper: Revised Edition of Searching Writing.* Portsmouth, NH: Boyn-ton/Cook.

"National Survey of Internet Usage: Teachers, Computer Coordinators, and School Librarians, Grades 3-12." 1997. *The Heller Report* 2, no. 9 (March).

Oatman, Eric. "Blogomania." *School Library Journal.* Available: www.schoollibraryjournal.com/article/CA632382.html (accessed April 13, 2008).

Richardson, Will. "Metablognition," *Weblogg-Ed.* (April 27, 2004). Available: www.weblogg-ed.com/2004/04/27 (accessed October 1, 2008).

CHAPTER 3

Experiencing History Through Podcasts

PART 1: IDEAS AND INSIGHTS

It has been said that in October of 2004 a Google search returned less than 6,000 results for the term "podcasting." Today, a similar search yields more than 857,000 results. As with any new technology, getting started is the hardest part. Educators hear the word "podcast" or "Webcast" and duck their heads and look in the opposite direction. However, teachers who have really involved themselves in using podcast technology have made the following comments regarding the ease of it: David Warlick (Landmarks for Schools; www.landmark-project.com) says, "All you need is a computer, access to the Internet, and a microphone that you can buy from Toys 'R' Us." Kathy Schrock (Nauset Public Schools; http://nausetschools.org/podcasts.htm) says, "Just the word podcast scares teachers away. There are a lot of misconceptions." She feels so strongly about using this technology that she gives workshops for teachers on using podcasting in the classroom.

Podcasting is becoming highly popular, especially with the younger generation. According to a phone survey conducted by the Pew Internet and American Life Project (Rainie and Madden, 2005) between February and March of 2005, approximately 29 percent of the 22 million people who owned iPods or other MP3 players had downloaded podcasts (more than 6 million people). There has been a corresponding increase in the number of podcasts that are available. On feedburner.com, an Internet news delivery system, for instance, the number of podcasts grew from about 200 in November 2004 to 13,782 in August 2005 (Crofts et al., accessed 2008). And, according to eMarketer, a respected market research firm, 2007 was a banner year for podcasting in that the U.S. podcast audience grew to 18.5 million in 2007 and is on track to increase 251 percent to 65 million in 2012. These statistics suggest that it is time for educators to take a look at this technology (Petersen, accessed 2008).

Objectives of This Chapter

This chapter is designed for use by social studies educators at both the elementary and secondary levels. Teachers in other subject areas can adapt the unit plan in Part 3 to their subject. After reading Chapter 3 and working through the exercises, teachers and librarians will be able to:

- guide students in Internet research and transform the research into a product;
- understand the basics of podcasting and why to use podcasts;
- find and listen to podcasts on the Internet;
- organize their own podcasts; and
- create a unit using podcast technology.

Many educators today are familiar with conducting research on the Internet and, if they are not, most of their students are. Information from different sites reveals many different viewpoints on the same historical figure or event and requires students to think critically about the validity and bias of the information. In addition, schools can now take advantage of the newer technology and analyze and synthesize their research into new formats employing audio and video, thus enhancing instruction for all learning styles.

> ➤ *For examples in other subject areas and different grade levels, go to Bev's Web site at www.neal-schuman.com/webclassroom.*

Glossary

Review the following terms before starting the chapter to fully understand the concepts discussed.

Audacity: A free digital audio editor application.

digital media player: A consumer electronics device that is capable of storing and playing digital media such as blogs, podcasts, and wikis.

download: To transfer a file from the Internet or other computer to your own computer.

GarageBand: A software application that allows users to create music or podcasts.

host: The person who introduces the podcast and each of its segments.

ID3 tags: Allows information such as the title, artist, album, track number, or other information about the file to be stored in the file itself.

iTunes: A free digital media player that runs on your computer.

Levelator: A free application that adjusts the audio levels within an audio segment.

MP3: A popular format for digital audio.

podcast: A series of digital media files which are distributed over the Internet using RSS feeds for playback on MP3 players and computers.

storyboard: A representation to present and describe interactive events, including audio and motion, for the purpose of previsualizing the final product.

upload: To transfer a file from a computer to the Internet.

Introduction

One of the so-called Web 2.0 technologies is the podcast. Podcasting can be an important tool in education because the technology is easy to use and allows students, teachers, librarians, administrators, and parents to share information at any time. Podcasts can be used in a variety of ways. Teachers can create a podcast of a lesson so that absent students can keep up to date with content they have missed. Podcasts provide the vehicle for keeping in touch with parents on their students' progress, homework assignments, and special events at the school. Administrators use podcasts for school announcements. Librarians create book talks as podcasts. Podcasts enhance the curriculum in a range of ways from broadcasting interviews, sending pen-pal letters, publishing oral presentations, and more. Video podcasts, to a lesser degree, are also used.

In addition, podcasts enhance cooperative learning, allowing students in small groups to interact with one another, learn from each other, solve problems together, and use one another as resources. The unit plan in Part 3 requires students to work together to organize the project and delegate tasks among group members. They will have to listen to one another's ideas and comments, ask questions of each other, respect the opinions of others, and share ideas and thinking. Only by helping each other can groups create successful podcasts.

Part 1 of this chapter examines podcast technology—what it is, why use it in education—and provides examples to illustrate its use in the classroom with today's curriculum. Part 2 provides tips on equipment, services that educators suggest, and steps to put together a podcast. Finally, Part 3 lays out a step-by-step unit plan with objectives, activities, and evaluation. Two sets of exercises are included. One exercise after Part 2 involves educators practicing what they have learned about the technology, and the other after Part 3 has them formulate plans to create their own podcasts in a curriculum area. Tables containing Web sites for the unit and general Web sites to visit for more information on podcasts complete the chapter.

What Is a Podcast?

The word "podcast" combines two words to make a new word: (1) POD from the well-known music player iPOD or "playable on demand," and (2) broadcast. Podcasts are one-way, non-interactive communications. According to Wikipedia (http://en.wikipedia.org/), "a podcast is a collection of digital media files which is distributed over the Internet, often using syndication feeds (e.g., RSS or Atom feeds) for playback on portable media players and computers." Thus, a podcast can be downloaded automatically using software capable of reading RSS or Atom feeds. A podcast is audio or visual content that is automatically delivered over a network via free subscription. Once subscribed to, podcasts can be regularly distributed over the Internet or within a school's network and accessed with an iPod or a computer. The essential element of a podcast, what makes it "subscribable," is an RSS (Really Simple Syndication) feed. If you have a Web site or podcasting host that creates an RSS feed for you, you don't have to worry about this technical aspect of podcasting. (See Chapter 2 for more about RSS feeds.) The most common type of audio podcast is an MP3 file. Enhanced podcasts can have images to go along with the audio.

Why Use Podcasting?

There are many educational benefits both for teachers and students in using podcasts. Children acquire social skills by working together, learning to write, organizing and delivering information when they have an authentic audience, and they enjoy themselves in the process. More specifically,

- Podcasting easily engages a population of diverse learners.
- Students can work together to script, record, and edit a podcast that can be stored and easily shared with a potentially worldwide audience. Knowing that there is a real-world audience gives students purpose and motivation to create a spectacular product.
- When students create a podcast to present an argument and provide the specific details to support it, they are learning to think, to be logical, and to process information effectively, as well as to communicate.
- When creating a podcast, they are also building twenty-first-century skills such as problem solving, collaboration, and the ability to gather and analyze data.
- Students can edit and revise until what they say and how they say it is perfected.
- Students can save the podcast for other students, friends, and family members to listen to, learn from, and enjoy.
- For teachers, evaluating podcasts of the information students share can offer a very natural formative assessment tool. Teachers can assess student skills from the effectiveness of the arguments, use of technology, and presentation skills.
- The process of putting together an audio recording is extremely valuable in that it brings together different curriculum areas, such as language arts, science or social studies.

Classroom Podcast Examples

An important aspect of beginning work with a new technology is to view examples where the tool is being integrated into a lesson. This provides a model from which to get ideas for your own podcast. The following examples provide models for different grade levels and subject areas.

Example 1: Kidcast in the Classroom

The idea initiated by Dan Schmit is now a worldwide project. Entitled "Where in the World?" this project is a global geography podcasting quiz. The goal is to learn about geography, culture, and community (see Figure 3-1).

Figure 3-1. Kidcast

Where in the World?
A global geography podcasting quiz!

We are about to launch a new podcast quiz show created by students from all over the world focused on learning about geography, community, and culture. We want your students to be a part of it!

To participate in the *creation* of a "Where in the World?" podcast just follow these directions:

1. Plan and create a short podcast featuring your students giving creative clues about where they are in the world. You may choose your actual location OR you can choose to describe somewhere else in the world. You can use the scaffold below to help guide your production.

Students plan and create a short podcast in which they give clues about where they are in the world, either their actual location or somewhere else in the world. Instructions on the Web site at www.intelligenic.com/where/where.pdf tell schools how to participate, from what the podcast should contain to how to submit and subscribe to the podcast, and participate in the quiz show. Listening, deductive reasoning, and geography skills are required to solve the puzzle.

Example 2: ColeyCasts

Mr. Brent Coley teaches fifth grade at Tovashal Elementary School and has involved his students in creating podcasts in a number of subject areas. His students have created a podcast to describe space including planets, constellations, the sun and galaxies, another for poetry, one for weather and a culminating activity for their immigration unit on Ellis Island. Check this site at www.mrcoley.com/coleycast/index.htm for examples in different subject areas, as well as many tips to get started. Notice the different podcasts in Figure 3-2.

Example 3: Coulee Kids

At Longfellow Middle School in La Crosse, Wisconsin, seventh grade students have created the Coulee Kids' Podcasts. The Coulee teachers have organized the La Crosse curriculum into monthly themes, questions, and problems for students to explore. Since the curriculum takes place in an integrated learning environment, content from social studies, science, and math are often included in language arts activities. Coulee kids have created podcasts for several years ranging from adaptations to Shakespeare plays (e.g., *Romeo and Juliet*, *Hamlet*, and others), how the first day of seventh grade is different from other years, a genetics symposium, as well as podcasts about ants and crayfish. Students write storyboards, conference about the content, edit, perform, analyze the raw footage, combine the audio with photos or video, work in teams, and meet the class deadlines. They develop higher-order thinking skills, their ability to write, select facts, develop and organize ideas and content, and communicate orally. For example, for one podcast students wrote adaptations of each act and scene of a play and then performed the play. Review Coulee Kids' podcasts at www.sdlax.net/longfellow/sc/ck/index.htm to see a list of podcasts and listen to some of the excellent presentations (see Figure 3-3).

Figure 3-2. ColeyCasts

ColeyCast #26 *Enhanced Podcast
Spotlight on Poetry
"Fortunately, Unfortunately" Poems
Posted February 26, 2008

Click to subscribe
in iTunes

ColeyCast #25 *Enhanced Podcast
Early English Settlements in North America
Henry Hudson, Roanoke, Jamestown, and the Pilgrims
Posted December 8, 2007

Click to download
iTunes

ColeyCast #24 *Enhanced Podcast
Space
Galaxies, Constellations, the Sun, and Nine Planets
Posted December 8, 2007

Click to download
QuickTime

States & Capitals
State Report
Science
Art
iPod Flash Cards
Club Ed
WHC
Student of the Week
Parents
Calendar
Lunch Menu
Student Links
Teacher Links
Classroom Taxes
Class Info
Website FAQs
Meet Mr. Coley
E-Mail Mr. Coley
E-Mail Mrs. Coley
Tovashal

Source: Used by permission of Brent Coley; www.mrcoley.com.

Figure 3-3. Coulee Kids' Podcasts

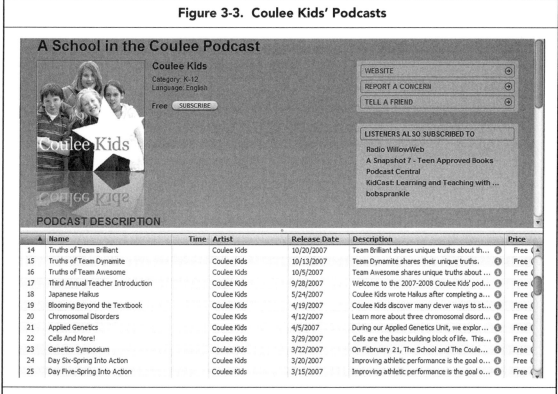

Source: Used by permission of Jeanne Halderson and Elizabeth Ramsay; http://www.sdlax.net/longfellow/sc/ck/index.htm.

In addition, the Coulee kids, in conjunction with the League of Women Voters in La Crosse, created a series of podcasts about women who made a difference titled, "The Road She Traveled." The site contains: docudramas about the women and interviews with the special women by the Coulee students. Coulee students donated this series to the community of La Crosse.

> ➤ Find URLs for additional examples at various grade levels at Bev's Web site at www.neal-schuman.com/webclassroom.

PART 2: GETTING STARTED

One educator said, "All it takes to create a podcast is (GarageBand included with iLife for a Mac computer), a built-in microphone, and your students' creativity." Actually, although the technology is easy to learn, preparation is important. Educators must train students to know their audience, pick a theme, research their point, organize the presentation and, of course, practice. As in writing an essay, a podcast must have a beginning, middle, and end. Research may be necessary and preparing the podcast requires students to work together.

Steps to Create a Podcast

Six simple steps will enable you to create your first podcast. Here's how it works.

Step 1: Select Your Equipment

To create a podcast, all you need is your own microphone, some software, and the ability to talk into that microphone. Here's the equipment needed:

- *Recording equipment.* No matter what type of microphone you choose, try to find one that cancels background noise. A good microphone won't eliminate all of the background noise, but it will help to keep it to a minimum. Background noise can destroy a recording, so it is important to filter out as much as possible. Moreover, student presenters will talk at different volumes; thus, some will be louder than others. One of the good solutions to level out discrepancies in volume is the Levelator from The Conversations Network (www.conversations network.org/levelator/). It is free and easy to use, by just dragging the podcast files into the Levelator icon on your desktop.
- *Editing equipment.* Some of the most popular editing equipment includes the following:
  - **Audacity** is a free software tool that can be used to edit in a Windows or Mac environment (http://audacity.sourceforge.net). See Figure 3-4.
  - **GarageBand**, popular with educators, comes free with Macs. (www.apple.com/ilife/garageband).
  - **VoiceThread**, also free, provides premium accounts to educators with unlimited bandwidth and lets students comment from home, via audio or text, about pictures or documents (www.voicethread.com). See Chapter 7 for more information.
- *Music.* Music can announce the introduction to your podcast, supply background, and provide transitions between different segments. Often, music is copyrighted and cannot be used without incurring cost. However, sites abound with royalty-free sounds including Soundzabound (www.soundzabound.com), RoyaltyFreeMusic.com, The Music Bakery (www.musicbakery .com), and The FreeSound Project, a collaborative database of licensed sounds with a Creative Commons license (http://freesound.iua.upf.edu/index.php).
- Other equipment for uploading podcasts for distribution is also needed.

Figure 3-4. Audacity

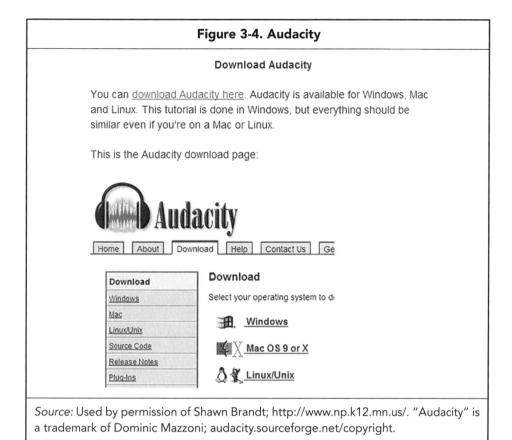

Source: Used by permission of Shawn Brandt; http://www.np.k12.mn.us/. "Audacity" is a trademark of Dominic Mazzoni; audacity.sourceforge.net/copyright.

- **Feedburner** (www.feedburner.com), recently acquired by Google, sends more than 1.1 million "feeds" to nearly 600,000 users. By signing up for feeds, any educator can keep tabs on what's happening in any other classroom across the country (see Figure 3-5).
- **iTunes** (www.itunes.com) for PC or Mac is a digital media player application for playing and organizing digital music and video files.

Figure 3-5. Feedburner

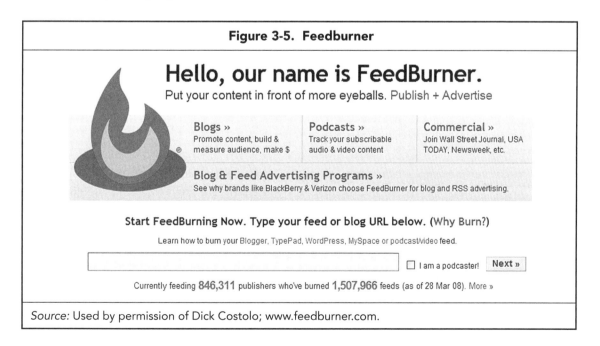

Source: Used by permission of Dick Costolo; www.feedburner.com.

Step 2: Plan for Recording

Before students even think of stepping up to the microphone, much planning must be done. In fact, preproduction may take over three-quarters of the time to produce a podcast. Planning puts the focus on learning, not on the technology. Several things need to be considered:

- *Consider the audience.* Who will listen to the podcast? Is it everyone in the school? Is it parents? Is it students in another state or at another grade level? Determining who exactly the audience is should help focus the podcast.
- *Name the podcast.* The podcast will need a name—the more creative, the better. Since listeners search podcasts on the Internet, an intriguing name can catch the eye of a prospective listener. Often names are added to each segment of the recording to emphasize the theme of the podcast.
- *Decide on the format.* Who will actually be heard in the recording? Should you have a host? What segments do you plan for the show?
- *Consider the length.* This will be based on your content and audience. Some teachers have everyone pair up in class. The pairs all write segments. Then the pairs present the segments to the entire class. The teacher and students then select which segments should be included in the podcast. This way everyone is involved, the podcast gets the best segments, and the recording will be an appropriate length.
- *Write a storyboard.* A script will allow students to know exactly what they are going to say, when they will speak, and whether they will speak alone or with a partner. Additionally, music and visuals should be planned at this time.

Step 3: Record the Podcast

- Before students record, they should practice reading their scripts out loud, paying special attention to speaking loudly, clearly, and slowly. The speaker must learn to control his/her volume, speed, and fluency.
- Technically, speakers should start with a few sample recordings to test the software, adjust volume levels, and make sure everything works.
- Consider the following tips when recording:
  - Know your segment very well. Have it close to memorized.
  - Speak slowly and clearly so that your audience can understand you.
  - Do not touch or move the microphone. You will hear it on the recording.
  - Be quiet if you are not the speaker. The microphone is sensitive and will pick up any little noises in the background.
  - Avoid rustling your papers when at the microphone. Put the paper on the table if you need to read from it.
  - Be interested in what you are saying—your voice will show it if you're not.
  - Do not move around when speaking into the microphone; plant your feet.
  - Do not get too close to the microphone. It will distort your voice and your audience won't be able to understand you.

Step 4: Postprocess the Recording

- Now it's time to edit. In most cases, that means cutting out mistakes and long stretches of silence. Edit the recording wisely and rerecord sections where necessary. Check files for length as typical student podcasts should run about 10 minutes at a time so listeners do not get bored. Remove dead spaces when no one is talking (see Figure 3-6).

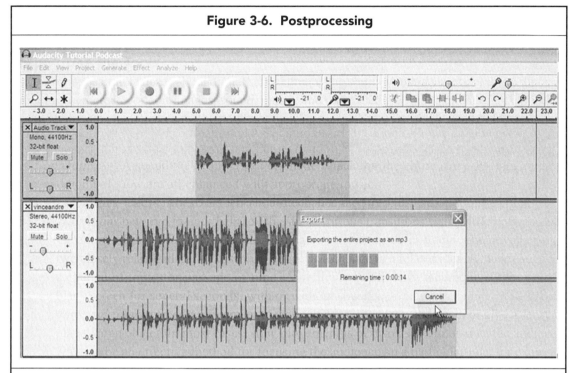

Figure 3-6. Postprocessing

Source: Used by permission of Shawn Brandt; http://www.np.k12.mn.us/. "Audacity" is a trademark of Dominic Mazzoni; audacity.sourceforge.net/copyright.

- Add music to introduce the podcast. You might consider music between segments if there are different types of speeches such as on a radio broadcast.
- Once the podcast sounds just the way you want it, it is time to upload the podcast.

Step 5: Upload the Podcast

- Convert the audio file to MP3 format. MP3 is the standard format being used in podcasting.
- Upload the podcast files that include a description of your podcast, a link to the corresponding MP3 file, and other information. There are a number of Web sites that will hold your recording for free. Create a blog on a free Web site (e.g., Blogger, Word Press) and post your material there so it is available for others. If your school has a Web site, this is another place to create a specific directory for the podcast. See Chapter 2 to see how to create the blog.
- An MP3 file contains information about the artist, album, genre, etc., stored in ID3 tags. iTunes and Windows Media Player use these tags to organize the MP3s, so you may want to add this information before uploading it.
- Test all files using any MP3 player to make sure they are ready for distribution.

Step 6: Publish the Podcast

- Create a newsfeed for your podcasts. These are RSS files describing your podcasts that contain information for each and link to the MP3 files you have created.
- To help attract an audience to your podcast, submit your link to podcast directories such as iTunes or promote it on sites such as the educational Podcast Directory. Such sites include links for downloading your podcast. By submitting your podcast to one of these directories, your podcast can be accessed by a large group of people.

> ➤ *Review additional details about storyboarding and recording a podcast at Bev's Web site at www.neal-schuman.com/webclassroom.*

Teacher Exercises: Now You Try It . . .

You have completed Parts 1 and 2 where you learned about the new technology of podcasting and how it might help you teach your students. Take a moment now to get some hands-on practice with what you have learned. Complete the following exercises so you have a good understanding of the technology before putting it together with the educational aspects of creating a lesson.

1. Explore some of the tutorials for either GarageBand (www.apple.com/support/garageband/) or Audacity (http://audacity.sourceforge.net/help/documentation). Write basic step-by-step instructions that you and your students can use to learn how to use the software.
2. Visit a couple of free music sites, listen to several clips, note the names if they seem appropriate for introductory music. Try downloading a music clip.
3. Visit each of the example podcast sites in Part I and listen to the student podcasts. Reflect in your Web 2.0 notebook, identifying what you like about the podcast, how you think your students might react to participating in one and what you might do to prevent any unforeseen difficulties from arising.
4. If you really feel confident, sign up using RSS to receive one of the podcasts that you find most meets your needs and with which you feel most comfortable.

Now that you have had some personal experience with these technology tools, it's time to put them together with the important part, the educational value of integrating the technology with a content-based unit plan.

> ➤ *More exercises are available at Bev's Web site at www.neal-schuman.com/webclassroom.*

PART 3: PRACTICAL APPLICATIONS

Immigration has become an extremely controversial topic in the news, in political circles, and among countries. The United States has, from its beginnings, been a magnet for immigration all over the world. It has continued to provide ethnic groups with a haven from political, religious, and cultural persecution. Many immigrants have come to the United States to achieve the "American Dream." But, what is the American Dream? How does one achieve it? How does a person know when he/she has achieved it? Is it the same for all Americans? How has the American Dream changed over time?

Unit Plan for Social Studies on Immigration

This unit on immigration is designed to get students involved in activities in which they can research an immigrant through primary source materials, including newspapers, photos, interviews, diaries, autobiographies, and other resources. Before doing the research on their person, they will explore the American Memory site on the Internet to view some primary sources that show backgrounds of immigrants when they arrived in this country, their experiences at Ellis Island, where they chose to live, and what their dreams were in coming to America. Once students feel comfortable with the source material, they will begin the first of two projects.

The first project begins with the broad study of a historical character, for example, an African-American slave, a western pioneer, or a nineteenth-century European immigrant. This will require research into the background of the characters—where did they migrate from? Where did they settle? What factors caused them to come to America? Why did they settle in a particular area and how did the area where they lived contribute to the persons they became? What events may have triggered success and what is meant by success? Have they achieved the "American Dream"? The person will be studied in historical context so students understand the economic, social, and political conditions of the times. A podcast interview between the immigrant and the interviewer will be the culminating activity.

Based on what students learned from their research into the past and what immigrants faced in the nineteenth century, the second project requires students to reflect upon their personal dreams for themselves and the nation—what they consider to be success and how they can achieve it. Does today's generation have an American Dream? What advice would they give future generations? The culminating activity for this project will also be a podcast.

This unit bases activities and tasks on national standards and state framework goals and objectives. It illustrates some of the resources that are available for projects on the Internet, offers suggestions on how to integrate them into the social studies curriculum and requires that students become familiar with Web 2.0 technology. Finally, it provides a model for creative teachers to use as they review their own subject matter for other units and as they tailor the activities to meet the needs of their own students. There are five steps in this unit:

1. Apply framework standards.
2. Identify general goals and specific objectives.
3. Gather materials including Web sites.
4. Create sample activities to be used throughout the lesson process.
5. Provide for evaluation.

Step 1: Apply Framework Standards—What Should Be Taught?

An important area in courses in American history is the study of major social and cultural changes that have taken place as the United States developed. One major change has occurred in immigration policies, especially the recent reopening of America's borders to immigrants from Asia and Central America.

Study of immigrants can be traced throughout the K–12 curriculum. In second grade, children listen to stories about men and women from other cultures who have made contributions in America. In fifth grade, as part of U.S. history and geography, students learn more about immigrants who came to this country, the hardships they faced and where they settled. In eleventh grade, students explore in more depth the significance of immigration in producing more cultural diversity. Thus, the curriculum provides for an integrated and sequential framework from the elementary grades through high school.

Standards accommodated in this unit include these:

- Understands issues concerning the disparities between ideals and reality in American political and social life
- Gathers and uses information for research purposes
- Connects learning of the past with the present
- Supports a variety of content-appropriate teaching methods that engage students actively in the learning process
- Emphasizes critical thinking skills, reading, writing, speaking, and listening as stressed in the language arts

This unit combines content about immigration with language, the medium for all learning. Additionally, the *National Educational Technology Standards for Students and Teachers* (NETS) (2007), which are necessary to work and live in the twenty-first century, are also an integral part of this unit.

Step 2: Identify General Goals and Specific Objectives

As part of their growth and development throughout their school careers, students will work independently, competitively, and cooperatively on tasks and projects. During this unit, the primary focus will be students working cooperatively to create the podcast.

Goals

At the end of this unit, students will:

- explain the factors that caused immigrants to come to America in the nineteenth century and compare those with reasons why today's immigrants come;
- brainstorm the reasons that have sparked increased immigration to the United States in recent times;
- use technology for research and presentation; and
- investigate life stories of recent immigrants to explain the reasons for their decisions to emigrate from their homelands and the challenges they face in moving to a new land.

Content-Related Objectives

After performing activities in this unit, students will be able to:

- identify contributions of different ethnic groups;
- conduct research on issues and interests by generating ideas and questions, and by posing problems. They will gather, evaluate, and synthesize data from a variety of sources (e.g., print and nonprint texts, artifacts, people) to communicate their discoveries in ways that suit their purpose and audience;
- use a variety of technological and information resources (e.g., libraries, databases, computer networks, video, audio) to gather and synthesize information and to create and communicate knowledge;
- develop ideas and content, organization, word choice, voice, sentence fluency, conventions, and presentation;
- determine new immigrants' common experiences;
- write a script for their podcasts;
- define, present, and defend in their podcast their ideas about what the American Dream has been through the decades; and
- present in a podcast what they have uncovered from inquiry and research relevant to their own American Dream.

Technology Objectives

The *National Educational Technology Standards for Students* (2007) includes standards for using technology. Based on these new standards, students will:

- organize their own podcast on the topic of immigration;
- work together to create the podcast;
- record their podcast segment on the topic of immigration;
- create a visual to accompany the audio;

- use their vocal abilities as an effective tool to portray a message; and
- use the technology to publish their podcast.

Note: Depending on the age of the students, the teacher may need to edit the podcast.

Step 3: Gather Materials

For this unit, educators will have students look at different resources to collect information for two podcasts they will create. Some resources may be found on the Internet or in the school or public libraries. Students will find:

- Primary source material including photos of immigrants, audio where they speak about their experiences, maps to locate their countries of origin, newspapers, and other historical documents (see Table 3-1 for URLs to check)
- Secondary sources such as oral interviews with relatives, family members and friends, as well as pictures, records, and other documents

Table 3-1. URLs for Immigrant Unit	
URL	**Description**
http://lcweb2.loc.gov/learn/lessons/psources/types .html	Types of primary sources
http://memory.loc.gov/learn/features/immig/interv/toc.php	Interviews with immigrants
www.pbs.org/wnet/americannovel/video/ANamericandream.html	Video of comments on the American Dream
http://library.thinkquest.org/20619/Past.html	Stories of immigrants of the past
http://memory.loc.gov/cgi-bin/query/r?ammem/papr:@filreq%28 @field%28NUMBER+@band%28lcmp002+m2 a10987%29%29+@field%28COLLID+newyork%29%29	Film of immigrants landing at Ellis Island
http://library.thinkquest.org/20619/Eivirt.html	Immigrant remembrances at Ellis Island
http://library.thinkquest.org/20619/Timeline.html	Timeline on U.S. immigration
http://library.thinkquest.org/20619/Present.html	Stories from present immigrants
www.pbs.org/independentlens/newamericans/for educators_lesson_plan_09.html#HistoryAssignment	Sample immigrant interview
www.pbs.org/now/transcript/transcript_alhibri.html	Bill Moyer interview with Muslim scholar
www.pbs.org/independentlens/newamericans/newamericans .html	Stories of new immigrants
www.pbs.org/independentlens/newamericans/sharestories.html	Immigrant stories
www-lib.iupui.edu/kade/unit19/apen19-h.html	German immigrant story
http://memory.loc.gov/ammem/papr/nychome.html	Immigrants landing at Ellis Island
http://lcweb2.loc.gov/ammem/wpaintro/exinterv.html http://lcweb2.loc.gov/ammem/wpaintro/indlore.html	Interview excerpts with immigrants
www.clarkhumanities.org/	Oral histories and interviews written by students about immigrants

Step 4: Create Sample Activities

There are four basic aspects to the unit:

1. Learning about primary source materials
2. Understanding the problems, contributions, and conditions existing in the United States when different ethnic groups came to America and why they came
3. Comparing and contrasting "American Dreams" of the immigrants they researched and their own dreams and how they might achieve them for themselves and their country.
4. Using the Web 2.0 tool—a podcast—to present information

Activities to Introduce the Unit

At the beginning of the unit it is important to draw upon students' prior knowledge. These tasks will review some of the concepts about different ethnic groups that students learned in earlier grades and increase their knowledge of immigration and primary sources. As a class students will:

- *Review primary sources.* Review several types of sources (e.g., published documents, unpublished documents, photographs and interviews) (http://lcweb2.loc.gov/learn/lessons/psources/types.html). Use questions (Figure 3-7) to analyze the sources they reviewed.

Figure 3-7. Questions About Primary Sources

Directions: When you review primary sources, you should not take everything you see or hear at face value. You should look analytically at photographs, historical documents, or maps. Look carefully at the document, and try to answer the following questions to help judge its authenticity, quality and usefulness.

A. Quality of Document

- Who created the source and why? Was it created through a thoughtful, deliberate process?

  _____

- Did the creator have firsthand knowledge of the event? Or, did the creator report what others saw and heard?

  _____

- Was the creator a neutral party, or did he/she have opinions or interests that might have influenced what was recorded?

  _____

- Verify the dates and places mentioned in the document?

  _____

- Compare the information with other primary and secondary sources. Is it valid?

  _____

- Did the recorder wish to inform or persuade others? (Check the words in the source. The words may tell you whether the recorder was trying to be objective or persuasive.) Did the recorder have reasons to be honest or dishonest?

  _____

- Was the information recorded during the event, immediately after the event, or after some lapse of time? How large a lapse of time?

  _____

(Cont'd.)

Figure 3-7. Questions About Primary Sources *(Continued)*

B. How useful is the document for your topic?

- What information is useful for developing your topic?

  _____

- How will you use the information in your research?

  _____

- Is any information biased or incorrect?

  _____

- *Watch a short video.* Watch the video on PBS where immigrants comment on what makes the American Dream.
- *Discuss the American Dream.* Discuss what the term "American Dream" means to them and what kinds of qualities the characters have that relate to the American Dream.
- *Create a cluster diagram.* Map out all reasons they can think of why immigrants came to America, what they planned to achieve, what they were leaving behind, and what they expected when they arrived (see Figure 3-8).

Figure 3-8. Immigrant Cluster

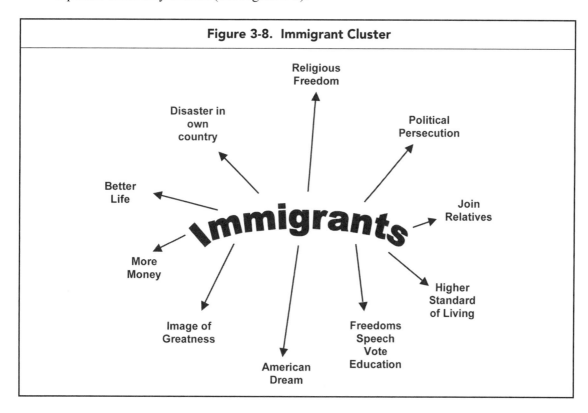

Activities to Use During the Unit

Activities to be completed during the unit will be based on both the content and technology objectives. In teams of four, students will:

- *Read immigrants' stories.* Select five (5) stories of immigrants that have the same ancestry, if possible. Stories might describe coming to Ellis Island, settling in a specific part of the country, trials or successes they encountered.

- *Compare/contrast immigrants' pasts and present.* Select at least five (5) interviews from "Interviews with Today's Immigrants." Select at least two (2) from the regions that their ancestors came from and three (3) from a completely different area of the world. As students listen to the interviews, they will make a checklist of questions (see Figure 3-9) that the interviewees answered, identify reasons the immigrants came to the United States, and see if they can tell what the immigrants' American dreams are.

Figure 3-9. Oral Interview Guide Sheet

Interviewer: _____

Immigrant: _____

Q: What country are you originally from?
A: _____
_____

Q: Why did you leave this country?
A: _____
_____

Q: What were the conditions in the country when you left?
A: _____
_____

Q: Why did you choose the United States? Why not some other country?
A: _____
_____

Q: What changes in lifestyle did you make when you came here?
A: _____
_____

Q: What were your hopes for yourself (and/or your family) when you came here? Have you realized these hopes?
A: _____
_____

Q: Were your expectations of America met? Was your idea of America the same as the reality?
A: _____
_____

Other possible questions:
- When did you leave your home country? How old were you at that time?
- What was your first impression of the United States? Has this initial impression changed over time?
- What are some of the differences/similarities you've noticed in the cultures here and in your home country?
- How were you treated when you first arrived in the United States? How are you treated now?
- Who came with you when you emigrated? Who did you leave behind? What did you leave behind?

- *Identify the American Dream.* Based on the stories and research, consider what immigrants think about the idea of the "American Dream." They will consider what the American Dream is, if anyone still believes in it, if it is still achievable, what drives people to pursue it, and do they think they have achieved it.

- *Create interview questions.* In pairs, assume the role of the interviewer and immigrant in order to write questions that the interviewer will ask the new immigrant and the answers the immigrant will give. This conversation forms the basis of their podcast script. These questions will be based on the research they did, as well as interviews they conducted.
- *Write answers for the interview questions.* Based on their reading, each pair will create answers to the questions. Both questions and answers will be used during the podcast. See a sample interview at www.pbs.org/independentlens/newamericans/foreducators_lesson_plan_09.html#HistoryAssignment.
- *Write the segment including the storyboard.* Make sure that you introduce the broadcaster/host at the beginning of the segment and each of the participants.

Plan the podcast. Preplanning activities are the most important part of creating the podcast. The goal is to get all students to participate, whether in writing the script, presenting the material, or postprocessing or publishing. During these activities students will work on the technical aspects of the podcast. Students will work together in pairs to:

- *Assume a role in the podcast:* write a segment, host the podcast, name the podcast, write the teaser that introduces the podcast, deliver a segment or assume other possible roles (e.g., compiling visuals).
- *Select music for the podcast* and determine where it will be placed (e.g., beginning, between segments, end).
- *Assemble equipment*, including the room in which to broadcast, download software, if necessary, decide where to locate the podcast, create an account with iTunes.
- *Practice* once the script is finalized until it is almost memorized.
- *Prepare the site* to host the podcast, including text and visuals for it.

While two students are creating the immigrant script, the other group members will:

- Research the immigrant's country of origin, the area or town where he/she settled in the United States and the time period. The introduction should show some knowledge/understanding of the person's country of origin. Create an introduction for the podcast that provides some background on the person and some specific details about the topic.
- Compile at least two or three graphics (e.g., map showing the immigrant's journey, photos of immigrants, person at work or with family, the town of origin or destination). These will be used as part of the podcast page where audio is placed.

Note: Check some free Web sites like Sloganizer (www.sloganizer.net/en/) or the PC man Web site's Free Slogan Creator (www.thepcmanwebsite.com/free_slogan_creator.php) to help create a name for the podcast.

> ➣ Activities in science and language arts are available at Bev's Web site at www.neal-schuman.com/webclassroom.

Activities to Be Used as Follow-Up
As an extension activity, have each group of students try one of the following:

- Divide into teams and dramatize being processed at Ellis Island. Have each team member select a role (e.g., immigrants, nurse, processing agent). Each group will portray a different country of origin.

- Write questions and interview an immigrant (e.g., relative, friend) to talk about the American Dream.
- Use a modern newspaper editorial on immigration as a springboard into exploration of that issue. Show how immigration issues today are different from and similar to feelings toward immigration in the past. Ask students to make predictions about the future of immigration based on what they have read in contemporary editorials.

Step 5: Evaluate What Was Learned

Educators who are currently using podcasts in their classrooms have found that students like this activity. Because there are several different types of activities, evaluation needs to take place as students are performing these various tasks. You will be assessing the content they learned about immigration, their interaction in groups, and their ability to use both Web resources and podcasting. It is also important for students to participate in the evaluation process. Some possible evaluation strategies for each task in this unit include:

- *Primary sources.* Have students write a response to a primary source (speech, news article, photo) taking the position of someone who lived at the time the source was created. Other possible evaluation tasks based on primary sources include:
  - Write on the class blog about a primary source document. Explain how the source supports or challenges a commonly accepted conclusion about a time in history.
  - Based on analysis of several primary sources, prepare an oral presentation taking a stand on an issue in history.
  - Select primary source documents to create a museum display about a historical topic. Write captions for the items and justify the documents that were selected.
  - Write a response to a primary source (speech, news article, sermon), taking the position of someone who lived at the time the source was created.
  - Prepare a visual display (poster, magazine cover, illustrated timeline) that highlights the most important points to be gained from the primary sources under study.
- *Podcast.* Use the Podcast rubric to assess the four parts of the podcast (see Figure 3-10):
  - Content and organization, writing quality of the interview, including the introduction, questions and answers, and conclusion.
  - Visuals and music.
  - Technical side of the podcast, including recording, podcast Web page, and delivery.
  - Group work, including working well with teammates, contributing to team effort, and equally to the workload.
- *Self-Reflection.* Complete the Self-Reflection Checklist so students identify how well they accomplished various tasks in the unit. See Figure 3-11.

Summary

This chapter combines not only the new technology of podcasting but also the two Web 2.0 tools we learned about in Chapter 2—blogs and RSS feeds. Podcasts can be set up on blogs and when a listener subscribes to a podcast via an RSS feed, if a new podcast episode is published, it will automatically be downloaded to the subscriber's computer. All three tools work together to make communication among educators and their students an easy process.

Teacher Exercises: Now You Try It . . .

Now that you've reviewed in detail a unit plan that incorporates podcasts, try the following exercises. Be sure to focus your attention on how the technology can enhance student learning.

Figure 3-10. Podcast Rubric			
A podcast has four main sections that need to be evaluated—the content (e.g., the script); the total presentation (e.g., visuals, music, editing); the delivery, and teamwork. This rubric identifies different parts of each section listed. Separate rubrics could also be created for each section.			
Category	**Exemplary** **9 points**	**Proficient** **6 points**	**Partially Proficient** **3 points**	**Incomplete** **0 points**

Category	**Exemplary** **9 points**	**Proficient** **6 points**	**Partially Proficient** **3 points**	**Incomplete** **0 points**
Interview content and organization	Catchy and clever introduction. Provides relevant information and establishes a clear purpose engaging the listener immediately.	Describes the topic and engages the audience as the introduction proceeds.	Somewhat engaging (covers well-known topic), and provides a vague purpose.	Irrelevant or inappropriate topic that minimally engages listener. Does not include an introduction or the purpose is vague and unclear.
	Tells who is speaking, date the podcast was produced, and where the speaker is located.	Tells most of the following: who is speaking, date of the podcast, and location of speaker.	Alludes to who is speaking, date of the podcast, and location of speaker.	Speaker is not identified. No production date or location of the speaker is provided.
	Creativity and original content enhance the purpose of the podcast in an innovative way. Accurate information and succinct concepts are presented.	Accurate information is provided succinctly.	Some information is inaccurate or long-winded.	Information is inaccurate.
	Keeps focus on the topic.	Stays on the topic.	Occasionally strays from the topic.	Does not stay on topic.
	Conclusion clearly summarizes key information.	Conclusion summarizes information.	Conclusion vaguely summarizes key information	No conclusion is provided.
Delivery	Well rehearsed, smooth delivery in a conversational style.	Rehearsed, smooth delivery.	Appears unrehearsed with uneven delivery.	Delivery is hesitant and choppy and sounds like the presenter is reading.
	Student uses a clear voice and correct, precise pronunciation of terms.	Student's voice is clear. Student pronounces most words correctly.	Student's voice is low. Student incorrectly pronounces terms.	Student mumbles, incorrectly pronounces terms, and speaks too quietly to be heard.

(Cont'd.)

	Figure 3-10. Podcast Rubric (Continued)			
Category	Exemplary 9 points	Proficient 6 points	Partially Proficient 3 points	Incomplete 0 points
Visuals and music	The visuals used create a unique and effective presentation and enhance what is being said in the podcast and follow the rules for quality graphic design.	The visuals relate to the audio and reinforce content and demonstrate functionality.	The visuals sometimes enhance the quality and understanding of the presentation.	The visuals are unrelated to the podcast. Artwork is inappropriate to podcast.
	Music enhances the mood, quality, and understanding of the presentation.	Music provides supportive background to the podcast.	Music provides somewhat distracting background to the podcast.	Music is distracting to presentation.
Presentation	Presentation is recorded in a quiet environment without background noise and distractions.	Presentation is recorded in a quiet environment with minimal background noise and distractions.	Presentation is recorded in a semi-quiet environment with some background noise and distractions.	Presentation is recorded in a noisy environment with constant background noise and distractions.
	Volume of voice, music, and effects enhance the presentation.	Volume is acceptable.	Volume is occasionally inconsistent.	Volume changes are highly distracting.
	Podcast length keeps the audience interested and engaged.	Podcast length keeps audience listening.	Podcast length is somewhat long or somewhat short to keep audience engaged.	Podcast is either too long or too short to keep the audience engaged.
Teamwork	Performed all duties of assigned team role and contributed knowledge, opinions, and skills to share with the team. Always did the assigned work.	Performed nearly all duties of assigned team role and contributed knowledge, opinions, and skills to share with the team. Completed most of the assigned work.	Performed a few duties of assigned team role and contributed a small amount of knowledge, opinions, and skills to share with the team. Completed some of the assigned work.	Did not perform any duties of assigned team role and did not contribute knowledge, opinions or skills to share with the team. Relied on others to do the work.

- Review several more podcasts in your subject areas and grade levels to get ideas on how other educators are using podcasts in their classrooms. Check the General URLs in Table 3-2.
- Sign up for a podcast service.
- Create a simple lesson plan that focuses on either language arts or history objectives. This should be one that you think you can implement in your classroom at your grade level.

> ➤ Review additional exercises at Bev's Web site at www.neal-schuman.com/ webclassroom.

Figure 3-11. Self-Reflection Checklist

Reflect on the work that you did to create the podcast, including writing the script, delivering the podcast, working on the technical end of creating the presentation, and working with your teammates. Then, answer the questions below.

I. About the Podcast:

- What I heard that surprised me was

  _____

  _____

- Something I learned from the podcast was

  _____

  _____

- One thing I thought was important from the interviews was

  _____

  _____

- From what I heard and read, I have a question or would like to know more about

  _____

  _____

II. Assess group participation, determining whether the student worked well with teammates, contributed to the team effort, and shouldered work equally. Students will answer the following questions:

- Did you do your best?

  _____

  _____

- Did you work hard, enjoy the project, and feel good about what you completed?

  _____

  _____

- How much did you contribute to the group's project?

  _____

  _____

- Did you finish your work on time?

  _____

  _____

- If you had to do it again, would you do anything differently?

  _____

  _____

CONCLUSION

To make podcasting a success at a school, educators must incorporate podcasting into the classroom routine and motivate their students to produce podcasts regularly. The goal is to make students look forward to creating them. Thus, podcasts need to be included as part of lesson development. Podcasts are a great way to expand the learning environment of your class, and a surefire way to make the learning experience authentic and personally meaningful for your students.

Table 3-2. General URLs for Podcasting	
URL	**Description**
http://eaglecreekkinderteacher.podomatic.com/	Podcast about a book by a kindergarten class
www.downsfm.com/	Radio show created by students at an elementary school
www.sandaigprimary.co.uk/radio_sandaig/index.php	Radio show from Glasgow, Scotland
www.apple.com/education/resources/podcastingvideos/video/video2.html	A teacher talking about and showing student podcasts
www.apple.com/support/garageband/podcasts/	Tutorials and tips for using software on MAC
www.jakeludington.com/podcasting/20050222_recording_a_podcast.html	How to use Audacity software on a PC
http://audacity.sourceforge.net/manual-1.2/index.html	Tutorials for using Audacity software from Sound Forge
http://comtechlab.iupui.edu/tutorialsfolder/garageband.html	GarageBand tutorials from Com Tech Lab
www.learninginhand.com/podcasting/index.html	The site developer suggests resources and discusses the four phases of production.
www.educational-feeds.com/showrss.php?category=Class%20Podcasts%3A%3AK-6%20Class%20Podcasts	Lists of podcasts created by K-12 classes
www.k12handhelds.com/mashups/?p=17	Secondary student podcasts on different subjects
www.epnweb.org/index.php?view_mode=questions	The Education Podcast Network contains podcasts at all grades

REFERENCES AND FURTHER READING

California State Department of Education. 1987. *English—Language Arts Framework for California Public Schools: Kindergarten Through Grade Twelve.* Sacramento: California State Department of Education.

California State Department of Education. 1988. *History—Social Science Framework for California Public Schools, Kindergarten Through Grade Twelve.* Sacramento: California State Department of Education.

Crofts, Sheri, Jon Dilley, Mark Fox, Andrew Retsema, and Bob Williams. "Podcasting: A New Technology in Search of Viable Business Models." *First Monday*, 10, no.9. Available: www.firstmonday.org/issues/issue 10_9/crofts/index.htm (accessed October 1, 2008).

Deubel, Patricia. "Podcasts: Where's the Learning?" *T.H.E. Journal* (June 7, 2007). Available: www.thejournal.com/articles/20764 (accessed October 1, 2008).

National Educational Technology Standards for Students and Teachers. 2007. The International Society for Technology Educators.

Rainie, Lee, and Mary Madden. 2005. Data Memo RE: Podcasting, Pew Internet and American Life Project (April), p. 2. Available: www.pewinternet.org/pdfs/PIP_podcasting.pdf (accessed October 1, 2008).

Petersen, Alan. "2007 Was a Very Good Year for Podcasting." EzineArticles.com Expert Author. Available: http://ezinearticles.com/?2007-Was-A-Very-Good-Year-For-Podcasting&id=1061321 (accessed May 31, 2008).

CHAPTER 4

Creating Literature Wikis in the Classroom

PART 1: IDEAS AND INSIGHTS

In Chapter 2, you read about blogs and blogging in the English/language arts. Teachers are also using wikis in the English classroom and are quite excited about their students' participation and enthusiasm for learning literature. Teachers show their enthusiasm about using wikis:

> "I have used countless technological tools—but I have never found a tool so useful in the educational process." (Vicki Davis, Westwood Schools)

> "Wikispaces has been great so far. It is an amazing thing to learn through community building activities in an online environment that encourages the free exchange of ideas and emphasizes high level, clear communication and critical thinking." (David Conlay, Estancia High School)

> "There is just nothing out there that is so simple to use!" (Leigh Blackall, Blended Learning)

According to *Education Week* (Davis, 2007), in the last three years, there has been an enormous increase in wiki use in K–12 education. In January 2006, one of the hosts of wikis, Wikispaces, decided to offer their Plus Plan free to K–12 teachers to help teachers see how easy it was to use wiki technology. Since then over 10,000 educational wikis have been set up through Wikispaces. Excitement among teachers, librarians, students, and now administrators to use wikis to meet educational goals has sparked the increased enthusiasm to introduce wikis into the classroom.

Objectives of This Chapter

This chapter explores ways to integrate wikis into English and language arts content instruction. It is designed to be used by English/language arts educators and library media specialists at both the elementary and secondary levels. By the end of this chapter, in addition to content goals, educators will be able to:

- define a wiki and differentiate it from a blog;
- describe the characteristics of a wiki and why it is useful in the K–12 classroom;
- set up a wiki; and
- create a literature unit that includes the use of wikis.

English/language arts educators expose students to literature in the form of fiction, nonfiction, poetry, and drama. They require students to create meaning from texts they read. They also provide opportunities for students to speak in small groups and to the whole class about their experiences with literature. And, they create assignments that require students to write about their thoughts and experiences, and analyze ways that literature provides meaning for their own lives. Now they are also adding wiki technology to their tools.

Part 1 of this chapter provides an introduction to wikis and examples of how teachers are using them in the classroom. Part 2 suggests how to get started, including tools and rules for using wikis in education. In Part 3, a sample unit plan illustrates how to use this technology as part of a literature project at the secondary level.

> ➤ Other subject areas are illustrated at Bev's Web site www.neal-schuman.com/ webclassroom.

Glossary

authentication mechanism: A user login to edit the wiki so that every post or edit can be attributed to an individual student.

backup feature: A wiki that backs up each night to prevent lose of data.

rollback feature: Used by administrators to repair any deletions of information of the wiki or misuse as required.

sandbox: A place to try editing a WikiPage created by others.

signature tool: A tool that creates a link to the wiki page of the user editing a wiki.

wiki: A collection of Web pages designed to enable anyone who accesses it to contribute or modify content.

Wikipedia: An online encyclopedia with over 200,000 contributors.

Wikiword: Two or more words with initial capitals, run together. Wikiwords are topic names.

Introduction

Wiki, wiki. You've probably heard this word and wondered what strange language your students are speaking. Actually, wiki comes from the Hawaiian word meaning "quick" or "fast" and was coined by Ward Cunningham, a Portland, Oregon, programmer, who created the first wiki software to help programmers from different locales communicate effectively. Now wikis are being used in the classroom for everything imaginable—group study guides, online lesson plans, classroom notice boards, collaborative essays—all come alive through wikis. As you explore this chapter, you will understand why the technology was given this name because a wiki is so simple to set up and easy to use.

What Is a Wiki?

A wiki is a collaboratively developed and updated Web site. Web site pages are created and edited directly in the Web browser (e.g., Firefox, Internet Explorer) by anyone who has been granted editing rights. Wikis can provide users with both author and editor privileges. This means that any visitor to the wiki can change its content if they desire.

One of the wikis most known by librarians and teachers is Wikipedia, the online encyclopedia, which has over 200,000 contributors (see Figure 4-1). Wikipedia, however, has its share of advocates and skeptics. Some educators worry about its quality and accuracy. One teacher comments on one of its strengths: "Wikipedia provides a teaching opportunity for teachers to talk to students about reliability and to teach them about being critical of sources and where information comes from."

What is the difference between a wiki and a blog? Chapter 2 provided comprehensive information about blogs. However, these terms are often confused. A blog, or Weblog, shares writing and multimedia content in the form of "posts" and "comments" to posts. While members of the blog or the general public can comment on a post, no one is able to change a comment or post made by another. Blogs are a good forum for individuals to express their own opinions. Wikis, on the other

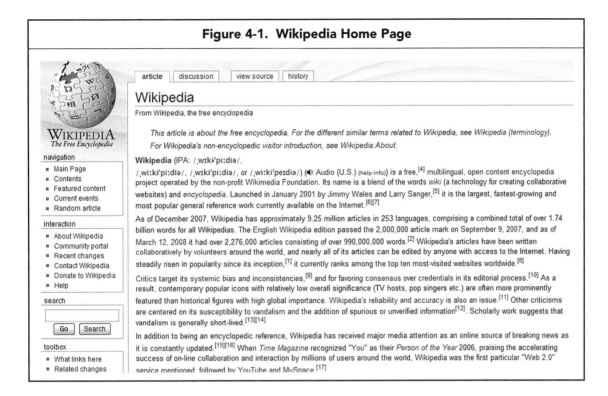

Figure 4-1. Wikipedia Home Page

hand, have a more open structure and allow others to change what one person has written. In fact, group consensus may override individual opinion.

Criteria for Selecting a Wiki

A teacher who is contemplating using a wiki in the classroom should do so only after considerable thought. Following are some points for educators to consider when they decide to start a wiki.

- Some host sites have ads on the wiki; others do not. A host site without ads is best, if possible, so educators have full control over what information students are exposed to in their classrooms or libraries.
- Choosing a site that is easy for students to navigate lets students focus on learning the class topic not figuring out how to find the material or understand the technology.
- Some hosts offer the ability to use a wide range of learning media. For example, teachers and students should be able to easily incorporate text, color, images, video and audio into their wiki pages to meet all learning styles.
- A monitoring capability is vital. Teachers need to be able to monitor what individual students are doing on the wiki. The classroom wiki must support individual log-ins for each member of the class, so that every edit made by students has their user names attached. This allows the teacher to track the progress on the wiki.
- Important also is the need for the wiki to be safe from intruders with good mechanisms for keeping out vandals and spammers. The wiki provider should have a clearly stated privacy policy (e.g., www.wetpaintcentral.com/pageSearch?contains=Privacy+ &+Terms+of+Use&t = anon).
- Students will work individually on some projects and collaborate in groups on others so separate areas should be available on the wiki site.
- Teachers will want to provide external Web links as resources for students so that linking to external Web resources will be easy.

- Support from the wiki host should include an enthusiastic user community to help teachers share ideas on how to make the best of their classroom wiki.
- As part of the wiki, teacher aids are essential, for example, notifying teachers by e-mail or RSS (see Chapter 2) when a change is made to the wiki, keeping statistics on use by individual students, a commenting ability directly on students' wiki pages, and calendars that lay out what is expected of students and by when.

Of course, the best classroom wiki is free. Several sites described later offer all or most of these criteria.

Why Use Wikis in the Classroom?

The question, then, is why should educators want to use wikis in their classrooms and why are students so excited to participate? Wikis, like any tool for learning, are limited in use primarily by the creativity of the teacher or designer. Ten reasons suggest pedagogical importance for using wikis. Wikis:

1. enable team members to work on an assignment at any time, from any location with an Internet connection;
2. encourage student involvement;
3. offer a powerful yet flexible collaborative communication tool for developing content-specific Web sites;
4. provide a central place for groups to form around specific topics;
5. provide students with direct (and immediate) access to a site's content, which is crucial in group editing or other collaborative project activities;
6. show the evolution of thought processes as students interact with the site and its contents;
7. promote pride of authorship and ownership in a team's activities;
8. showcase student work;
9. encourage collaboration on notes; and
10. promote concept introduction and exploration.

Wiki-enabled projects can provide various levels of site access and control to team members, offering a fine-tuning element that enhances the teaching and learning experience. Because wikis grow and evolve as a direct result of people adding material to the site, they can address a variety of pedagogical needs such as student involvement or group activities. Wikis are also well suited to reflecting current thoughts. In addition, wikis are helpful as e-portfolios, illustrating their utility as a tool for collection and reflection.

Classroom Examples of Wikis

Teachers and librarians nationwide have begun to explore the role of wikis in classroom settings—and the possibilities appear endless.

Example 1: Flat Classroom Project

One goal of this award-winning wiki project, created by Vicki Davis from the Westwood Schools in Georgia and Julie Lindsay now at Qatar Academy, was to challenge students to have a deeper understanding of the effect of information technology on the world (see Figure 4-2). Another was to "flatten the classroom walls" so that students in Georgia and Bangladesh could work together on a project using Internet tools to analyze the ten societal trends from *The World Is Flat* by Pulitzer Prize–winning author Thomas Friedman.

Figure 4-2. Flat Classroom Project Home Page

Source: Used by permission of Vicki Davis and Julie Lindsay; http://flatclassroom.project.wikispaces.com.

Objectives of the project included:

1. To understand, analyze, and evaluate the trends highlighted in *The World Is Flat*
2. To create a project wiki page that details this investigation and synthesis of the material
3. To use the wiki to facilitate collaboration, as well as to create a final project

Each student was paired with an overseas partner. To start the project, every student posted a podcast introduction (see Chapter 3). After "meeting" their partners, students planned their topic using tools such as the discussion tabs on the wiki pages, MySpace, e-mail, and instant messaging. See Figure 4-3 for student reactions.

A project outcome was to show that the single-classroom research that emphasizes the effectiveness of collaborative learning, genuine assessment, and project-based learning can occur when students have partners that are never in class at the same time. The wiki linked Davis's Georgia students with students in Bangladesh to collect and present information on globalization and outsourcing, virtual communication, and how the Internet has changed the world. To evaluate the project, classroom-specific, criterion-based rubrics allowed each classroom to assess its cumulative end-of-semester project.

Additional projects are forthcoming based on *The World Is Flat*, including The Horizon Project with three new classrooms in Austria, China, and Australia. You can view lesson plans, worksheets, rubrics and more from the project at:

http://flatclassroomproject.wikispaces.com/Lesson+Plans
http://flatclassroomproject.wikispaces.com/space/showimage/Flat_Classroom_LL_August07.pdf

Example 2: Villagewiki for Social Studies

From high school students to first graders, wikis can be used by all grade levels and in all subject areas. Created by the Village K–6 Elementary School, the Villagewiki showcases student work on curriculum topics they are studying. It is the intent of this wiki to gather research, create the wiki, and add to it over time so that others will be able to benefit from this information and edit it as

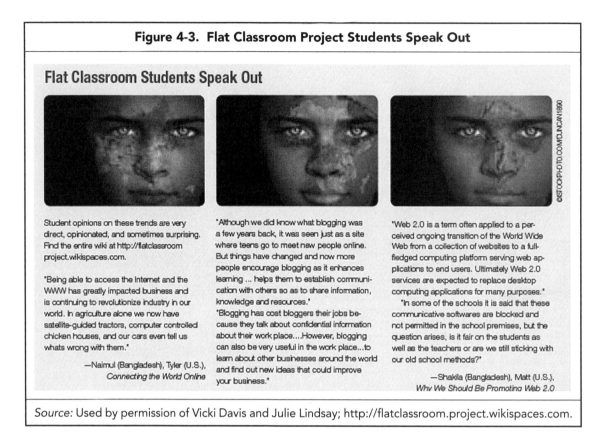

Figure 4-3. Flat Classroom Project Students Speak Out

Source: Used by permission of Vicki Davis and Julie Lindsay; http://flatclassroom.project.wikispaces.com.

needed. The first example is about penguins. First graders created fact sheets about penguins using the Inspiration mapping tool and movies with audio and their own original pictures. They also had to read the script for the movie, providing reading practice for the first graders (see Figure 4-4).

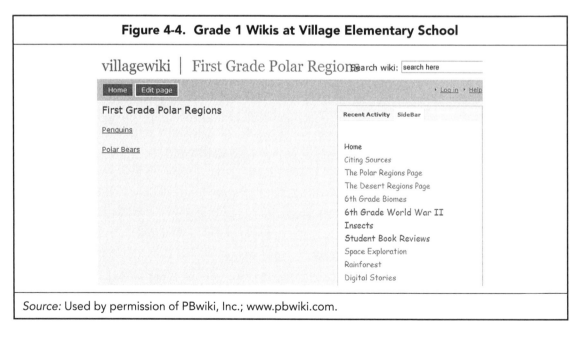

Figure 4-4. Grade 1 Wikis at Village Elementary School

Source: Used by permission of PBwiki, Inc.; www.pbwiki.com.

The sidebar contains a list of topics and the grade level that created them. Topics include the polar region, insects, space exploration, digital stories, and much more. Review other topics, see movies, and listen to students tell about their topics at http://villagewiki.pbwiki.com/.

Example 3: Wikis in Different Subject Areas

Wikis for Collaborative Storytelling

Teachers at Bellaire Primary School in Geelong, Victoria, Australia, constructed projects where group members learned from collaborating through the writing process. The following exercise illustrates how a writing project enables students to build on one another's contributions. The wiki mentioned here is a project from grades 3–4. The story is the adventures of a tennis ball called Terry. Started by their teacher in 2006, students continued to add to it. View the story in Figure 4-5. The story is available at http://terrythetennisball.wikispaces.com/.

Figure 4-5. Collaborative Storytelling

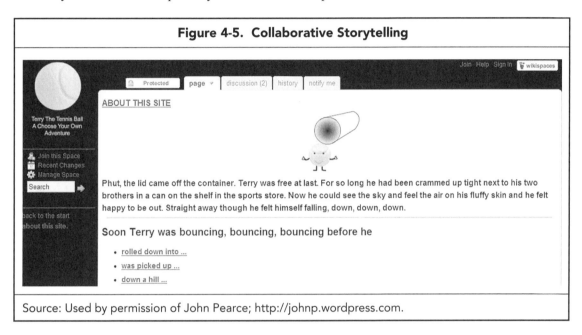

Source: Used by permission of John Pearce; http://johnp.wordpress.com.

Wikis for Social Studies

In this example, students make notes about the different units they are reading to help consolidate their knowledge around the concepts they are learning. In this social studies class, students learned about ancient humans, ancient Egypt, ancient Rome, feudal Europe, and European colonization. Wiki pages are available on each topic to which students can add, modify, or delete content. See topics covered at http://studyingsocietiesatjhk.pbwiki.com/.

Wiki Ideas in Science

Some of the ideas schools have employed using wikis in science are listed here:

- A student-made glossary of scientific terms with illustrations and definitions added by the class (using original digital photos or those from other online Creative Commons sources, such as Flickr). Linking to separate pages with detailed information allows the main glossary list to remain reasonably short.
- A taxonomy of living things with information about each branch in the study of Biology over a full year.
- Designs of experiments (and resulting lab reports) for a chemistry class.
- Observations from field sites, such as water testing in local streams, weather observations from across a state, or bird counts during migratory season. This activity would also work well as a collaboration with other schools in different states.
- Detailed and illustrated descriptions of scientific processes: how mountains form, etc.

PART 2: GETTING STARTED

Using any technology tool requires thought, preparation, and experimentation prior to using it with students. Administrators and parents must be advised and school policies need to be adhered to. It is also a good idea to seek out other educators who have been working with the new technology to hear about their experiences. Some basic questions, to name a few, that the teacher or librarian must consider include: What service should I use? How will the tool fit into my curriculum or my library? Are my students capable of using it? Do the advantages outweigh the disadvantages? How is security handled?

Preparing for a Wiki
The following steps will organize the process for the novice starting out.

Step 1: Keep the Administration Informed
Check your school's Acceptable Use Policy (AUP) about using wikis and inquire about the following:

- Is it permissible to post student work to the Web?
- What is the policy on posting students' names? (Initials? Pseudonyms?)
- What is the policy on posting pictures of students or class scenes?
- What is the policy on posting any information that might identify the wiki class?
- Can these policies be met through security settings, parent and student agreements?
- Does the district filtering prevent access to the wiki tools from school? If so, will your administrator facilitate unblocking the wiki's exact URL?

The response of the administration will help you decide if a wiki tool has the capabilities and security you need for it to be successful for your classroom. It is also useful to set up short, simple usage guidelines, written in a positive tone. In addition, it would be helpful to illustrate how other schools are using wikis in their classrooms to allay administrative concerns. See Figure 4-6.

Step 2: Make Basic Decisions About Setting Up the Wiki
Before you start your wiki with your class(es), consider the following questions:

- How do you envision using the wiki? (How will you explain it to parents?)
- Who will be able to see the wiki? (Other schools? The class? Group members? Parents?)
- Who will be able to edit the wiki? (Other schools? The class? Group members?)
- Who will be able to join the wiki? (Students only? Parents? Invited guests? The public?)
- What parts of the wiki will you "protect" (lock from changes)?
- Who will moderate the wiki for appropriateness, etc?
- Will you, as the teacher or librarian, be notified of all changes?

Here is one teacher's thoughts: Karen wanted a way to quickly engage her students online without opening her classroom to outside visitors. Today, she advises teachers to address this concern by creating an easy-to-use, private site on PBwiki. All PBwikis require a password to edit, and private sites take it one step further, requiring a password to gain entrance to the site. For teachers, PBwiki's notification system allows the administrator to see who has logged in and who is contributing to the Web site. For students, the ability to quickly upload or edit information provides strong motivation to participate inside, as well as outside, the classroom.

Step 3: Choose a Host Using Specific Criteria
Several criteria should be considered in selecting a wiki service to host your wiki. These criteria include:

Figure 4-6. Wiki Sample Contract

The following contract must be signed before students may participate in the class wiki.

Purpose of the wiki

The members of [name of class] class at [name of school] will be participating in a class wiki for the purposes of [include all that apply, and delete others; e.g., Practicing taking varied points of view on a topic]

_____

_____

_____

_____

_____

Safety

This wiki will be created using a wiki tool at [paste URL of wiki here].
In the interest of students' safety, the following restrictions have been configured on the wiki: [e.g., only registered members can see the wiki]

_____

_____

_____

_____

_____

Terms and Conditions

Read the terms and conditions carefully before signing the contract.

- _____
- _____
- _____
- _____
- _____
- _____

Consequences of violating the Warranty

Any violation of the above terms and conditions shall make the violator subject to both immediate termination from the wiki, **with all related sacrifice of points** toward grades and to discipline through the school code of conduct, where applicable. At the teacher's discretion, a warning may be given in the case of minor infractions.

Signatures

I agree to the terms and conditions of the class wiki for (name of class here) for the (add dates) school year and permit my student to participate in the wiki project.

_____   _____
Student signature   Date   Parent signature   Date

- *Easy to use.* Ideally, how to add material to a wiki can be learned in a matter of minutes, even for young elementary students, as long as they can find letters on a keyboard.
- *Cost.* There are many free wiki hosts on the Web. Most fund their existence through advertising that appears on the wiki pages. This can be very distracting or even inappropriate for students who inevitably click on the enticing links.

- *Appearance.* The wiki should be easily navigated so it is simple to find information within the wiki and the overall look can be adjusted. Graphics can be used as needed adding to the message. Graphics should not be distracting but used where needed to further explain a topic.
- *Security.* The wiki should follow school policy. If the entire wiki needs to be in private view (visible and editable only by members), then it must be set up that way.
- *Usage guidelines.* The wiki should have usage guidelines that are short, simple, and written in a positive manner. The guidelines should encourage users to be considerate of others and be active and friendly in their wiki posts.

Step 4: Select the Wiki Host That Meets the Criteria

Three sample hosts on which to create wikis are listed below. Each service meets the criteria already discussed (see Figure 4-7).

Figure 4-7. Wiki Comparison

Legend	free option	hosted	download	WYSIWYG	wiki features	own domain	Notifications	private	Multi media	html	Layouts	Income	S.E.O.	https
Central Desktop	✓	✓	X	✓	✓	X	✓	✓	X	X	X	X	X	X
ClearWiki	✓	✓	X	✓	✓	X	✓	✓	X	✓	X	X	X	✓
Confluence	✓	✓	✓	✓	✓	✓	✓	✓	✓	✓	✓	✓	✓	✓
cyn.in	✓	✓	X	✓	✓	X	✓	✓	✓	✓	X	X	X	X
editme	X	✓	X	✓	✓	✓	✓	✓	✓	✓	✓	✓	+/-	✓
Legend	free option	hosted	download	WYSIWYG	wiki features	own domain	Notifications	private	Multi media	html	Layouts	Income	S.E.O.	https
Netcipia	✓	✓	X	✓	✓	X	+/-	✓	✓	X	✓	✓	✓	X
PBwiki	✓	✓	X	✓	✓	X	✓	✓	✓	✓	✓	+/-	✓	X
Socialtext	✓	✓	✓	✓	✓	✓	✓	✓	✓	✓	✓	X	X	✓
stikipad	✓	✓	X	+/-	✓	✓	✓	✓	X	X	✓	✓	X	✓
Legend	free option	hosted	download	WYSIWYG	wiki features	own domain	Notifications	private	Multi media	html	Layouts	Income	S.E.O.	https
TWiki	✓	X	✓	✓	+/-	✓	✓	✓	✓	✓	✓	✓	✓	✓
wetpaint	✓	✓	X	✓	✓	✓	+/-	✓	✓	X	+/-	X	+/-	X
WikiDot	✓	✓	X	X	✓	✓	✓	✓	✓	X	✓	X	X	✓
wikispaces	✓	✓	X	✓	✓	✓	✓	✓	✓	✓	+/-	✓	X	✓
Legend	free option	hosted	download	WYSIWYG	wiki features	own domain	Notifications	private	Multi media	html	Layouts	Income	S.E.O.	https

- *Wikispaces* (www.wikispaces.com/help+teachers) is a place where you can create a wiki, or a simple-to-use collaborative Web site to use in your classroom and your school. In January 2006, Wikispaces offered their Plus Plan to K–12 teachers free of charge. They were interested in helping teachers use wiki technology in the classroom. Now over 10,000 educational wikis are set up and free. Secure, advertising-free wiki space is being offered to educators until they reach 100,000 teacher wikis.
- *Wetpaint* (www.wetpaint.com/category/education/?zone=module_e3) offers free, ad-free, secure classroom wikis, no matter the size. A special page for education enables you to see tutorials, ask questions of the "Education Ambassador" and see how other educators are using their wikis.
- *PBWiki* (http://pbwiki.com/education.wiki) is the world's largest provider of hosted business and educational wikis. They host over 400,000 wikis and serve millions of users every month.

The first version of PBwiki was written by Stanford Computer Science graduate David Weekly at 26 years of age. The service offers free, ad-free, secure wikis for education.

> ➤ *Additional information about other wiki hosts can be seen on Bev's Web site at www.neal-schuman.com/webclassroom.*

Wiki Feature Comparison will enable educators to compare some of the important features before selecting the appropriate service for their school (see Table 4-1).

Table 4-1. Wiki Feature Comparison			
Wiki Services	**PBWiki**	**Wikispaces**	**Others (WetPaint)**
Able to upload images			
Tracks edits and updates			
Authentication mechanisms			
Signature tool			
Rollback feature			
Backup feature			
Help			

Note: Check the glossary at the beginning of this chapter for any words with which you are not familiar.

Step 5: Decide How to Use the Wiki

Students can use wikis to create a set of documents that reflect the shared knowledge of the learning group. Wikis can also be used to facilitate the dissemination of information, to enable the exchange of ideas, and to facilitate group interaction.

Wikis have two states, *read*, the default state, and *edit*. In the *read state* the wiki page looks just like a normal Web page. When users want to edit the wiki page, they must access the wiki's *edit state*. To edit a wiki, users click the edit button or link featured on each wiki page. For example, Wikipedia (www.wikipedia.org/) provides a tab style format at the top of each page, which contains a clickable link entitled "edit this page," that users can click to access Wikipedia's *edit state*.

Other features shown as tabs at the top of wiki pages are important as well. The Discussion tab lets users communicate about a page without having to actually edit the page. For example, a student can post new poetry on their page, and others can offer "comments" in the discussion area. The History tab enables users to view changes that have been made to an entry, as well as return to a previous version of the wiki page, in case of accidental or intentional undesired changes. For formative evaluation teachers can use the "compare" feature to measure change over time in a student product. The Notify Me tab can save the educator time by keeping track of when someone makes changes to the wiki either via e-mail notification or through an RSS feed. Finally, users can keep informed about current content of interest by using the Watch tab at the top of any wiki page. The watchlist provides a list of changes to those pages that the user can track and review.

Setting Up a Wiki

Here is an example using Wetpaint to show you how easy it is to set up a wiki. Other wiki hosts (e.g., PBWiki and Wikispaces) are equally easy to begin. With Wetpaint there are six steps to follow.

- *Step 1: Name and describe your wiki.* The first step is to create a site name, a URL address, a description of the wiki, and indicate who can view the wiki and who can edit the wiki. See Figure 4-8.

Figure 4-8. Name and Describe the Wiki

Source: Wetpaint is a trademark of wetpaint.com, inc. Used by permission; www.wetpaint.com.

- *Step 2: Select a style for the wiki.* There are a number of wiki templates available from which to choose. At this point you can preview and customize your wiki name. See Figure 4-9.

Figure 4-9. Select a Wiki Style

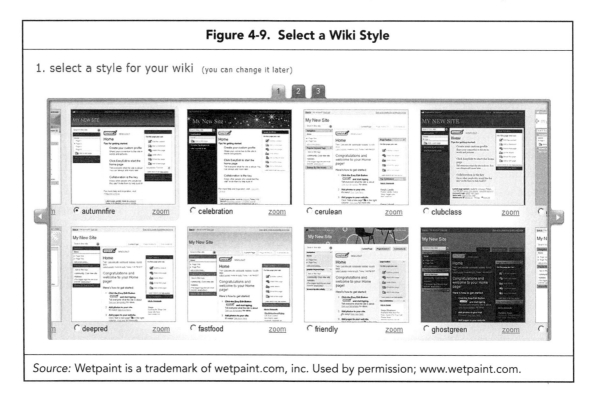

Source: Wetpaint is a trademark of wetpaint.com, inc. Used by permission; www.wetpaint.com.

- *Step 3: Preview the wiki.* Review the name and description of the wiki.
- *Step 4: Create a Wetpaint account.* Complete the screen entering data needed to set up the account. See Figure 4-10.

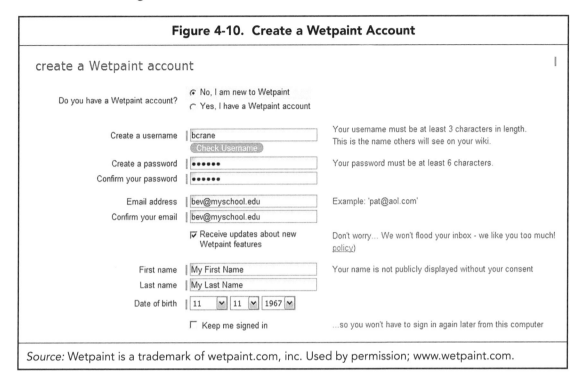

Figure 4-10. Create a Wetpaint Account

Source: Wetpaint is a trademark of wetpaint.com, inc. Used by permission; www.wetpaint.com.

- *Step 5: Invite participants to your wiki site.* Identify the role you want them to play (e.g., writer, viewer) and enter their e-mail addresses. Once you have invited others to participate, click the link to set up the account. See Figure 4-11.

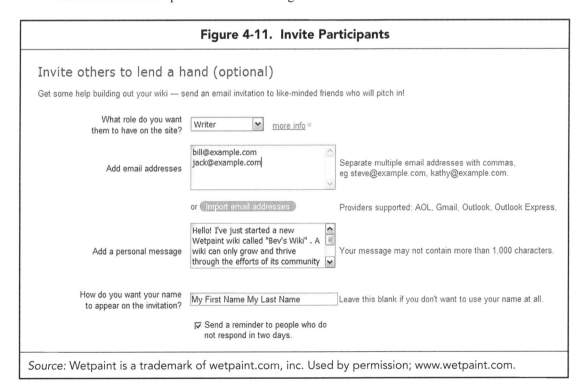

Figure 4-11. Invite Participants

Source: Wetpaint is a trademark of wetpaint.com, inc. Used by permission; www.wetpaint.com.

- *Step 6: Get going.* Your wiki is set up. Now you're ready to place some content on your wiki and have your friends collaborate with you.

Teacher Exercises: Now You Try It . . .

Before trying to use a wiki in your classroom, you will need to become familiar with how it works. There is no better way to do that than with hands-on practice. Try some of the following exercises to get you started:

1. Visit several wiki sites listed in Part 1 of this chapter. Select different subject areas and grade levels and explore the content of the wiki: how the content is presented and different technology used on the sites. In your Web 2.0 journal, note what you like about each host site, ideas you could use on your own wiki, and concerns you might have.
2. Now go to the Web sites for wiki services mentioned in Part 2 (e.g., Wikispaces, PBwiki, Wetpaint). Read the news, take a tour to see how they work, and compare the characteristics. Then write your comments on the Comparison Wiki Sheet (Table 4-1).
3. Check the comments that educators have provided at http://edutechation.wordpress .com/2007/08/03which-wiki-to-use/ and compare their reactions to each wiki to what you saw at the wiki sites. You might even want to submit a comment or ask a question.
4. Now, if you really feel confident, sign up for one of the wikis that you find most meets your needs and with which you feel most comfortable.

Completing these tasks should give you practical experience in what you have been reading about in Parts 1 and 2 of this chapter, and you will be ready to tackle Part 3—an actual example incorporating a wiki into a unit plan on literature in English/language arts.

> ➤ Look for more exercises to practice what you learned at Bev's Web site at
> www.neal-schuman.com/webclassroom.

PART 3: PRACTICAL APPLICATIONS

Team learning is an effective method for developing and strengthening content area abilities. Students and teachers will use the wiki in this unit for collaboration in their reading and writing activities. Before beginning the unit, you will need to create a classroom wiki. We have already described some of the details about setting up a wiki in Part 2: Getting Started.

An English/language arts curriculum has the responsibility to teach students to listen well, speak effectively, read and think critically, and write clearly. To accomplish these tasks, we, as English/language arts educators, have students read biographies, Shakespeare plays, historical novels, and poems. As students read and respond to literature, their abilities to think critically, interpret, and explain what is written will improve. As part of daily classroom activities, we have students participate in Readers' Theater, act out roles in plays, and write and present haiku poetry. These assignments require students to analyze ways that literature mirrors events in their own lives.

Many of us also incorporate technology into our English/language arts classrooms. We have students search the Web for sources for research projects, use tools like Microsoft Powerpoint to create class presentations and write their essays using word processing. Web 2.0 tools provide additional diversity so that educators can craft assignments that will engage students as they work together and collaborate to produce the results for a project.

Multidisciplinary Unit Plan for English Literature

This unit offers students a way to investigate the themes of the 1920s, while at the same time drawing parallels to the modern era in which they live. Students assume roles that prompt them to report their findings from a unique perspective. Students will work independently and collaboratively. All pieces must fit together to make the culminating product a success. All teams' work will be available for review through one central Web 2.0 tool—the wiki. The unit is designed as a multidiscipline activity involving language arts, history, and technology.

> ➤ *See activities using wikis in other subject areas at Bev's Web site at www.neal-schuman.com/webclassroom.*

This unit focuses on the novel *The Great Gatsby* by F. Scott Fitzgerald, and specifically on its characters. It is a novel often read in eleventh grade American literature classes. However, any work of literature, drama, or poetry could be used at any grade level. The activities in this unit model the types of tasks that educators can create for their own classes.

Step 1: Apply Framework Standards—What Should Be Taught?

This unit supports *Standards for the English Language Arts*, created by the National Council of Teachers of English (NCTE) (www.ncte.org/about/over/standards/110846.htm). The unit encompasses the use of print, oral, and visual language and addresses six interrelated English language arts: reading, writing, speaking, listening, viewing, and visually representing as follows:

- The research will illustrate interdisciplinary connections between English literature, history, and the performing arts.
- Activities gathering and using the Internet will develop students' research skills.
- Students will use analysis and synthesis to think critically as they research modern day comparisons to the characters of a novel.
- Students will read a wide range of print and nonprint texts to build an understanding of texts, of themselves, and of the cultures of the United States and the world; to acquire new information; to respond to the needs and demands of society and the workplace; and for personal fulfillment. Among these texts are fiction and nonfiction, classic and contemporary works.
- Students will apply a wide range of strategies to comprehend, interpret, evaluate, and appreciate texts. They will draw on their prior experience, their interactions with other readers and writers, their knowledge of word meaning and of other texts, their word identification strategies, and their understanding of textual features.

The unit will also reinforce the technology standards from the International Society for Technology in Education (ISTE), which include:

- improving familiarity with and use of Web 2.0 tools; and
- incorporating technology into classroom content projects.

Step 2: Identify General Goals and Specific Objectives

In addition to English/language arts standards, the California History-Social Science framework acts as a guide for standards in this unit. The goals and specific objectives that follow form the basis for the content and skills of this unit.

Goals

When searching for information on the characters in the novel *The Great Gatsby*, students will:

- use Internet technology to find information;
- locate, gather, analyze, and evaluate written information for a variety of purposes, including research projects, real-world tasks, and self-improvement;

- build critical thinking skills by analyzing and synthesizing collected research;
- demonstrate competence in the general skills and strategies of the writing process;
- interpret character traits based on the context of the entire story;
- collaborate with classmates; and
- understand, when reading a novel, how character analysis plays a part in understanding the novel.

Objectives

More specifically, as part of each goal, in the area of *Content Objectives in English and History*, students will:

- draft, revise, and edit their writing as part of the writing process;
- write with a command of the grammatical and mechanical conventions of composition;
- gather and use information effectively for research purposes;
- apply a variety of response strategies, including rereading, notetaking, summarizing, outlining, and relating what is read to their own experiences and feelings;
- read critically and ask pertinent questions regarding character roles in *The Great Gatsby*;
- synthesize historical research and draw conclusions; and
- synthesize and evaluate historical sources.

And in the area of *Technology Objectives*, students will:

- demonstrate competence in using a wiki for collaborative writing.

Step 3: Gather Materials

Students will already have read *The Great Gatsby*. Using their knowledge of characters in the novel, they will research real-life persons whom students feel exhibit the personalities, hopes, and dreams or other attributes of their character. Some possible resources are listed in Table 4-2.

Table 4-2. URLs for the Gatsby Unit	
URL	**Description**
www.thesolutionsite.com/lesson/1603/ gatsbycharacters.ppt	Introduction to the characters in *The Great Gatsby*, PowerPoint created by Pamela Fuller of Capital High School
www.geocities.com/BourbonStreet/3844/index .html#nick	Beginner's Guide to *Gatsby*
http://www.huffenglish.com/gatsby/index.html	*The Great Gatsby* Web page
http://en.wikipedia.org/wiki/The_Great_Gatsby	Wikipedia entry
www.webquest.org/questgarden/lessons/25768- 060531185118/task.htm	WebQuest lesson using a wiki to compare life in Gatsby's time to life today
www.kn.pacbell.com/wired/fil/pages/webtheroarch.html	The Roaring 20s WebQuest
www.fcps.k12.va.us/westspringfieldhs/academic/ english/1project/99gg/topics.htm	List of character synopses written by students

Step 4: Create Sample Activities

This unit requires that students think about the novel, not in isolation, but by analyzing the characters and identifying characteristics that they might identify in a person they know or have read about, such as political leaders, sports figures, entertainment personnel, and others whom they might know more personally. Students will have already discussed and researched the 1920s during their reading of the novel. Each of the searches that students must now complete will require them to employ increasingly higher levels of critical thinking as they analyze the characters from the novel, compare their traits with real-life persons, and synthesize the material into a concise writing.

In addition, on the class wiki students will be working first in pairs where they will read and comment on each other's writing about their Gatsby character and, second, add comments and questions to student pairs who have researched the same or other characters.

Activities to Introduce the Unit

The focus of this unit is to reinforce what students learned in their literature review and emphasize the value and relevance that literature has for their own lives. These initial tasks require students to think about the novel as a whole; then narrow the focus to the novel's characters. Students should now be able to look at the timeframe, which is in the 1920s, and understand the different events that were happening and the effects that they had on people's lives. To draw upon their prior knowledge, students in pairs will:

- Review the characters in *The Great Gatsby* and select the character they are most interested in knowing better. Main characters include: Nick Carraway, Daisy Fay Buchanan, Jordan Baker, George Wilson, Myrtle Wilson, Jay Gatsby, and Tom Buchanan. Pairs can choose other minor characters with the teacher's approval.
- Brainstorm personality traits about their character and then locate from their reading the following information about their characters: three adjectives about physical appearance; three adjectives about personality; one quote from another character about their character; and one quote by their character that is indicative of his/her personality. Note page numbers and quotes that they think exemplify their character's traits (see Figure 4-12). Students should divide the above tasks.

Figure 4-12. Character Analysis Log

Instructions: On your wiki use this form to identify personality and physical traits of one of the main characters from the novel *The Great Gatsby*. Also include quotes from the novel to support selected character traits.

_____ (name of character you have chosen)

Example:

Daisy

married a man whom she does not love
physical traits and social status similar to Myrtle
husband unable to fulfill her romantic needs and therefore she marries him only for wealth and social status
engaged in a loveless marriage   Quote

Character Trait	Quote to support it

Note: The teacher should model an example of personality traits of a famous person most students would recognize, such as Michael Jordan or Barack Obama or Hilary Clinton.

- Categorize their characters into the following areas: nouveau riche, old money, middle class, and blue collar.
- Write a draft analysis of their character for the wiki.

The Wiki. The class wiki will be the central repository for all of the information collected by each pair, including notes about the characters, drafts of their character analysis, and the final writing. Throughout the initial process, students will use the wiki to:

- collect their notes about the Gatsby character;
- choose at least three (3) other pairs' characters to read about and add at least three comments and/or questions on that character to the wiki;
- collect photos and other artifacts that represent the Gatsby character;
- discuss the notes about their character made by other classmates before writing the draft character analysis;
- review at least five (5) pairs' draft analyses and based on their own knowledge from reading the novel add, delete, and modify the analyses; and
- write the final Gatsby character analysis, taking other students' revisions into consideration.

Activities During the Unit

During the introductory activities, students have reinforced their knowledge of characters in *The Great Gatsby*. They must now complete a number of tasks to compile sufficient information to convince class members of the similarities between their Gatsby character and the "real-life" person they will choose. In groups of four students will:

- brainstorm a list of persons the group thinks fits the description of their Gatsby character using the Character Analysis Log created earlier;
- create a similar map of the "real-life" person (e.g., personality, class, accomplishments, etc.);
- collect photos and other memorabilia that represent the time period of the real-life character; and
- research the "real-life" person to find three adjectives about physical appearance, three adjectives about personality, one quote from another person about the "real-life" person, and one quote by the "real-life" person that is indicative of his/her personality (see Figure 4-13 for another example).

The Wiki. Throughout this part of the activity, groups will use the wiki to keep track of all information, photos of the time period and more that represent the real-life character. Groups will do the following:

- Divide their wiki space in half using one side for traits on their Gatsby character and the other side for the "real life" character, making sure supporting page numbers and quotes or URLs are listed.
- Collect the group's notes on the wiki, have teams read the notes and add to them, and begin writing the character sketch of the "real-life" person.
- Identify photos, pictures, and other memorabilia that represent the "real-life" character.
- Have each group review the character sketches of other groups making their changes and suggestions on the wiki.
- Write a final draft character analysis of their "real-life" person incorporating other students' suggestions.

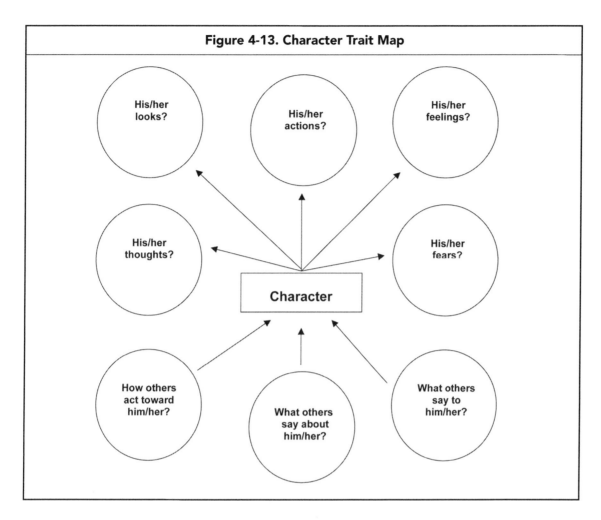

Figure 4-13. Character Trait Map

- Present the final character analyses on the wiki, complete with pictures that are appropriate to the character type and the time period in which both the fictional and nonfictional characters lived.

Note: It is a good idea for each student in the group to assume a role (e.g., *research coordinator* assists others in finding key quotes, pictures, primary sources, etc.; *archive manager* uploads all files to the wiki page, etc.).

Activities to Be Used as Follow-Up

The Great Gatsby is all about achieving the "American Dream." As extension activities, have groups try some of the following:

- Write about their vision of the American Dream. If their American Dream is fulfilled, what will they be doing when they are Nick's age (30)? Have students create self-portraits of themselves as adults who realize their American dreams. Alternatively, have students write monologues from the perspective of themselves as fulfilled thirty-year-olds.
- Role play the fictional and "real-life" characters they wrote about to capture personality traits.
- Perform on a panel to help a group of radio listeners understand the American Dream in the 1920s by comparing and contrasting the values of F. Scott Fitzgerald's characters in *The Great Gatsby* to the values and attitudes in our culture today.
- Write a three- to five-page essay on the following topic: What is your American Dream? Compare and contrast your dream to the dream of a character from *The Great Gatsby* (your

choice). What do our dreams reveal about us? Do you plan to make your dreams come true? How? Does your character have his/her dream come true? Why or why not?

Include the following in your essay:

- characteristics of people who work toward the American Dream;
- paths toward achieving the American Dream;
- obstacles people face when working toward the American Dream;
- emotions people experience when working toward the American Dream; and
- whether or not everyone who aspires to achieve the American Dream achieves it and what happens when it doesn't work out.

Step 5: Evaluate What Was Learned

It is important to evaluate both students' work (the product) and students' working (the process). For this unit evaluation will be based on:

1. Assessment of the analyses of the characters from *The Great Gatsby* and the "real-life" characters (see Figure 4-14)

Figure 4-14. Wiki Rubric				
Category	**4**	**3**	**2**	**1**
Content	Covers topic in-depth with details and examples. Subject knowledge is excellent.	Includes essential knowledge about the topic. Subject knowledge appears to be good.	Includes essential information about the topic but there are 1-2 factual errors.	Content is minimal or there are several factual errors.
Organization	Content is well organized, using headings or bulleted lists to group related material.	Content is logically organized for the most part.	Content uses headings or bulleted lists to organize, but the overall organization of topics appears flawed.	There was no clear or logical organization but a lot of facts.
Attractiveness	Makes excellent use of font, color, graphics, effects, etc.	Makes good use of font, color, graphics, effects, etc.	Makes use of font, color, graphics, effects, etc. But occasionally these detract from the presentation content.	Makes use of font, color, graphics, effects, etc. But these often detract from the presentation content.
Contribution to the group	Contributes greatly to the development of the class wiki.	Contributes adequately to the development of the class wiki.	Contributes moderately to the development of the class wiki.	Contributes minimally to the development of the class wiki.
Accuracy	No misspellings or grammatical errors. No broken links or missing images.	Three or fewer misspellings and/or mechanical errors. No more than two errors in the student's contribution to the wiki.	Four misspellings and/or mechanical errors. No more than four errors in the student's contribution to the wiki.	More than four misspellings and/or mechanical errors. More than five errors in the student's contribution to the wiki.

2. Thorough research on the "real-life" person as compared to the Gatsby character
3. Participation in creating the wiki content
4. Collaboration among team members in reviewing and revising their own fictional character analysis and "real-life" character descriptions and those of other groups on the wiki (see Figure 4-15 for a collaborative rubric)

Figure 4-15. Group Participation Rubric				
Name: _____				
Date Observed: _____				
Feature	**Mastered**	**Developed**	**Developing**	**Not Developed**
Time on Task	Always on task	Mostly on task	Sometimes on task	Completely off task
Verbal Response	Elicits others' opinions	Accepts others' opinions	Ignores others' opinion	Rejects others' opinions
Participation	Actively participates in group goals	Occasionally participates in group goals	Sometimes participates in group goals	Does not contribute to group goals
Interaction	Listens and gives nonverbal feedback	Exhibits attention to others	Exhibits inattentive behavior	Exhibits rude behavior
Attitude	Encourages participation of others	Accepts participation of others	Discourages participation of others	Ridicules others

5. Self-evaluation of students' knowledge of wikis (see Figure 4-16)

Figure 4-16. Wiki Self-Evaluation Checklist				
Category	**Beginning**	**Developing**	**Accomplished**	**Exemplary**
I can distinguish wiki sites from other Web sites.				
I can describe several key characteristics of wikis.				
I can identify several ways in which wikis can be used in my assignments.				
I can create a wiki page and/or create my own wiki.				
I feel confident about creating a wiki as part of my assignment.				

Use the Wiki rubric to evaluate the work students accomplished throughout this unit on *The Great Gatsby* in which they used the wiki as an integral part of collecting material, collaborating with classmates, and presenting the finished product.

Summary

This unit used *The Great Gatsby* characters as a starting point to make students think about literature as it relates to their own experiences and/or research. They used listening, reading, writing, and researching to accomplish the tasks of this unit. They incorporated some of the latest technology—creating and using a wiki—for easy collaboration, revision of their writing and presentation of their projects to classmates. As a result, they improved their critical thinking and saw how literature relates to their own lives. Finally, students are now familiar with using a wiki for collecting information, talking about and revising writing, and publishing their work.

Teacher Exercises: Now You Try It . . .

To prepare to create your own lesson using a wiki, complete the following exercises:

1. Start a collection of Web sites, which are used for educational purposes. Write the URLs in your Web 2.0 notebook. Go to http://coollessons.wikispaces.com/Administrator_Academy_Read-Write-Web and select at least two wikis in your subject area and grade level to review. Select a third wiki that appears to have a different purpose (e.g., an administrative site). Write a brief description of the sites in your notebook and reflect on how a wiki can be used in your classroom.
2. Search for a subject that interests you discussed on a wiki and add a comment to it. (Hint: add the word wiki to your keyword search.)
3. Write a short description explaining how you would incorporate a wiki into one of your lessons. How/what would the wiki add to your class? Review the URLs in Table 4-3.
4. Create a wiki with content using a free wiki-hosting Web site.
5. Reflect on the following questions about wikis:
    - How might you use a wiki in your instruction?
    - Would using a wiki benefit your students?
    - What hurdles might impede your using a wiki?
    - Is it possible to remove the hurdles?
6. Create a personal wiki that you can use to reflect on the Web 2.0 tools that you are learning about in this book. Invite colleagues to participate.

> ➤ *Additional exercises at Bev's Web site at www.neal-schuman.com/webclassroom will give you more confidence in using wikis.*

CONCLUSION

When starting out with your wiki, keep the activity very simple, whether you have seniors or second graders. At first have students access the wiki in class. Listen to what other educators who are using wikis in their lessons have to say:

- At Olde Columbine High School in Longmont, Colorado, Bud Hunt began an experiment last spring using a wiki to teach writing. "The quality of writing across the board was better than any of the work they had done previously," he says. "I think it was because the students had an authentic audience. They knew others were looking."
- At Cranbrook School in Bloomfield Hills, Michigan, music teacher Alex Ruthman has encouraged kids to share their solutions to composition problems on a wiki. "A lot of teachers want to have all the control, and I didn't want that," he says. "I wanted students to be empowered."

Table 4-3. General Wiki URLs	
URL	**Description**
http://www.wikispaces.com/site/tour#introduction	Tutorial showing how to use Wikispaces
http://www.wikispaces.com/site/for/teachers100K	Sign up for Wikispaces for free
http://edutechation.wordpress.com/2007/08/03/ which-wiki-to-use/	Blog showing comparisons between wikispaces and pbwiki
http://www.wikispaces.com/site/tour#introduction	An introduction to wikispaces, including how to get started
http://www.newmediaworkshops.com/tripleAlecture/editwiki/ editwiki.html	Tutorial on how to use PBWiki
http://www.readwritethink.org/lessons/lesson_view .asp?id=979	NCTE Read, Write and Think lessons
http://www.schoollibraryjournal.com/article/ CA6277799.html	Library Journal Wiki article
http://www.wikihow.com/wikiHow:Tour	Wiki How to Tour
http://www.wikihow.com/wikiHow:Tour/Understand-the-Writer %27s-Guide	Wiki Guide
http://coollessons.wikispaces.com/Administrator_Academy_ Read-Write-Web	Cool lessons for wikis at all grade levels and subject areas
http://cte.jhu.edu/techacademy/web/2000/kajder/ wqeval.html	Scoring rubric on American Dreams
http://www.grandviewlibrary.org/ThirdGradeWikis.aspx	Sarah Chauncey's library wiki

- Wikis have also been used to help students gain insights into world events. At West Hills High School in Santee, California, teams of students in Dan McDowell's world history courses spent two weeks last June piecing together the history of the Holocaust. "The wiki's features of easy collaboration and easy Web publishing made the project possible," McDowell says. "Overall it worked great. The students took information and built their understanding of [the topic] themselves."
- As Michael Stephens, the special projects librarian at the St. Joseph County Library in South Bend, Indiana, and a consultant on digital tools, comments: "If you show media specialists what a wiki is, I think they'll fly with it. The school librarian who gets it and starts doing it and showing teachers and administrators how to do it—that person will be a superstar."

REFERENCES AND FURTHER READING

The American Heritage® Dictionary of the English Language, Fourth Edition. 2000. Boston: Houghton Mifflin Company.

California State Department of Education. 1987. *English—Language Arts Framework for California Public Schools: Kindergarten Through Grade Twelve*. Sacramento: California State Department of Education.

Davis, Michelle R. 2007. *Digital Directions*. "Wiki Wisdom: Lessons for Educators." (September 12). Available: www.edweek.org/dd/articles/2007/09/12/02wiki.h01.html (accessed October 1, 2008).

Friedman, Thomas L. 2006. *The World Is Flat*. New York: Farrar, Straus and Giroux.

Leuf, B., and W. Cunningham. 2001. *The Wiki Way: Quick Collaboration on the Web*. Upper Saddle River, NJ: Addison Wesley.

National Educational Technology Standards for Students and Teachers. 2007. The International Society for Technology Educators.

Oatman, Eric. 2005. "Make Way for Wikis." *School Library Journal* (November 1). Available: www.school libraryjournal.com/article/CA6277799.html (accessed October 1, 2008).

Powazek, D. M. 2002. *Design for Community. The Art of Connecting Real People in Virtual Places*. Indianapolis, IN: New Riders.

Wiki. Wikipedia contributors. *Wikipedia, The Free Encyclopedia*. Available: http://en.wikipedia.org/wiki/Wiki (accessed October 1, 2008).

CHAPTER 5

Digital Storytelling: Cross-Curricular Connections

PART 1: IDEAS AND INSIGHTS

Storytelling has been a part of culture from the time that cavemen wrote on walls, Native Americans passed oral stories down through the generations, and the Egyptians wrote their hieroglyphics. Each culture has its own stories. But, why do we tell stories? What motivates us to tell and listen to stories?

Stories are a way to engage the imagination of a reader or listener. Stories can teach lessons. Stories warn us of the consequences of our actions to ourselves and to others. Stories help us understand ourselves a bit better. Stories provide insight into someone's history and culture, forcing one to look at a situation from another's point of view. These and many more reasons illustrate why storytelling is so popular. It is how we share experience, understand one another, and create community.

Although digital storytelling has been around for a few years, educators are now implementing the process with the availability of easy-to-use technology. Many books have been written describing this new writing process, and there is a wealth of material on the Internet about it. In this chapter we want to review the basics of storytelling, emphasize the importance of storytelling as a writing process, familiarize educators with digital storytelling, and illustrate how digital media can enhance writing for K–12 students.

Objectives of This Chapter

This chapter describes digital storytelling and illustrates ways to create digital stories for science content instruction, specifically energy sources and energy conservation. It is designed for use by science educators and library media specialists at both the elementary and secondary levels. By the end of this chapter, in addition to content goals, educators will be able to:

- define digital stories and describe the components comprising digital stories;
- explain why they are useful in the classroom;
- identify how they address different learning styles; and
- create a digital storytelling unit, including writing storyboards and scripts, filming and more.

Background as it relates to storytelling is also included so that all curriculum areas understand the basics of writing stories and how they can be incorporated across the curriculum in subject areas such as science and social studies.

Glossary

Review the following terms to become familiar with energy terms used in the unit plan and words related to creating digital stories.

biomass: Organic material that has stored sunlight in the form of chemical energy. Biomass fuels include wood, straw, manure, and many other by-products from agricultural processes.

digital storytelling: Uses new digital tools to help ordinary people tell their own "true stories" in a compelling and emotionally engaging form.

dissolve: A gradual transition from one still image to another.

energy: The ability to do work or the ability to move an object.

fade: Gradually darken and disappear.

Fair Use: Allows limited use of copyrighted material without requiring permission from the rights holders, such as use for scholarship or review.

fossil fuels: Materials that were formed from ancient plant and animal life that were compressed underground over millions of years. Examples are coal, oil, and natural gas.

Movie Maker: Video creating and editing software bundled with the Microsoft Windows operating system.

nonrenewable energy: Fuels that cannot be made (or renewed) in a short period of time. Nonrenewable fuels include oil, natural gas, and coal.

pan: A camera shot in which the photographer moves slowly from one side of an image to the other side.

protagonist: The main character or the central figure of a story.

renewable energy: Fuels with limitless quantities or that can be used over and over again. Renewable fuels include solar, wind, hydropower, biomass, and geothermal energy.

soundtrack: Recorded music accompanying and synchronized to the images or the physical area of a film that contains the synchronized recorded sound.

storyboard: Graphic organizers such as a series of images displayed in sequence for the purpose of visualizing an interactive media sequence.

zoom: A camera shot where the photographer moves in for a closer shot of the subject.

What Is Digital Storytelling?

Digital storytelling is an engaging means of integrating technology into the curriculum, whether the technology includes digital movies or online storybooks. This phenomenon uses technology to accelerate students' oral, visual, and written communication skills to express what they know and understand to others. Stories can be created by people everywhere, on any subject, and shared electronically all over the world. Storytelling projects help improve student's reading and writing skills. These same projects can also enhance cross-curricular learning to improve math, social studies, and science learning.

Digital storytelling, however, has nebulous definitions. Some educators' definitions include:

> "Digital stories derive their power by weaving images, music, narrative and voice together, thereby giving deep dimension and vivid color to characters, situations, experiences, and insights." (Leslie Rule, Center for Digital Storytelling)

> "Digital storytelling takes the ancient art of oral storytelling and engages a palette of technical tools to weave personal tales using images, graphics, music and sound mixed together with the author's own story voice." (Bernajean Porter, *DigiTales*)

Story Elements

Good stories contain essential elements, and digital stories are no different. However, because digital stories are so short, usually from two to five minutes, authors do not have the same space to expand upon their message; therefore, some components become more important than others when creating digital stories.

- *Digital stories are personal.* The creator of the digital presentation is in the story in a key way—as the narrator and sometimes also as the protagonist. The story is usually written using the "I" point of view. Although many digital storytelling projects feature third person, the narrator is encouraged to personalize the tale, making it clear how the people or events in the story impacted his or her life. The audience should be able to sympathize with the character's feelings, and the story should be appropriate to listeners.
- *The story or script is most important.* Each story should have a single theme that is clearly defined. The plot should be well developed with a beginning, middle, and end. Furthermore, the story should be told in a way that allows the audience to identify with it, remember it, and be changed by it.

    Other aspects of the story include: developing intrigue or tension around a situation that is posed at the beginning of the story and resolved at the end, sometimes with an unexpected twist. Using a unique event to start the story provides a hook that leaves the viewer wondering how the story will unfold and how it will all end. The tension of an unresolved or curious situation engages and holds the viewer until the story reaches a memorable end. Pacing helps to sustain story tension. Figure 5-1 provides a general story outline.

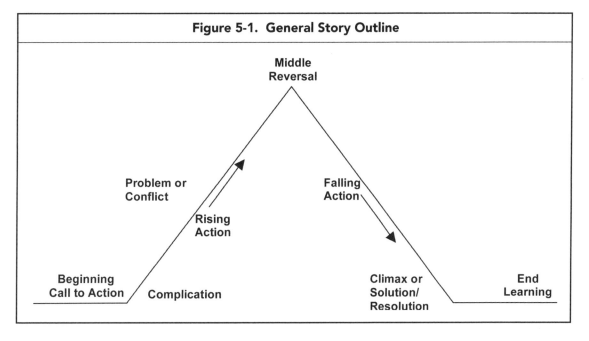

Figure 5-1. General Story Outline

- *"Show—don't tell."* Students should write using "observations." They must describe the characters and settings and help the listeners sympathize with the character's feelings. Stimulating the audience's senses so they feel, smell, touch, and listen enables the reader to see vivid pictures. This is also the art of good writing.
- *Collaboration is involved.* Once participants have a draft of the story, they give and receive feedback on their scripts. Peer revision is crucial to the final product.
- *Technology enhances story meaning.* A good story incorporates technology so that it communicates with images, sound, voice, color, white space, animations, design, transitions, and special effects. All media elements are selected to illustrate the meaning of the tale rather than being used to "decorate" the story.

Creating digital stories, students can connect the past with the present, relate personal narratives and improve their reading, writing, and technology skills, while enjoying themselves at the same time. Since these stories can focus on a scientific event or a historical figure, they lend themselves to cross-curricular connections as well.

> ➤ *Learn more about storytelling at Bev's Web site at www.neal-schuman.com/ webclassroom.*

Story Types
There are a variety of story types that educators can use as assignments for their students in the classroom or library.

- *Circle story:* A tale that follows a circular pattern, ending just as it began. The main character learns by the end, for example, that he or she is the best or the strongest.
- *Cumulative tale:* A chain tale in which a new part is continuously added.
- *Fable:* A brief story with a moral, usually with animal characters, such as *Aesop's Fables.*
- *Ghost story:* A story about the supernatural, usually a ghost or an apparition where often the ghost returns because of some unmet need—revenge, lost love—to give a warning or to retrieve a misplaced meaningful object.
- *Scary story:* A type of tale that focuses on common fears, such as the horror story.
- *Tall tale:* Exaggerated stories about extraordinary people (e.g., Paul Bunyan or Pecos Bill).
- *Why story:* A tale that explains the origin of some trait (e.g., why cats have nine lives) or fact (e.g., why ocean tides come in and out each day).
- *Myth:* A story, usually about gods or demigods, that explains a natural event or the creation of the world or a race of people. Myths differ in scale from why stories. The latter tells the origins of traits or situations; the former deals with the creation of worlds or natural phenomena.

Examples of Digital Storytelling in the Classroom
Many digital stories have been created in the last few years with a number of teachers and librarians pioneering the technique. Students in health classes have created public service announcements on addiction; English classes have created visual poetry; and history students have interviewed their parents about their own ancestors. As part of preparing the digital story, students develop critical questions to address in their presentations. Digital stories have many purposes from relating a personal story, to describing a place, to examining a historical event, to informing or instructing, to taking a position on a current issue. Educators have embraced this technology at all grade levels and in different subject areas as shown in some of the following examples.

Example 1: Study of Heroes
In Scott County schools in Georgetown, Kentucky, one high school teacher had her seniors create projects related to a study of heroes in literature. The students picked their own heroes from real life and created digital stories about them. They learned to write scripts no longer than one double-spaced page and to focus on one event or situation to illustrate their point. They then recorded sound tracks, digitized images, and edited their narratives into short, filmed digital stories. In the same school district as part of a primary-grade project, another teacher had her students agree on their five favorite holidays. They then worked collaboratively to write a whole-class script and turn it into a digital story. Figure 5-2 shows other stories by students in Scott County (www.dtc.scott.k12 .ky.us/technology/digitalstorytelling/studentstories.html).

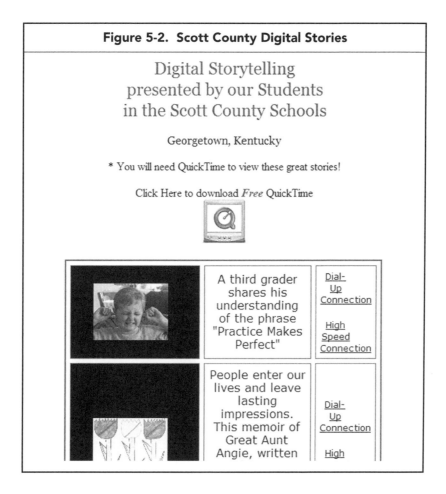

Figure 5-2. Scott County Digital Stories

In Scott County digital storytelling has widespread support. The Scott County Digital Story-telling Center is a collaboration between the public library and the school district where they teach patrons how to create digital stories. Moreover, each year Scott County holds a Digital Storytelling Festival where teachers, students, and community members come together to share their stories.

Example 2: The Power of One

The Power of One is a particularly powerful digital story illustrating how one vote has changed the direction of countries, states, and peoples. The story describes how one vote put Hitler in power; one vote made Jefferson president; and one vote led the United States into war. And, the theme of the story is that everyone should vote because every vote matters. See Figure 5-3: The Power of One. View this story and many others at http://sfett.com/html_movie/Ican4/the_power_of_one.html.

Example 3: Walled Lake School District Digital Stories

Two sixth grade teachers in Walled Lake School District in Michigan collaborated on a digital story-telling unit to improve the communication and writing of their students. Students used different forms of media as part of their stories. They wrote their personal narratives, created a storyboard, collected music, photos and other elements needed for the presentation, and worked all parts into their two- to three-minute digital stories using multimedia tools. Some stories focused on a relative—a grandparent or sibling or pet; others on an event such as moving to another location or a scary happening. See Figure 5-4: Walled Lake Digital Stories and view the stories at http://walledlake .k12.mi.us/aal/digstorytelling/Examples.htm. Many tools on the Web site exemplify the process the class went through to create their stories.

Figure 5-3. The Power of One

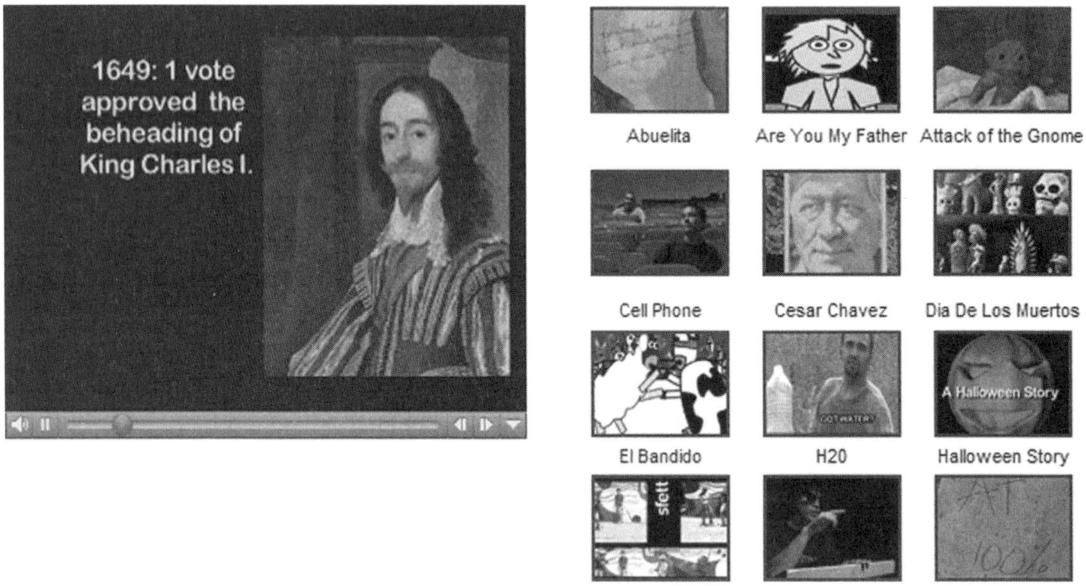

Source: Used by permission of SFETT, the San Fernando Education Technology Team; sfett.com/html_movie/lcan4/the_power_of_one_html.

Figure 5-4. Walled Lake Digital Stories

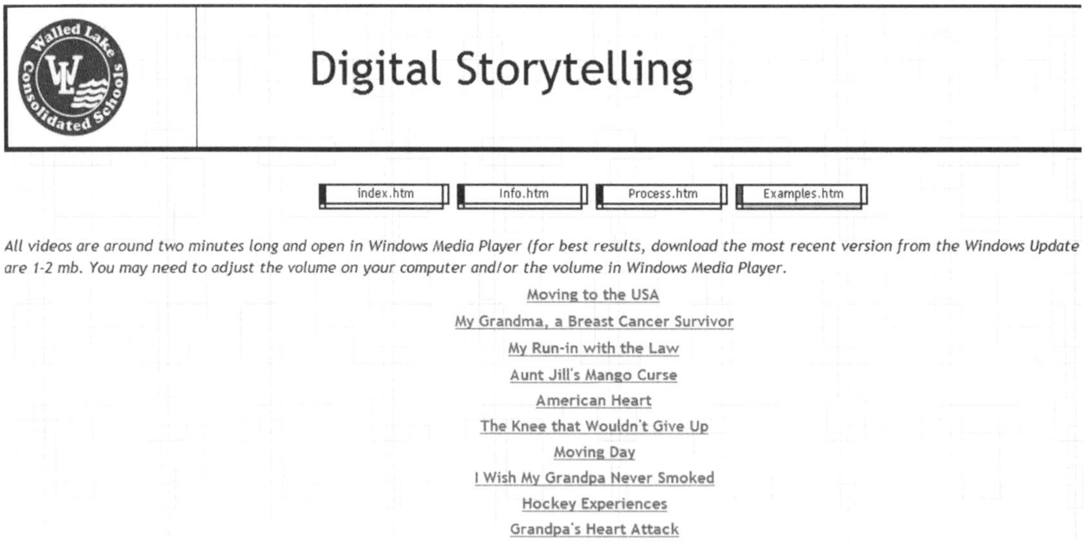

Source: Used by permission of Pam Shoemaker; http://walledlake.k12.mi.us/aal/digstorytelling/Example .htm.

Example 4: Elementary Grade Stories

Another class at Village Elementary School in New York created their own digital stories. Each was written, illustrated, and recorded by one or more students. Story titles (see Figure 5-5) like "Lost in the Big Apple," "Yankee's Dream," and "Monkeys to the Rescue" illustrate the diversity of story lines. Read the stories at http://villagewiki.pbwiki.com/Digital+Stories.

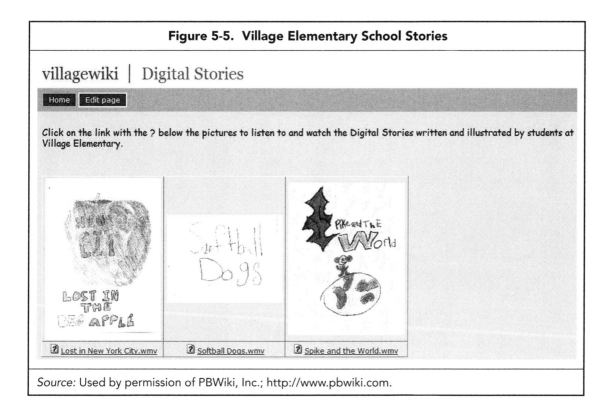

Figure 5-5. Village Elementary School Stories

Source: Used by permission of PBWiki, Inc.; http://www.pbwiki.com.

Example 5: KQED Digital Storytelling Initiative

KQED, an educational TV station in California, has sponsored a number of digital storytelling contests. "Coming to California," for example, illustrates autobiographical stories by high school students, such as the story by the granddaughter of a Japanese man who immigrated to America to experience the American Dream and died in a Japanese internment camp in Arizona during World War II.

> Visit URLs and read more about how educators are using digital storytelling at Bev's Web site at www.neal-schuman.com/webclassroom.

Other stories celebrate Black History Month and Women's History Month. Even as young as kindergarten, children have stories to tell. An imaginative story about the girl who invented a diaper-changing machine because she didn't like the smell of 100 dirty diapers is one of those. Review other stories at http://dsi.kqed.org/index.php.

PART 2: GETTING STARTED

Although writing stories in English and language arts classes is an essential part of the curriculum, writing across the curriculum is equally important. Thus, the curriculum tie-in to digital storytelling is integral to the activity. As was mentioned, the most important aspect of digital storytelling is the story and how students interact in creating the parts of it. However, the technology can enhance the story and motivate students to create a story that they otherwise would never have been excited to begin.

A digital story encompasses three phases of production. First and foremost is the preproduction, which includes creating the story itself. Second is the production stage where all elements are gathered together and media is introduced. Finally, during postproduction, students put the story together and present it to the audience. Figure 5-6 describes the steps in the process. We'll take a look at each phase next.

Figure 5-6. Video Production for Kids

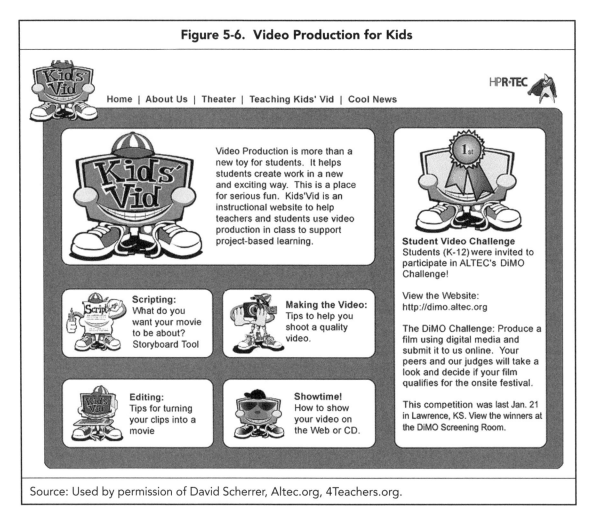

Source: Used by permission of David Scherrer, Altec.org, 4Teachers.org.

Preproduction

Preproduction forms the basis of building a digital story. Idea-sharing takes place, responsibilities are assigned, and sketches and text evolve as students write the storyboard. This phase is most important to the rest of the production and usually takes the longest to complete. During this phase it is helpful if the educator develops a set of steps, promotes expectations for each step, and assigns roles and responsibilities.

Step 1: Draw Upon Prior Knowledge

Assigned to groups, students should review several examples of digital stories and participate in cooperative learning activities to discuss the stories. These tasks allow them to gain confidence in sharing their own ideas. Prompts like those in Figure 5-7 can elicit ideas so that students can begin to think about their own experiences as a story.

Step 2: Start with an Idea

Students should begin with an idea that is both personal and meaningful to them. They must also think about the purpose of the story: Are they trying to inform, convince, provoke, question? How has this particular topic touched the author's life? The idea can also focus on their interests in a content area. For example, a young boy who loves insects can create his story around his interest in science; a student fan of the Civil War can use the historical period as a backdrop for a digital story; or a young girl with a new baby sister in the house can pour out her personal feelings in a story. One's

---

Figure 5-7. Story Prompts

- Think about a time you had to grow up, made a friend, lost a loved one.
- Pay tribute to a family member.
- Tell the story of a special place.
- Write a memoir.
- Identify a hero in your life.
- Relate a personal decision that will change a life forever.
- People enter our lives and leave lasting impressions.
- "Practice Makes Perfect"
- Does a mom really know best?
- Share a favorite holiday
- Trying new things for the first time can be scary!
- Where does your strength come from?
- How do you deal with thoughtless comments?

---

imagination is the only limiter to the story. The primary concern, however, is encouraging thoughtful and emotionally direct writing. Each story is told in first person so students' own storytelling voices narrate the tale.

Step 3: Gather Resources

Finding resources entails researching the Web, reading articles, interviewing, or going to the library. In addition, the digital story includes sounds and images. For example, a personal story might need photos of a family member. Besides gathering the sources, it is also necessary for students to evaluate what they have obtained, selecting only those images that enhance the story quality. Copyright rules must be adhered to and checking Creative Commons licenses is important (http://creativecommons.org) (see Chapter 1). Remember, too, that government resources are usually in the public domain, meaning they can be used without specific permission although the owner should be identified. Some sources have a more lenient copyright (Fair Use) if they are used for educational purposes. Nonetheless, it is still important to ask and credit the source.

For a three-minute story, students should select a maximum of fifteen images. This achieves two goals: first, it forces students to make decisions on the value of the photos to the story and results in the use of only the best photos or drawings. Second, it focuses their attention back to the story. Students must rely on the story driving the images, instead of the images taking over the story. Flickr.com (www.flickr.com) is a good place to look for vivid artistic images. Students should create individual folders on the class computer in which to place all sources they have gathered.

Step 4: Create a Storyboard

When students have written their stories, discussed them with their classmates, and made the necessary revisions, they are ready to create a storyboard. It is important to plan out their stories and using a storyboard helps to coordinate all parts of the story. Storyboard templates are graphic organizers that allow authors to visualize and detail all aspects of their story—narration, images, titles, transitions, special effects, music, and sounds. The storyboard lets them organize their thoughts before they go to the computer to type the story. When an idea for the digital story is firm, the storyboard starts and continues throughout the process. As students connect their ideas in the storyboard, they will see where they need new resources and how the direction of the story is proceeding.

Storyboarding allows students to "structure" their stories and synchronize the images to words. It is a place to plan out the visual story in two dimensions. The first dimension is time: what happens first, second, and last. The second is interaction: how does the audio, the voiceover narrative of the story and music, interact with the images or video? In addition, a storyboard can be an effective roadmap of where and how visual effects, transitions, animations, and organization of the screen will be used. The storyboard also promotes revision of the story when students see how the words work with the images.

The storyboard starts with the actual text from the script along with the images and titles being planned. Transitions and special effects fill in the storyboard. Sound effects and music are added last, even though ideas may be forming along the way. Finally, good storyboards display pictures and text and lead each group into production.

There are several effective methods of storyboarding. The storyboard can be as simple as a poster board with sticky notes placed where photos will be in the story. On the computer Microsoft PowerPoint can provide a quick and easy version, or a template from Microsoft Word using text and image boxes will also work. All students need to do is insert images in order and copy and paste the corresponding narration. See Figure 5-8.

Figure 5-8. Storyboard

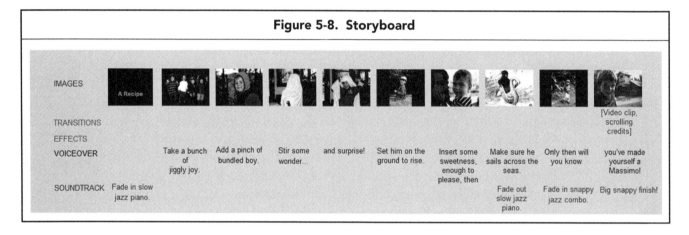

Step 5: Organize the Resources

Managing all the files—text, images, sound, music, and final product—is an important and often overlooked piece of the process needed to ensure everything is where it needs to be for each student's product. Each student needs his or her own folder containing all media elements. If preproduction has been successful, students are ready to "produce" the digital story. This includes delivering the written script as voiceover and combining it with visual and audio effects as shown on the storyboard.

➤ See additional tips to use in preproduction of digital stories at Bev's Web site at www.neal-schuman.com/webclassroom.

Production

During the production phase students will use the media to film and/or photograph, download files, if necessary, digitize images or sound, draw pictures, and select music. Editing media resources also occurs during this phase.

Step 6: Practice the Delivery of the Voiceover

Part of any delivery is enthusiasm, animation, variety in the voice, facial expressions, pacing, and sincerity. Students should practice their narratives a number of times before recording. Their narratives will become the voiceovers for their stories. The delivery is important because the audience needs time to process images, and a slower pace—at least most of the time—is much more effective. Also, blocks of time with no narration can add dramatic appeal. The voiceovers should be created first as separate audio files.

Step 7: Use the Tools

One of the appealing features about digital storytelling is the ability to use a variety of tools. Students should gather, create, or edit images, sound, music, and other media with the intention of extending the understanding and increasing the power of their message. There are also a number of techniques they can use.

1. *Soundtrack*—A soundtrack can have a dramatic impact on the entire story. Pacing, emotion and point of view are all enhanced with appropriate music.
2. *Visual effects*—Less is best. Effects should enhance the story instead of dominating it.
   - *Transitions* between images help tell the story. Various transitions signal different pauses in the action of the story. For example, having no transition serves to quickly move between two closely related ideas. A "dissolve" suggests a change to a related idea. A "fade" suggests a change of topics or passage of time. A particularly effective technique is the use of a black screen for several seconds: with or without sound.
   - *Pans and zooms* can add movement to static images, focus the audience, or give a sense of place for an object. In most cases, slow movement is best so as not to distract the audience.
   - *Text* can be an effective method for focusing the audience on a particular line, for example, by using actual text on the screen. Selected lines that are particularly important can be used in lieu of narration.

Walled Lake School District teachers at (http://walledlake.k12.mi.us/aal/digstorytelling/Directions. pdf) have written detailed, step-by-step instructions on using MovieMaker 2 to digitize photos, import pictures, and add voiceover to prepare to put together the movie. Note that if these digital projects are to be distributed outside the classroom, it is very important to adhere to copyright standards. Setting up a copyright free library for sounds and pictures is helpful.

> ➤ *Learn more about visual effects to produce digital stories at Bev's Web site at www.neal-schuman.com/webclassroom.*

Postproduction

While a storyboard provides the initial decisions and elements, in the postproduction phase it is time to combine the elements together in a compelling and memorable story that illuminates understanding for the audience.

Step 8: Putting It All Together

There are two parts in postproduction. The rough draft provides the author with the first view of the story, which includes the voiceover and sequencing of images/video and titles. It illustrates how the story will flow. This draft has no music or sound, no transitions or special effects. Authors can review the draft to determine if anything is missing or if additional material or text is needed. Now is the time, too, to have other students provide feedback about the tone and design of the story.

The final product contains all parts—music, sounds, transitions—that appeared in the storyboard. Authors should review their effects as they relate to the purpose of the story, remembering that each element illustrates and extends the message.

Teacher Exercises: Now You Try It . . .

Part 1 focused on the digital story itself and Part 2 on how to create it. Review the following exercises to familiarize yourself with both stories and media.

1. Review at least three or four digital stories. You can use the stories given as examples or check some of the other URLs in Table 5-1. In your Web 2.0 notebook, jot down what you like best about the story, what you like least. Evaluate how well you think your students would handle writing a digital story.

2. Think about an experience you've had and would like to share with your students and/or colleagues. Write a two-minute script using one of the storyboards listed in Part 2.

Table 5-1. General URLs for Digital Storytelling	
URL	**Description**
www.umass.edu/wmwp/DigitalStorytelling/How%20to%20Create%20a%20digital%story.htm	Storytelling Info
www.umass.edu/wmwp/DigitalStorytelling/Steps%20to%20Creating%20a%20Digital%20Story%20in%20MovieMaker.doc	Steps for using MovieMaker to create a digital story
www.umass.edu/wmwp/DigitalStorytelling/Lesson%20Plans%20for%20Digital%20Storytelling.htm	Lesson plans
www.picosearch.com/cgi-bin/ts.pl	Storytelling search engine
www.folktale.net/openers.html	Folktale openings
www.folktale.net/endings.html	Folktale endings
www.timsheppard.co.uk/story/storylinks.html	Story links of all kinds
www.timsheppard.co.uk/story/tellinglinks.html#Articles:%20story%20in%20education	Great site with excellent links to all aspects of storytelling
http://pblmm.k12.ca.us/PBLGuide/MMrubric.htm	Multimedia rubric
http://falcon.jmu.edu/~ramseyil/storyhandbook.htm	Handbook for storytellers
www.storycenter.org/cookbook.pdf	Center for digital storytelling
www.mcli.dist.maricopa.edu/learnshops/digital/examples.php	Examples of digital stories
www.dtc.scott.k12.ky.us/technology/digitalstorytelling/studentstories.html	K-12 digital stories in the Scott County Schools
http://cinedelagente.com/html/muves.htm	Digital story examples from all over the world
www.dtc.scott.k12.ky.us/technology/digitalstorytelling/studentstories.html	Student digital stories
www.digitales.us	DigiTales
www.jasonohler.com	Jason Ohler.com
http://techszewski.blogs.com	Techszewski
http://tech-head.com/dstory.htm	Tech Head Stories
www.techteachers.com/digstory/gradclass/rubrics.htm	Sample rubrics for storytelling
http://jdorman.wikispaces.com/digitalstorytelling	Everything you wanted to know about digital stories and media

3. Explore at least two or three music and image sites to see what the sites contain and what is needed to use them in your classroom.

> ➤ *Visit Bev's Web site at www.neal-schuman.com/webclassroom for more exercises on creating digital stories.*

PART 3: PRACTICAL APPLICATIONS

Digital storytelling lends itself to cross-curricular activities at all grade levels because stories are so versatile. As mentioned earlier, a story can be personal, describe historical events or characters, or illustrate events in science. This unit on energy incorporates the steps outlined in Part 2 so that students can create digital stories with a science focus. It also reinforces learning from Chapter 3 as students create podcasts about their energy sources.

Unit Plan for Science on Energy Sources and Conservation

Energy is a topic that children as early as the third grade are supposed to understand so that they can describe some forms of energy and talk about ways energy is produced and conserved. They start by studying sources of energy, such as wind, sunlight, nuclear power, water, fossil fuels (coal, oil, natural gas, and wood). By the time students are in the upper elementary grades, they should be able to compare and contrast all forms of energy and list the advantages and disadvantages of each.

Energy and energy conservation are important to countries around the world, and students of all ages can do their share to help conserve energy. This unit has two parts: Project A requires students to learn about energy sources and create a podcast explaining what they learned; Project B builds on the project just completed. Students will focus on energy conservation and create personal digital stories about their efforts to conserve energy. The digital stories that result from this topic emphasize cross-curricular areas to include language arts, science, and technology. Students will have already studied writing stories in their language arts classes prior to starting this unit.

Digital stories also integrate technology standards into the curriculum because they can be presented using video or still photos or pictures as video, and contain narrative, music, and other effects.

Step 1: Apply Framework Standards—What Should Be Taught?

This unit adheres to California standards in science and language arts for upper elementary students. English/language arts standards encourage an integrated curriculum in which students practice language skills in meaningful contexts and strive to promote the acquisition of speaking, listening, reading, and writing. Moreover, as part of the learning process in science, students should be developing skills necessary to think critically about issues.

Fourth and fifth grade frameworks for science include the following standards:

- In the fourth grade, science investigation and experimentation is particularly important. In addition, language arts also plays a part, which adds a cross-curricular component. Students will:
  - differentiate observation from inference (interpretation) and know scientists' explanations come partly from what they observe and partly from how they interpret their observations;
  - compare and contrast information on the same topic after reading several passages or articles;
  - use various reference materials; and
  - write summaries that contain the main ideas of reading selections and the most significant details.

- In the fifth grade students extend their knowledge of investigation and experimentation. Students will:
  - plan and conduct simple investigations based on student-developed questions and write instructions others can follow to carry out the procedure;
  - deliver focused, coherent presentations that convey ideas clearly and relate to the background and the interests of the audience;
  - discern main ideas and concepts presented in texts, identifying and assessing evidence that supports those ideas; and
  - distinguish facts, supported inferences, and opinions in texts.

Telling stories provides a way to practice and improve each skill. Moreover, the recently revised *National Educational Technology Standards* (NETS) emphasize the importance of children learning technology that they will be essential to them in the twenty-first century. The multimedia nature of a digital story lends itself well to using Web 2.0 tools that many students may have no access to outside the classroom. Also important is the way this media addresses all learning styles—visual, audio, and kinesthetic—and multiple intelligences, including musical, verbal-linguistic, visual-spatial, interpersonal, and intrapersonal.

In addition, most schools require that upper elementary-aged children engage in science fairs as a part of the science curriculum. A school science fair will provide the venue for students to demonstrate what they have learned in environmental education based on different types of energy sources and energy conservation and efficiency. Products from both parts of the unit will be presented at the Science Fair for the school and parents. As a result, the importance of energy sources and conservation will be delivered to the whole community.

➤ *For activities to create other types of digital stories, go to Bev's Web site at www.neal-schuman.com/webclassroom.*

Step 2: Identifying General Goals and Specific Objectives

Some of the main goals in upper elementary grades are to educate students about types of renewable sources of energy, how they use energy in their homes, and how to become responsible, smart energy users. This unit can be adapted for younger and older students. The goals and objectives develop student skills in science, technology, language arts, and critical thinking. Use the goals and specific objectives that follow as a basis for the content and skills developed in this unit.

Goals

In this digital storytelling unit that encompasses science goals related to energy sources and conservation of energy, students will:

- improve expressive language skills and inventive thinking;
- improve self-esteem and build confidence and poise when speaking before a group;
- use media to create a product;
- work cooperatively on a project while communicating in small groups;
- use resources from different sources to gather information for the project;
- address individual differences based on learning styles and multiple intelligences;
- identify sources of renewable energy and build good energy-saving habits; and
- protect natural resources for future generations.

Objectives

This unit provides content and strategies for students to achieve the following objectives in science and language arts while using Web 2.0 tools to enhance their learning. As a part of this unit, students will:

- read with a specific purpose in mind and learn how to make judgments about stories;
- learn to be respectful listeners and give constructive criticism;
- combine science content related to energy, language arts skills, and learning styles;
- use media including graphics, audio, video, animation, and Web publishing to present their digital stories;
- explain the importance of an energy source, how it is used, and where it comes from;
- learn basic Internet research skills;
- develop an awareness of how we use energy today in the community, at school, and at home; and
- encourage families to develop energy efficient practices to save money and energy.

Step 3: Gather Materials

Depending on the topic of the digital story, the types of materials needed may be very different. For example, a personal story may require students to find photographs of themselves or their relatives; however, a story on an environmental issue as in this unit may necessitate students doing Internet and/or research in their local community, taking photographs or conducting interviews about energy sources and energy conservation.

In addition, other technological materials are needed: a microphone, perhaps a digital camera or video recorder, plus software to create and edit the movie.

Step 4: Create Sample Activities

Activities will be divided into the three phases of production—preproduction (activities to introduce the unit), production (activities during the unit), and postproduction (activities as follow-up to the unit). You may also want to divide tasks so that students' specific learning styles are addressed.

Writing assignments have often taken the form of an assigned essay, a book, or a report to be completed by the end of a unit to test students' understanding. Digital storytelling, on the other hand, provides a powerful way for students to personalize their learning. Stories are designed to be engaging, to be personal, and to help viewers draw conclusions about their own lives or actions. Whether they are talking about their own experiences or something they have learned about in history or science, digital storytelling teaches them to ask important questions like: "Why am I telling this story?" "What is the main point I want to make?" "Where am I in this story?" "How do I relate to it?" Knowing that their writing exists for more than just the teacher can also be very motivating.

Activities to Introduce the Unit

At the beginning of any storytelling unit, it is important to stimulate students' prior knowledge of how stories are put together, learned in the language arts curriculum. A brief review of story types with examples, such as similarities, differences, which story is better and why, and writing patterns that repeat in each story, provides a model for students before they create their own story. Figure 5-9 illustrates the component parts to any story, as well as those components needed in a digital story, considering that the storyline occurs during the preproduction phase.

Next, students will turn to the topic of energy sources. In groups of four, students will do the following:

- Complete a K/W/L chart (what they know, what they want to find out, what they learned) together to help them access the extent of their background knowledge on the topic of sources of energy (see Figure 5-10).
- Read the introduction to the energy story found at www.energyquest.ca.gov/story/index.html. Each group researches sources to become an expert on a particular type of energy. Use the worksheet shown in Figure 5.11.

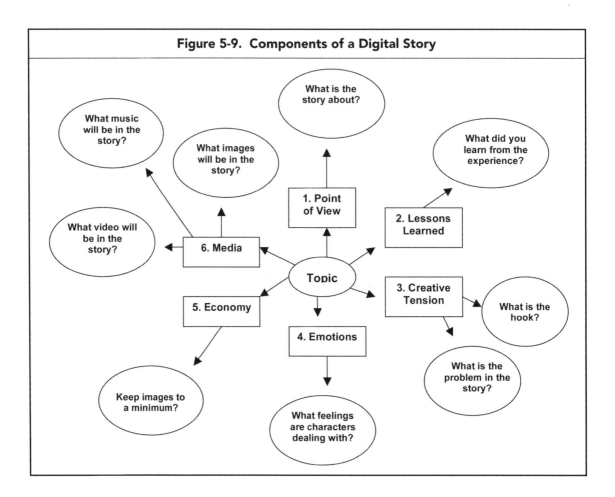

Figure 5-9. Components of a Digital Story

Figure 5-10. K/W/L Chart		
What You Know	**What You Want to Find Out**	**What You Learned**

- Discuss the following questions: "What energy source is the most important to us and why?" "Which is better: renewable or nonrenewable energy sources and why?" "Why don't we use more renewable energy sources?"
- Reflect on the following issues:
  ○ explain the difference between a renewable and nonrenewable energy source; and
  ○ summarize the key points of their review on energy sources (e.g., is the source renewable/nonrenewable? Where does the source come from? And how is it used?).
- Share K/W/L charts with another group.

Figure 5-11. Energy Sources Worksheet

Name: _____

Nonrenewable energy: _____

_____

Examples: _____

Renewable energy: _____

_____

Examples: _____

Do you think it is better to use renewable or nonrenewable energy sources? Explain:

_____

_____

What were your individual and group successes?

_____

_____

Were there any disappointments? Explain:

_____

_____

- Identify Planetpals (www.planetpals.com/planetpals_flash/ppintro1.html) to see the different kinds of problems we need to worry about on the planet. Each Planetpal (see Figure 5-12) represents one of the following: sun, clouds, water, garbage, earthman, green bean (living things), etc.

Figure 5-12. PlanetPals

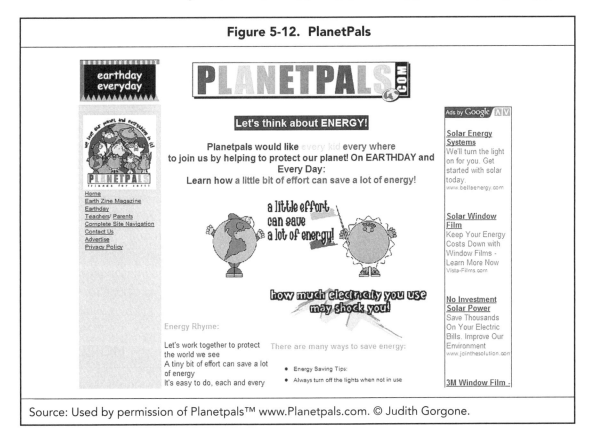

Source: Used by permission of Planetpals™ www.Planetpals.com. © Judith Gorgone.

As a result of completing these activities, students will have reviewed and reflected on their prior knowledge about energy and be ready to start their tasks about energy sources.

Activities to Use During the Unit

During the unit each group will select an energy source to research so that they can become the experts on that type of energy. Table 5-2 supplies Web sites appropriate for their research as do the links that follow.

Table 5-2. URLs for the Energy Unit	
URL	**Description**
http://teacher.scholastic.com/products/instructor/thinkgreen.htm	"Green" scavenger hunt
www.pbs.org/now/shows/413/index.html	Energy savings PBS
www.pbs.org/now/media_player/player.html?id=413ss&caps=low	Energy slide show
www1.eere.energy.gov/kids/roofus/	Roofus, the dog's efficient home
www.epa.gov/greenkit/student.htm	Sustainable energy for students/teachers
www.eirc.org/website/Programs-+and+-Services/Green-Apple-Program/Green-Classroom.html	Green classroom with lots of K-12 projects on energy
www.planetpals.com/partnerenergy.html	Energy saving ideas
www.planetpals.com/recyclefacts.html	Recycle center
www.planetpals.com/precycle.html	Precycle center
www.cnn.com/EVENTS/1996/earth_day/facts.html	Facts about energy
www.eere.energy.gov/	U.S. DOE Energy Efficiency and Renewable Energy
www.energyquest.ca.gov/story/index.html	Energy story
www1.eere.energy.gov/education/report_resources.html	Student resource section of the Dept. of Energy Web site
http://geocities.com/researchguide/energy.html#general	All about different types of energy, a comprehensive site with links

The two unit projects are intended to open up discussions about environmental responsibility and what it means to be an environmental-supportive citizen. Students should be challenged to find as many examples as possible of the energy sources they have learned about at school and at home to determine which one they are using the most. Students will also use Web tools for research and to keep up to date with the latest information on their source.

Project A. To learn about energy sources, groups will do the following:

- Assume the role of one of the Planetpals kids (e.g., Breezy, Earthman, etc.), who will describe energy facts (www.planetpals.com/partnerenergy.html);
- Read the introduction to the energy story and select a chapter that tells about the type of energy for the role the group has assumed (e.g., wind, solar) (www.energyquest.ca.gov/story/index.html). Each group researches sources to become an expert on a particular source of energy (see Figure 5-13).

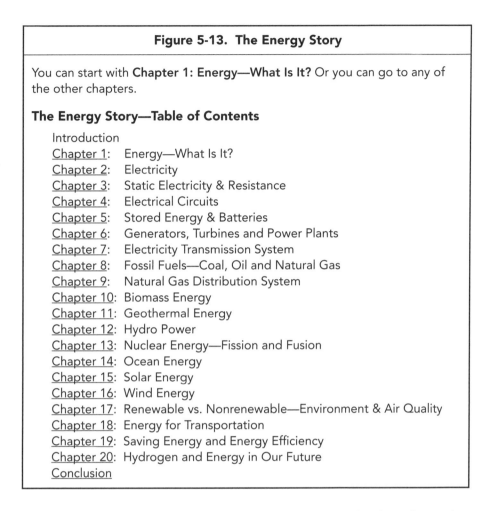

Figure 5-13. The Energy Story

You can start with **Chapter 1: Energy—What Is It?** Or you can go to any of the other chapters.

The Energy Story—Table of Contents

Introduction
Chapter 1:   Energy—What Is It?
Chapter 2:   Electricity
Chapter 3:   Static Electricity & Resistance
Chapter 4:   Electrical Circuits
Chapter 5:   Stored Energy & Batteries
Chapter 6:   Generators, Turbines and Power Plants
Chapter 7:   Electricity Transmission System
Chapter 8:   Fossil Fuels—Coal, Oil and Natural Gas
Chapter 9:   Natural Gas Distribution System
Chapter 10: Biomass Energy
Chapter 11: Geothermal Energy
Chapter 12: Hydro Power
Chapter 13: Nuclear Energy—Fission and Fusion
Chapter 14: Ocean Energy
Chapter 15: Solar Energy
Chapter 16: Wind Energy
Chapter 17: Renewable vs. Nonrenewable—Environment & Air Quality
Chapter 18: Energy for Transportation
Chapter 19: Saving Energy and Energy Efficiency
Chapter 20: Hydrogen and Energy in Our Future
Conclusion

- Listen to a podcast from the Willowdale Elementary School students about energy (www.mpsomaha.org/willow/radio/index.html) (see Figure 5-14).

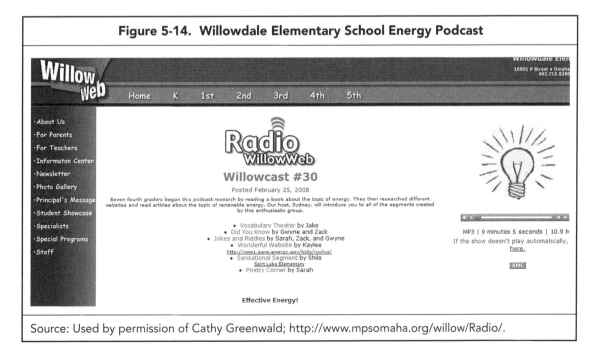

Figure 5-14. Willowdale Elementary School Energy Podcast

Source: Used by permission of Cathy Greenwald; http://www.mpsomaha.org/willow/Radio/.

Each group will collaborate to write the script for a podcast about their energy source. Group members will do the following:

- Contribute at least two facts for the script about their source (e.g., wind, solar, nuclear) and write them on the group storyboard (see Part 2 for details about creating storyboards); review and edit the script into final form.
- Divide the work in pairs so that one of the pair finds or creates visuals for the podcast while the other partner looks at music sites for background music and other transition effects (see Chapter 3 for details on creating podcasts). Students may want to select tasks that enhance a particular intelligence (e.g., musical, artistic).
- Practice presenting the script in their group, making sure that each student has a part in the oral presentations.
- Record the podcast incorporating the music and visuals; present to the class for comments and feedback.

Project B. To learn about conserving energy, students will do the following:

- Watch the short video from PBS about how one family is remodeling their house to conserve energy (www.pbs.org/now/media_player/player.html?id=413ss&caps=low).
- Review Roofus' house (www1.eere.energy.gov/kids/roofus/) and the energy used (see Figure 5-15). In conducting an energy audit, create a chart of energy "hogs" and discuss what uses the most energy so that students can see patterns in the data they compile.

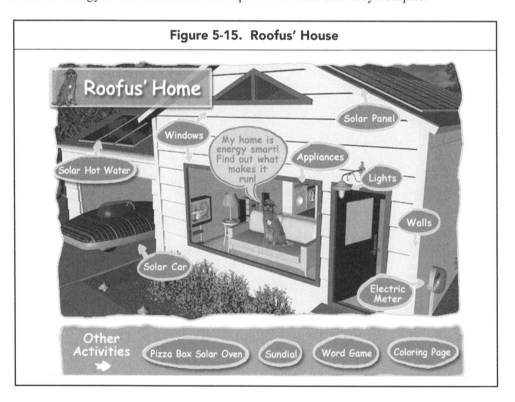

Figure 5-15. Roofus' House

- Discuss answers to the following questions in their groups based on the "energy audit":
  ◦ Why is a particular room the greatest energy user?
  ◦ How can the amount of energy used in this room be lowered?
  ◦ How can they save on the energy used in all the rooms?
  ◦ What form of energy is used the most?

- Why do we all need to save energy?
- How much of the energy used is renewable?

Note: Teachers can use this exercise as a pre-assessment task to be sure students understand ways to save energy and why it is important not to waste it.

- Subscribe to at least one (1) RSS feed containing energy conservation articles and ways to save energy in the home (http://home.howstuffworks.com/how-to-conserve-energy-at-home3.htm). See Chapter 2 for details on RSS.
- Do the following activities at home with their families after they complete the readings and discussions in class. These activities will encourage them to apply what they have learned in class to their own homes and help their parents reduce their monthly energy bills.
  - Complete the Energy Hog scavenger hunt (www.energyhog.org/pdf/ScavengerHunt.pdf). As a result of the hunt, have students identify four (4) ways that they can conserve energy in their homes.
  - See how the Energy Ninjas save on CO^2 emissions and make energy more useful. Try other energy games at www.sciencemuseum.org.uk/exhibitions/energy/site/EIZgames.asp.

Each group will collaborate to write a digital story about their experiences in conserving energy at home. Group members will do the following:

- Write the story collaboratively based on their personal experiences in conserving energy and put it on a storyboard; select visuals, music, and effects.
- Present the story to the class to obtain feedback, make revisions and final changes.
- Record the story integrating the audio, visuals, music, and transitions.

Note: See Part 2 of this chapter and also review the directions given at http://walledlake.k12.mi.us/aal/digstorytelling/Directions.pdf for details of production and postproduction.

Activities to Use as Follow-Up to the Unit

When each group has completed the two projects, it is time to distribute the podcasts and digital stories that students and educators have worked so hard to create.

The entire class should view all the podcasts and digital stories that were produced before setting up the Science Fair booth to showcase their efforts. This is also the time when students can give positive feedback to the authors.

Visitors to the Science Fair can hear and view each podcast and digital story at the class booth, and students will be available to explain how they created their presentations. In addition, sites on the Web such as School Tube (www.schooltube.com) allow students to post their stories to the world.

After each team experience, students should write journal entries and/or have a team conversation reflecting on the following four questions:

1. What did they learn?
2. What do they think about the process?
3. What questions do they have?
4. What advice would they give for designing student tasks with what they have experienced and now know?

Note: If the class has a wiki or blog, students can place their reflections on it.

Step 5: Evaluate What Was Learned

It is essential when evaluating this type of unit to perform assessment for both process and product. If teachers from different subject areas and library media specialists are working together to develop this unit, they should collaboratively decide on the evaluation at the time the unit is developed. Strategies for assessment can include:

- *Evaluate the final product.* Elements such as purpose of story, point of view, story content, clarity of voice, pacing, quality of images, meaningful audio track, economy of story detail, and grammar and language usage, all contribute when evaluating the success of a digital story. The rubric in Figure 5-16 provides examples of several components.

Figure 5-16. Digital Story Evaluation Rubric				
Category	**4 points**	**3 points**	**2 points**	**1 point**
Purpose of Story	Establishes a purpose early and maintains clear focus throughout	Establishes a purpose early and maintains focus for most of presentation	A few lapses in focus exist but purpose is fairly clear	Purpose is unclear
Clarity of Voice	Voice quality is clear and consistent throughout	Voice quality is clear and consistent through the majority of story	Voice quality is clear and consistent through some of presentation	Voice quality needs attention
Pacing of Narrative	Pace fits story line and helps draw audience into story	Occasionally speaks too fast or slow for the story	Tries to use pacing but noticeably does not always fit story	No attempt to match pace of the telling to the story or audience
Meaningful Audio Soundtrack	Music matches story line well	Music somewhat matches story line	Music is OK and not distracting but not coordinated well	Music is distracting, inappropriate or not used
Quality of Images	Images create distinct atmosphere	Images create an atmosphere that matches some parts of story	An attempt was made to use images to create a tone	Little or no attempt to use images to create tone
Economy of Story Detail	Exactly right amount of detail throughout	Composition is typically good but seems to drag somewhat	Story needs more editing	Story needs extensive editing

In addition, knowledge of content also requires evaluation. Figures 5-17 and 5-18 illustrate sample rubrics for assessing the energy sources podcast and energy conservation digital story.

- *Evaluate the process.* In a digital storytelling unit and when creating a podcast the process is as important as the product so it is important to assess the process in which students participated, how well students planned, how well they worked together in groups, and peer review of stories.

Using media involves taking risks and a self-assessment of the outcome. It also relies on learners sharing skills and insights. Self-evaluation rubrics in Chapter 3 can be used for self-assessment.

Summary

A digital story encompasses language arts, a content area such as science, and various technological tools. It requires that students work together, think critically about the process of putting all aspects

Figure 5-17. Rubric for Energy Sources Podcast				
Category	**4 points**	**3 points**	**2 points**	**1–0 points**
Pictures	Colored drawing of resource	Drawing of resource	Poorly drawn picture	No picture (0)
Facts	5 or more good facts	3 or more good facts	1 or 2 facts	No facts (0)
Content	Creative and applicable title; extra details, grammatically correct	Applicable title; 1–2 grammatical errors	Some type of title; 3-4 grammatical errors	No project completed (0)
Presentation	Presented very smoothly at an advanced level of understanding	Presented at the knowledge level	Presented a basic understanding of the concepts	Did not understand the material (1)
Teamwork	The workload is divided and shared equally by all team members	The workload is divided and shared fairly by all team members, though workloads may vary from person to person	The workload was divided, but one person in the group is viewed as not doing his/her fair share of the work	The workload was not divided OR several people in the group are viewed as not doing their fair share of the work (1)
Information Gathering	Accurate information taken from various sources in a systematic manner	Accurate information taken from a couple of sources in a systematic manner	Accurate information taken from a couple of sources but not systematically	Information taken from only one source and/or information not accurate (1)
Total				

Figure 5-18. Rubric on Conserving Energy Project				
Category	**4 points**	**3 points**	**2 points**	**1 point**
Conservation Methods	3 conservation methods clearly defined and explained	3 conservation methods mentioned, but not clearly explained	One conservation method was not completely met	More than one conservation method was not completely met
Energy Audit	Complete, clearly defined, and explained	Problems mentioned, but not clearly explained	Part of the audit not completed	Only one room of the audit completed
Resources	All resources conserved and named	Most of the conserved resources named	Several of the conserved resources not named correctly	Resources not named
Total				

of the story on the storyboard, research, write, read, speak, and listen. Students who create digital stories and use other technologies such as podcasts that meet all of these requirements have succeeded in real twenty-first-century learning.

Teacher Exercises: Now You Try It . . .

It is important to reinforce how to create digital stories, including writing the stories and producing them digitally. Before going on to Chapter 6, try some of the following activities:

1. Review Part 2 and how it fits together with the unit plan. Review Chapter 3 describing podcasts. Follow the process that students will take to complete the tasks in the unit. This will give you a feeling for what your students will experience as they complete each activity.
2. Take the story you wrote as part of the exercises at the end of Part 2 and create the actual story to use as a model. Include all components such as music, audio, transitions, and effects.
3. Identify several issues that you want students to explore. Divide students into groups and have them follow the process in the unit plan to create a storyboard they can use for the issue.
4. Reflect in your Web 2.0 notebook on the following:
   a. How will digital storytelling improve students' reading, writing, speaking, and listening skills?
   b. Is digital storytelling a good interdisciplinary project? Why or why not?
   c. What are some of your ideas for using digital storytelling in your school?

CONCLUSION

Advancements in technology have given everyone the opportunity to be a digital storyteller for an online, worldwide audience. Digital storytelling is an engaging means of integrating technology into the curriculum whether students are creating digital movies or online storybooks.

KOCE TV's Hall Davidson sees digital storytelling as one of several great ways for students to express themselves through media. "It's different from a video report where the objective is to convey information," he explains. "Stories definitely can teach, but they are also designed to be engaging, to pull at your heart as well as your head, and to help viewers draw conclusions about their own lives or actions."

Teachers who bring digital storytelling into the classroom are discovering what makes this vehicle for expression worth the effort. They watch students gain proficiency in writing and research, visual literacy, critical thinking, and collaboration. They see students experience a range of learning styles. Of course, they also see students make authentic use of technology, and they hear students discover the power of their own voice.

REFERENCES AND FURTHER READING

Gardner, Howard. 1983. *Frames of Mind: The Theory of Multiple Intelligences*. New York: Basic Books.

Porter, BernaJean. DigiTales: The Art of Telling Digital Stories. Available: www.digitales.us/ (accessed June 10, 2008).

Rule, Leslie. Center for Digital Storytelling. Available: www.storycenter.org/ (accessed June 10, 2008).

Saltpeter, Judy. "Telling Tales with Technology." (February 15, 2005). Available: www.techlearning.com/shared/printableArticle.php?articleID=60300276> (accessed June 13, 2008).

CHAPTER 6

Google in the Classroom—More Than Just Research

PART 1: IDEAS AND INSIGHTS

When we think of Google, the first thing that comes to mind is using the search engine for research. For example, if we want to find out about a medicine, want to search for information on the Civil War, or desire to locate an author's Web site, we "google" it. However, although Google's strength is in its search engine, it has broadened its array of tools to ones that are especially useful to the educational community. Here's what some educators say about Google Tools:

> "Collaborative features rock." (Google Docs) (Will Richardson, www.c4lpt.co.uk/ recommended/willrichardson.html)

> "I am really happy to have a tool like Google Docs for my students. It has changed the way I teach writing . . . for the better!" (Esther Wojcicki, Journalism teacher, Palo Alto High School)

> "I'm telling ya . . . if you haven't opened your Google Notebook yet, you're missing out! The BEST part is that I can access it from ANY computer ANYWHERE at ANY time." (Nancy Sharoff, Math teacher)

> "Google News is a great way to engage students in the election process and media analysis as the 2008 candidates make their run for the White House." (Cheryl Davis, Miramonte High School, Orinda, California)

Objectives of This Chapter

The tools in this chapter can be used by library media specialists and social studies content teachers at both the elementary and secondary levels. By the end of this chapter, educators will be able to:

- differentiate among the Google Tools, describing them and identifying their uses in the classroom;
- get started using Google Tools; and
- create a lesson that incorporates Google Tools.

Moreover, The International Society of Technology Educators (ISTE) recently revised its technology goals. After using tools described in this chapter, students will be able to:

- think creatively, construct knowledge, and develop innovative products using technology;
- employ digital media and environments to communicate and work collaboratively (including at a distance) to support individual learning and contribute to the learning of others;

- access, retrieve, manage, and evaluate information using digital tools; and
- employ critical thinking skills to plan and conduct research, manage projects, solve problems, and make informed decisions using appropriate technology tools.

Glossary

Google Alert: Notifies its users (by e-mail) about the latest Web and news pages of their choice.

Google Apps: A service from Google containing several Web applications with similar functionality, including Gmail, Google Calendar, Google Talk, Google Docs, and Google Sites.

Google Docs: A combination word processor, spreadsheet, and presentation tool that enables students to share their work easily, access it from any computer that has Internet access, and save their work automatically so they won't lose what they have written.

Google Earth: A free, downloadable application that combines satellite imagery, maps, 3-D terrain, and 3-D buildings to create a highly realistic virtual globe.

Google Groups: A free service from Google where groups of people have discussions about common interests.

Google Maps: A free Web mapping service application and technology that powers many map-based services.

Google News: Provides access to thousands of news sources, including archives going back 200 years.

Google Notebook: A handy tool that enables students to take notes while they are doing their research for a topic.

Google Reader: A Web-based aggregator, capable of reading Atom and RSS feeds online or offline.

Google Sites: A tool that can be used to centralize all types of information, such as videos, documents, spreadsheets, presentations, photo slide shows and calendars, directly onto Google Sites pages from other Google Tools.

Google Tools: List of Google products includes all major desktop, mobile, and online products.

placemarker: A marker placed on a map on Google Earth or Google Maps.

WebQuest: A learning activity used by educators where learners read, analyze, and synthesize information using the Worldwide Web.

Introduction

The list of Google Tools is too long to comment on each one in this chapter; however, the Google Web site for Educators (www.google.com/educators/tools.html) contains a comprehensive list. The site also describes the different tools, provides tutorials and videos showing how to get started using them. Some of these include: Page Creator (www.google.com/educators/p_pagecreator.html) to set up a Web page, Book Search (www.google.com/educators/p_booksearch.html) to search the full text of a growing list of books, Picasa (www.google.com/educators/p_picasa.html) to find, edit, and share pictures, and more. It also contains some examples that illustrate how educators are incorporating them into their own classrooms. It is a site you will want to bookmark and check often so you don't miss new tools, such as Google Sites, recently released, and projects like Doodle 4 Google.

This chapter describes some of the Google Tools, illustrates how educators are incorporating them into the curriculum, and demonstrates how the tools can be used together to create exciting and interesting lessons for students. A sampling of tools—Google Docs, Google Earth, Google Maps, Google Notebook, Google Groups, and Google News—described in this chapter is highlighted. Although Google Tools can be used in different subject areas, the focus of the unit in this chapter will be on the recent change of leadership on the island of Cuba, which is ideal for social studies, writing, and communicating across the curriculum. By reviewing the classroom examples and the detailed unit, educators will see how easy the tools are to incorporate into their lessons.

What Are Google Tools?

In an attempt to support educators, Google has created not only a site specifically for educators but a group of tools that will help educators do their job better and increase students' interest in learning. A newsletter and a discussion group (www.google.com/educators/community.html) designed to keep educators up to date on educational initiatives at Google are just some of the ways Google is supporting K–12 education. Several of the tools that are used as part of the unit later in this chapter are described here.

Google Docs (www.google.com/educators/p_docs.html) is a combination word processor, spreadsheet, and presentation tool that enables students to share their work easily, access it from any computer that has Internet access, and save their work automatically so they won't lose what they have written.

- The word-processing tool lets students collaborate during the revision process and keep track of the changes and who is making them through a Revision History tool.
- The spreadsheet helps educators organize grades, projects, or attendance sheets. Students can also use the spreadsheet, for example, to create a budget in math, keep track of the details of how a seed grows in a biology class, or watch candidates for the 2008 presidential election as shown in Figure 6-1.

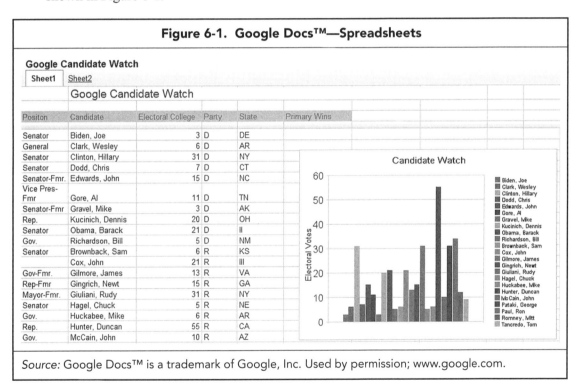

Figure 6-1. Google Docs™—Spreadsheets

Google Candidate Watch

Positon	Candidate	Electoral College	Party	State	Primary Wins
Senator	Biden, Joe	3	D	DE	
General	Clark, Wesley	6	D	AR	
Senator	Clinton, Hillary	31	D	NY	
Senator	Dodd, Chris	7	D	CT	
Senator-Fmr.	Edwards, John	15	D	NC	
Vice Pres-Fmr	Gore, Al	11	D	TN	
Senator-Fmr	Gravel, Mike	3	D	AK	
Rep.	Kucinich, Dennis	20	D	OH	
Senator	Obama, Barack	21	D	II	
Gov.	Richardson, Bill	5	D	NM	
Senator	Brownback, Sam	6	R	KS	
	Cox, John	21	R	III	
Gov-Fmr.	Gilmore, James	13	R	VA	
Rep-Fmr	Gingrich, Newt	15	R	GA	
Mayor-Fmr.	Giuliani, Rudy	31	R	NY	
Senator	Hagel, Chuck	5	R	NE	
Gov.	Huckabee, Mike	6	R	AR	
Rep.	Hunter, Duncan	55	R	CA	
Gov.	McCain, John	10	R	AZ	

Source: Google Docs™ is a trademark of Google, Inc. Used by permission; www.google.com.

- The presentation tool enables students to work together to create group presentations from any location and jointly present the topic.

Educators find Google Docs helpful because they can monitor student work while they are in the process of writing or revising in class and identify and work with students who are having major problems. Check the demos and click the download button to install Google Docs on your computer.

Google News (www.google.com/educators/p_news.html) provides access to thousands of news sources, including archives going back 200 years. Students can search for events, people, or ideas and see how they have been described over time. They can search articles in order of relevance to the query and see a historical overview of events and articles associated with the search on a timeline that is automatically created. The latter allows students to discover a variety of viewpoints across time periods. And, Google News is updated continuously throughout the day.

Google News Archive enables students to:

- search diverse sources from one place;
- browse timelines of events and stories related to specific queries;
- identify key time periods relevant to persons, events and ideas; and
- discover a variety of viewpoints across time.

Teachers, librarians, and students can also set up Google Alerts, e-mails automatically sent whenever there are additional news results about their saved search terms, allowing students to track developments in the news on an ongoing basis. Along with news alerts, there are five other types of Alerts: "Web," "blogs," "Comprehensive," "Video" and "Groups." Figure 6-2 illustrates how to set up an Alert.

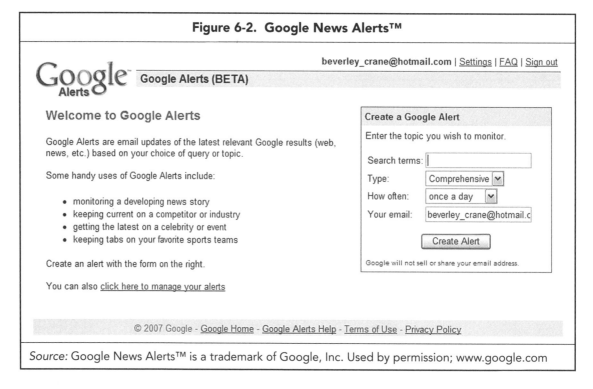

Figure 6-2. Google News Alerts™

Source: Google News Alerts™ is a trademark of Google, Inc. Used by permission; www.google.com

Google Groups (www.google.com/educators/p_groups.html) allows educators to set up their own place to communicate and collaborate safely and securely with their students. It is easy and quick to get started: create an account, name the group, and invite people to participate in private or public groups. Teachers can customize the look of the page and upload files to share students' work with others. Group members can also participate from any computer with an Internet connection. Teachers and librarians may also want to join the Google for Educators Discussion Group (http://groups.google.com/group/google-for-educators?lnk=gschg) to share ideas, ask questions, or tell their colleagues about teaching ideas they have created that have worked well.

Google Notebook (www.google.com/educators/p_notebook.html) enables students to take notes while they are doing their research for a topic. They can browse, clip, and organize information from across the Web in one online location that is accessible from any computer from the browser window. They can save and annotate clippings to return to later, share the notebook with specific persons, or publish it to make it public. Google Notebook allows users to organize their notes into several note-books and even search their notebooks. See Figure 6-3 for a sample page of a notebook.

Figure 6-3. Google Notebook™

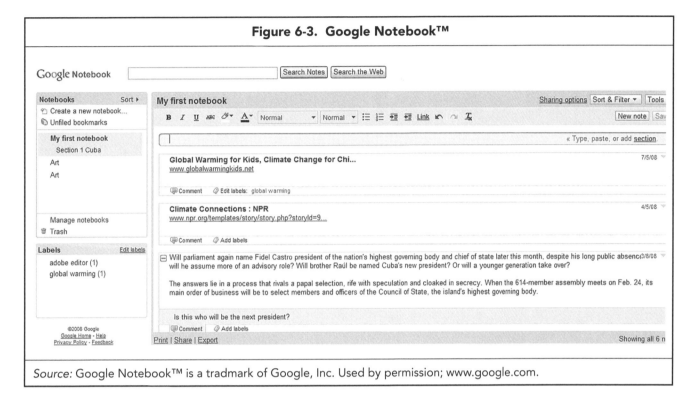

Source: Google Notebook™ is a trademark of Google, Inc. Used by permission; www.google.com.

Google Earth (www.google.com/educators/p_earth.html) is a free, downloadable application combining satellite imagery, maps, 3-D terrain, and 3-D buildings to create a realistic virtual globe. Teachers can create inquiry-based lessons using Google Earth to enhance understanding of topics such as earthquakes, volcanoes, erosion meteorite impacts, and more (see Figure 6-4).

Google Maps (ww.google.com/educators/p_maps.html), on the other hand, can be viewed right from your browser to view satellite imagery and shaded-relief terrain in a two-dimensional (overhead) view. These tools provide an uncomplicated means of combining satellite imagery with geological and geographic information to enable teachers to create learning environments that merge content, media, and geography.

Google Sites (http://sites.google.com/) is a fairly new tool that can be used to centralize all types of information directly onto Google Sites pages from other Google Tools, such as videos, documents, spreadsheets, presentations, photo slide shows, and calendars. Google Sites pages can be shared with just a few people, an entire school, or the world. Designations for owners, viewers only, and collaborators who have permission to edit the pages can be set up. See Figure 6-5 for an example of a teacher's team site.

Google Reader (www.google.com/reader/view/#overview-page) enables educators to collect all of their favorite sites in one convenient place. Google Reader constantly checks news sites and blogs they have selected for new content. Whether a site updates daily or monthly, users can be sure that they won't miss a thing. They can access their Google Reader

➤ *Review Bev's Web site at www.neal-schuman.com/ webclassroom to learn more about other Google Tools.*

account from any computer with online access. Sharing items from Google Reader with friends is also easy. A tour is available at www.google.com/intl/en/googlereader/tour.html.

Figure 6-4. Google Earth™

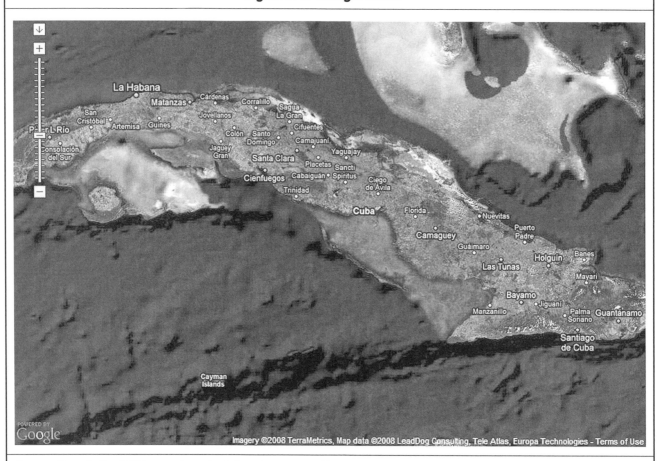

Source: Google Earth™ is a trademark of Google, Inc. Used by permission; www.google.com.

Why Use Google Tools in the Classroom?

Educators have already found many uses for Google Tools, both as a teaching aid and for administrative tasks like keeping track of grades. These free tools are easy to use, require little learning, and often are available from the desktop or through a quick download from the Google Web site. The wide variety of offerings enables teachers and librarians to use the tools as teaching aids and for collaboration and presentation, and they can be used with all grade levels and subject areas. The Educator's Web Site is loaded with teaching ideas and examples of uses in the classroom. Google Tools can be used to:

- practice research, evaluate sources, synthesize information, formulate opinions, and publish for an authentic audience (Google News);
- study natural and political maps, learn map reading and navigation (Google Earth, Google Maps);
- practice each phase in the writing process by getting quick feedback from many people and demonstrating editing skills (Google Docs);
- analyze and organize data and share data sets (Google Docs);
- study geography and mapping by finding locations all around the world (Google Maps); and
- share schoolwork such as book reviews with their peers, parents, and others; collaborate on projects and get feedback from others; keep a journal (Blogger).

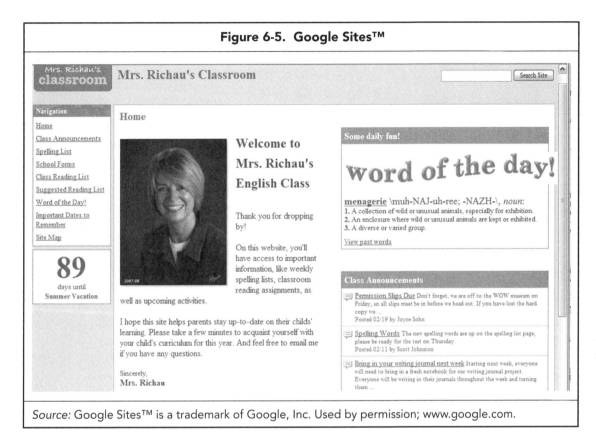

Figure 6-5. Google Sites™

Source: Google Sites™ is a trademark of Google, Inc. Used by permission; www.google.com.

The list of ways to use Google Tools in the classroom is extensive. As you proceed through this chapter, you will see illustrations of other ideas for Google Tools.

Examples of Google Tools for the Classroom

Besides the lessons on the Google site for each tool, several other sample lessons created by educators illustrate how easy the tools are to use, as well as emphasizing how well they can be integrated into the curriculum. A brief synopsis follows, describing the lesson, and the URL provides more information at the site.

Example 1: Social Studies and Google Earth

This lesson follows Sir Francis Drake's circumnavigation of the earth (see Figure 6-6). Using Google Earth, students can follow Drake's journey, view detailed information about each place he visited, and see a movie of the entire trip. In different parts of the unit students answer questions about Drake's trip, look at primary source material, gather evidence on Drake himself to determine if he was a hero or villain, and chart key points along the trip that might have been dangerous. The culminating activity is for groups of students to create their own trips using Google Earth. Details are available a www.activehistory.co.uk/Miscellaneous/free_stuff/google_earth/drake/index.htm.

Example 2: Google Earth in English Literature

This lesson using Google Earth has students build a Lit Trip as part of the process of reading a work of literature. By collecting Lit Trip content throughout the reading, students can focus on the kinds of details that make for rich classroom discussions during the reading. Group assignments include discussion starters with questions, as well as speculations and suggestions of connections to current real-world situations. Students should also collect URLs for images to enhance the comprehension of the setting, characters, plot, and/or themes, as well as images that improve comprehension of

---

Figure 6-6. Sir Francis Drake's Circumnavigation of the Globe

 Drake's Circumnavigation

Bookmark ...

| Online Games | Year 7 History (11-12 yrs) | Year 8 History (12-13 yrs) | Year 9 History (13-14 yrs) | GCSE History (14-16 yrs) | AS A2 IB History (16-18 yrs) | Search by Topic/Period | Your Account | History Shop [new!] |

Between 1577-1580, Francis Drake succeeded in becoming the first man to sail around ("Circumnavigate") the entire world.

In this lesson unit, you will investigate this extraordinary feat in a number of ways.

Step 1: Downloading the Google Earth Journey!

The core of this activity is a virtual "Flyover" of the journey using Google Earth (download it here).

Download the Google Earth Tour of the Circumnavigation here
[TIP: click the right-hand button of your mouse over this link, and choose "Save Target As" to save it to your desktop. This is a "Zipped" (compressed) file - so once it is downloaded, you will need to "Extract" it. Do this by double clicking on the folder icon which will appear on your desktop when it is saved, then choose "Extract all Files". When they are extracted, double click on the 'file.kmz' file to open up the tour in Google Earth!"].

Source: Used by permission of Russel Tarr; http://www.activehistory.co.uk/Miscellaneous/free_stuff/google_earth/drake/index.htm.

---

the historical, geographical, social, political, or other relevant subjects associated with the reading assignment. They can also put placemarkers on locations mentioned in the chapters. Many works of literature for all ages are listed on the site at www.googlelittrips.com (see Figure 6-7).

Example 3: Google Groups in the Writing Class

One English teacher used Google Groups (http://groups.google.com) to help students develop arguments for persuasive essays and speeches. This teacher created a different discussion thread for each topic being debated in class, such as illegal immigration or the death penalty. Students posted their opinions on assigned topics and included at least two links to Web resources (news articles, video clips, etc.) that supported

➤ *Explore other examples of educator Web sites using Google Tools at Bev's Web site at www.neal-schuman .com/webclassroom.*

their arguments. Each student was asked to respond to three other student messages with their own arguments and links for or against the issue and place their responses on Google Docs, which was accessible to all students at all times with an Internet access. Once the research was completed, students had a wide variety of opinions and resources to draw from before writing a persuasive essay or giving a formal presentation.

Teacher Exercises: Now You Try It . . .

Now that you've learned about the different Google Tools and ways they can be used for instruction, it is time to practice using them.

Figure 6-7. Google LitTrips

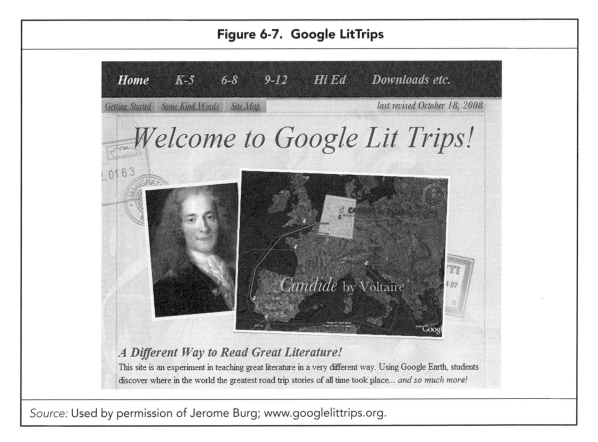

Source: Used by permission of Jerome Burg; www.googlelittrips.org.

1. Go to Google Maps (http://maps.google.com), which you can view through your browser, and enter your home address. Then select a destination you want to visit in the United States or elsewhere and enter that name. Get directions taking you from one site to the other.
2. Go to Google Notebook (http://notebook.google.com), create a new notebook and add a teaching tip and share it with another colleague.
3. Download Google Earth (http://bbs.keyhole.com/ubb/download.php?Number=151193) and then use it to take a virtual tour to Antarctica. Take notes in your Google Notebook on how this tour might be used with students.
4. Select a Google Tool that you are especially interested in; go to that Web site and review the tutorial on how to use it.

> *Try other exercises using Google Tools at Bev's Web site at www.neal-schuman .com/webclassroom.*

PART 2: GETTING STARTED

You, as a busy educator, have so many technology options to work with that it can be daunting at times. Google provides a couple of ways to get started. To implement a number of Google Tools to the entire school, Google has an education version of Google Apps—more about this later. Another method is for teachers or librarians to select the Google Tools that meet the goals and objectives of their education program or classroom lessons. Many of these tools were discussed in Part 1 of this chapter.

Starting with Each Tool

Each tool has its own process to set it up and get started. For some tools you must download the application to your computer (e.g., Google Earth); for others you can use your Web browser to get started (e.g., Google Maps, Google Notebook). So, just follow these five simple steps to get started with one or more Google Tools.

- *Step 1:* Go to the Google Site for Educators. Click "Tools for the Classroom" and scan the list of tools. Select those that you think you can use with your subject area and grade level. For example, Google Earth or Google Maps, ideal for science or social studies, allows you to explore the sky and see an exploding star; Google Docs enhances collaborative writing in an English/language arts class, enabling students to help classmates revise their work. Select at least two or three tools to get started.
- *Step 2:* Read the description of each tool you selected. For those that you think may meet your needs, follow additional links, and read the Frequently Asked Questions (FAQs).
- *Step 3:* If the tool needs to be downloaded, follow the instructions to download the tool that you think will enhance your lesson and provide the most interest and educational value to your students. For Google Earth you must download the program onto your computer from http://earth.google.com/. Take a virtual tour at http://earth.google.com/tour/index.html to see how to maneuver around the earth.
- *Step 4:* Practice using the tool with some simple exercises, for example, use Google Earth to identify your house or plan a trip that you have wanted to take. Experiment with some of the features including a visual overlay, add a placemark (a marker placed on the map) and share your work with a colleague.
- *Step 5:* Create a simple lesson that uses the tool, test it and use it with your students. Following the experiment, ask students to comment on the lesson. Of course, if you want to set up a blog (Blogger is a Google Tool), you can use it for the class dialogue about the new Google Tool. (See Chapter 2 for more on blogs.)

Notes:

- If you want to set up a blog, you can set up an account at Blogger at www.blogger.com/start?utm_source=en-cpp-edu&utm_campaign=en&utm_medium=cpp.
- To set up Google Docs, go to www.google.com/educators/p_docs_start.html to get started.
- Take a tour of Google Reader at www.google.com/intl/en/googlereader/tour.html.

> ➤ *Learn more about each Google Tool at Bev's Web site at www.neal-schuman .com/webclassroom.*

Getting Started with Google Apps

Google has a service for education called Google Apps that allows a school to have its own account for free communication, collaboration, and publishing tools. Google Apps provides access to a number of Google Tools, including Google Docs, Google Calendar, Google Sites, Google Talk, e-mail accounts on your school's domain (like student@your-school.edu), and help support (see Figure 6-8).

Note: Students can also get started for free with the Google Team Edition. A school e-mail address is needed to sign up.

Google has a guide to help you get started. Here's how:

- Go to the Google Apps page (www.google.com/a/help/intl/en/edu/index.html). Click the Compare Editions button and review the Education version features. You will note that the Education version contains many of the features of the Premier version, the difference being that the Education version is free to schools.
- To access the administrative control panel after signing up, sign in at www.google.com/a/your-domain.com. Replace "your-domain.com" with your school domain name. Then

---

Figure 6-8. Google Apps™

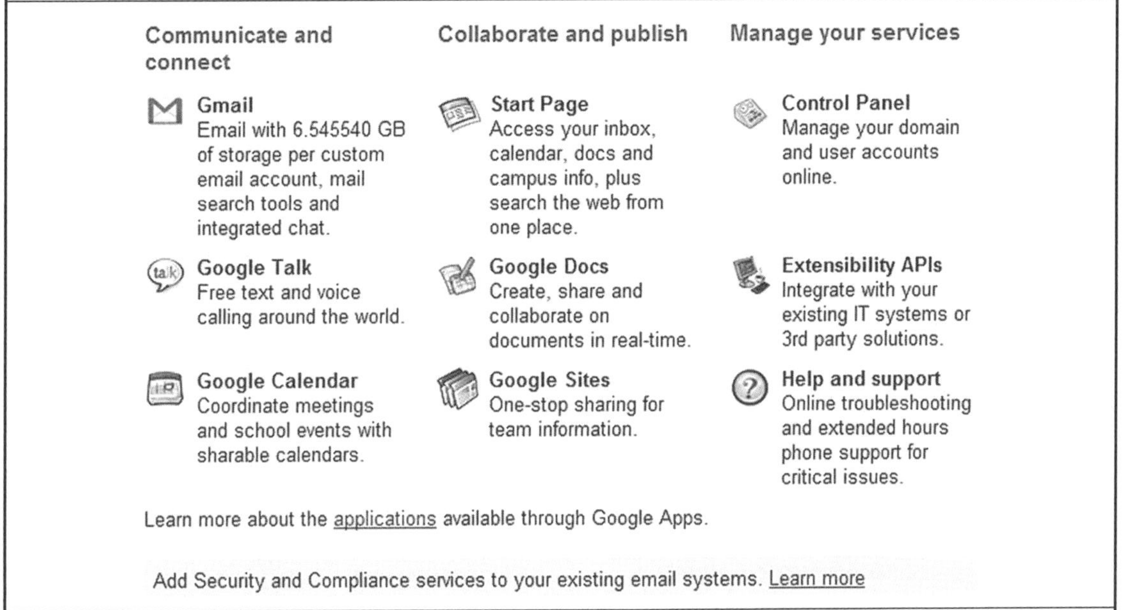

Communicate and connect

Gmail
Email with 6.545540 GB of storage per custom email account, mail search tools and integrated chat.

Google Talk
Free text and voice calling around the world.

Google Calendar
Coordinate meetings and school events with sharable calendars.

Collaborate and publish

Start Page
Access your inbox, calendar, docs and campus info, plus search the web from one place.

Google Docs
Create, share and collaborate on documents in real-time.

Google Sites
One-stop sharing for team information.

Manage your services

Control Panel
Manage your domain and user accounts online.

Extensibility APIs
Integrate with your existing IT systems or 3rd party solutions.

Help and support
Online troubleshooting and extended hours phone support for critical issues.

Learn more about the applications available through Google Apps.

Add Security and Compliance services to your existing email systems. Learn more

Source: Google Apps™ is a trademark of Google, Inc. Used by permission; www.google.com.

---

verify your domain name. The Google site at www.google.com/a/help/intl/en/admins/resources/setup/step_two.html provides two tests to verify the name.
- Customize Google Apps by applying a school logo, creating and publishing Web pages and configuring the Start Page. Instructions and demonstration tours are available to help in the process.
- Add users to your account either individually or all at once.
- Turn on the e-mail so that messages will be routed to your school domain. A number of instructive links provide all the information you need.
- Get your users started with Google Apps.

Now that your account is set up, Google also has training videos to get teachers, librarians and students started using Google Apps.

PART 3: PRACTICAL APPLICATIONS

The unit chosen for this chapter will illustrate using Google Tools in social studies. The unit is designed to incorporate a hands-on approach to learning and can be adapted for other grade levels and countries that might be part of the curriculum of study.

Unit Plan Using Google Tools in a WebQuest for Social Studies

The activity for this unit will be a WebQuest. WebQuests provide inquiry-oriented, engaging activities for accessing information and are designed to support learners' thinking at the levels of analysis, synthesis, and evaluation. A well-written WebQuest asks students to analyze a variety of resources and use their creativity and critical-thinking skills to create solutions to a problem. The problem is often "real world"—that is, one that needs a genuine and thoughtful solution.

Today's students will face a challenging world. In their jobs they will work in teams. Masses of information will be available to them, and they will have to sift through it, filtering the authentic from the opinion from the lies. Issues facing them will become more and more complex, and societal problems will resist easy solutions. WebQuests help build a solid foundation to prepare students for their futures, and Google Tools will facilitate the process.

As we have seen in the examples of classroom activities using Google Tools, they can be integrated into many subject areas at different grade levels. In this social studies unit plan at the secondary level, we will use several of the tools described at different stages of the WebQuest to explore a country—the island of Cuba, its history, geography, politics, and natural environment.

To compile this information, students will use the following Google Tools:

- GoogleEarth and Google Maps
- GoogleNews, archived news and Google Alerts
- Google Notebook
- Google Groups
- Google Docs

> ➤ *See other examples of using Google Tools in different subject areas and grade levels at Bev's Web site at neal-schuman.com/webclassroom.*

Step 1: Apply Framework Standards—What Should Be Taught?

This unit incorporates standards in English/language arts and history/social sciences, as well as taking into account the ISTE technology standards we discussed in earlier chapters. English/language arts standards encourage an integrated curriculum in which students practice language skills in meaningful contexts and improve their communication skills, both oral and written, through intensive practice.

In social studies, students are asked to consider historical events through a variety of perspectives and recognize how economic and social turmoil can affect ordinary people. The California History–Social Sciences Framework, for example, states that "history should be treated as a skill to be developed rather than as knowledge to be acquired." In other words, students should be taught to understand past and present connections in history so they can make meaning out of the future. The framework is further divided into strands so that teachers can achieve the framework goals.

The unit on Cuba incorporates:

- using primary-source documents to help students understand what people are saying and why they are saying it;
- integrating the teaching of history with other fields, such as language arts and science;
- incorporating a multicultural perspective that reflects experiences of men and women of different races, religions, and ethnic groups;
- engaging students actively in the learning process through collaboration, role-playing, and writing projects;
- including critical thinking skills at every grade level to learn to detect bias in print and visual media, to recognize illogical thinking and to reach conclusions based on solid evidence; and
- enhancing content using technology.

Step 2: Identify General Goals and Specific Objectives

The goals and specific objectives that follow form the basis for the content and skills of the unit.

Goals

Students will:

- link past to present;
- understand the increasing influence of other nations in the lives of American citizens;

- focus on Cuba and the United States with emphasis on cultural and political comparisons between these nations and their economic relationships today; and
- use Google Tools for research and technology for individual work, collaboration, and presentation.

Objectives

The activities and materials in this unit will contribute to a greater understanding of Cuba and the Cuban people. The unit will provide content and strategies so students will be able to:

Content:
- compare and contrast the Cuban economic, political, and social environment before and during the Castro regime;
- locate Cuba geographically in relation to the United States and South America;
- identify and describe specific sites of importance on the island of Cuba; and
- analyze and forecast possible changes to the economic and political structure of Cuba since Castro stepped down.

Technology—use the following Google Tools for their assignments:
- Google Earth and Google Maps to discover geographic areas and sites of interest on the island of Cuba;
- Google Maps to identify various types of flora and fauna endemic to Cuba;
- Google Notebook to keep track of and organize information for their projects;
- Google Docs to create a presentation incorporating research;
- Google Groups to share, collaborate, and edit their own and classmates' work;
- Google News, archives and Alerts for research on Cuba.

Step 3: Introduce the WebQuest

WebQuests comprise several components:

1. *Introduction* sets the stage and provides background.
2. *Task* provides a goal and focus for student energies.
3. *Information sources* direct students to information on which to make decisions.
4. *Process* is a series of steps that students will go through to accomplish the task.
5. *Guidance* helps students organize the information and determine how to structure the final project.
6. *Conclusion* reminds students what they learned and encourages them to extend their learning beyond the WebQuest task.

Outline the task. After almost 50 years, Fidel Castro has finally stepped down as the leader of Cuba. His brother Raul has taken the reins of control and is supported by the Cuban military. Most people have never been to Cuba. What do we know about this mysterious island just off the U.S. coast? Students need to find out as much as they can about its history, geography, economic situation, natural conditions, and how this change of leadership might affect its people and perhaps the people of the United States.

Task. You have been asked to serve on a special committee that will research Cuba's past and present in order to give the best recommendation for the structure of a future government. Your committee will present its findings to the newly appointed interim government under the leadership of Raul Castro.

In each group of four, there will be a historian/geographer, a political expert, a photojournalist, and an economist. Each person will research, take a virtual tour of the island, and provide the expertise for his/her topic:

- *Historian:* Research the history, before and after the Cuban Revolution and create a historical timeline based on more than 40 years of Cuban history.

- *Photojournalist:* Create a map of Cuba, highlighted with important sites (e.g., Havana, Guantanamo Bay) and areas of interest (e.g., Morro Castle). Collect pictures of natural flora and fauna for the map and compile facts about the island.
- *Economist:* Research economic trends before and after Fidel Castro came to power.
- *Politician:* Discuss the type of government pre-Castro and during Castro's time in office. Include Guantanamo Bay and its relationship to the United States.

> ➤ *Learn more about WebQuests and their use with Google Tools at Bev's Web site at www.neal-schuman.com/webclassroom.*

Step 4: Create Sample Activities

Included are activities to introduce the unit, use during the lessons, and follow up the lessons. Groups can check some of the URLs in Table 6-1 throughout the unit as they research their topics.

Table 6-1. URLs for the WebQuest Unit	
URL	**Description**
www.historyofcuba.com/history/baypigs/pigs2.htm	Invasion at Bay of Pigs
www.cia.gov/library/publications/the-world-factbook	CIA Fact Book
www.pbs.org/newshour/bb/latin_america/cuba/life.html	Life in Cuba
www.usaengage.org/index.php?option=com_issues&view=issue&id=12&Itemid=5	A business organization supporting policy changes toward Cuba
www.forbes.com/home/business/2008/02/19/cuba-castro-retirement-cx_0220oxford.html	Will Cuba change under Raul?
www.slate.com/id/2185087/	Will any changes occur with the passing of the baton?
www.canada.com/saskatoonstarphoenix/news/world/story.html?id=0cf307e8-533d-4d6e-983d-a1481387bee0	How do the young Cubans feel about the change? What do they wish for? What do Cuban bloggers say about the change?
www.reuters.com/article/worldNews/idUSN0738669420080207	Reuters: Cuban students openly challenge government
www.reuters.com/article/worldNews/dUSN2017089720080220	No end to repression says activist
www.reuters.com/article/worldNews/idUSN1926216920080219	Raul raises hopes for economic change in Cuba
www.nytimes.com/2008/03/01/world/americas/01cuba.html?em&ex=1204520400&en=83c44165cfcdf9e7&ei=5087%0A	Human rights violations in Cuba under Fidel Castro. Has anything changed since Raul Castro has taken office?
http://edition.cnn.com/TRANSCRIPTS/0205/12/sm.11.html	Carter goes to Cuba (2002)
www.usatoday.com/news/opinion/columnists/wickham/2002-05-21-wickham.htm	History, race must be factored into Cuban equation
http://edition.cnn.com/TRANSCRIPTS/0104/15/sm.12.html	Article on Bay of Pigs
www.guardian.co.uk/world/1959/jan/11/cuba	Cuba article from news archive from 1959

Activities to Introduce the Unit

Students and even most of their parents will have never visited Cuba and because it has been so isolated for over 40 years, it is important that students have some basic background on an island so close to the United States. As a group the class will:

- discuss what they have heard about Cuba, including politics, economy, and public opinion to draw upon their prior knowledge;
- discuss the people, including language, and read articles to provide background information on the differences of opinion about Cuba (www.historyofcuba.com/history/funfacts/embargo.htm) (Google News); and
- create a cluster diagram summarizing all of the facts they have discussed about Cuba (see examples of a cluster diagram in Chapter 3).

Activities to Be Used During the Unit

These activities will provide new information and reinforce the concepts that students have already attained. As part of groups of four, each student will be assigned one of four roles. The activities during the lesson will help students develop expertise to play their roles as follows:

Historian/geographer:
  ○ Use Google Earth to locate Cuba as it relates to the United States and South America. Create a map identifying major cities (e.g., Havana, Santiago) and historical sites (e.g., Morro Castle, Guantanamo Bay). Put placemarkers on the map at each site.
  ○ Use Google Maps (Figure 6-9) to calculate the distance between: Miami and Havana, Havana and Guantanamo or Santiago, Cuba and Central America, Cuba and South America.

Figure 6-9. Google Maps™

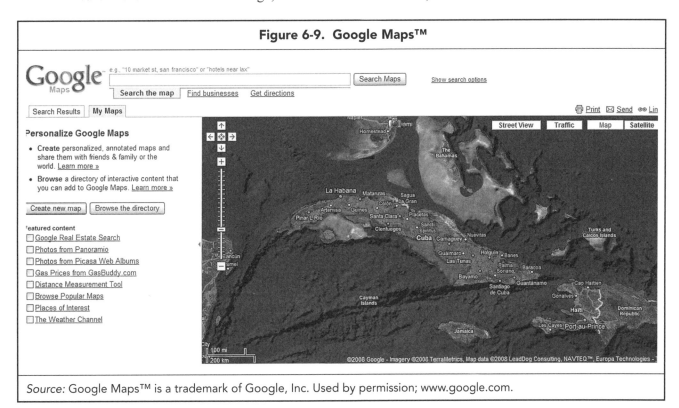

Source: Google Maps™ is a trademark of Google, Inc. Used by permission; www.google.com.

  ○ Use Google Docs to create a spreadsheet containing locations and distances of places and landmarks they have identified.

○ Use Google News and Archive News and the Google search engine to find other sites and compile a historical timeline of major events in Cuba's history.

Photojournalist:

○ Use Google Earth to find information on the flora and fauna of Cuba, particularly species that are endemic to the island environment. Using the map the Historian has created in Google Earth, place pictures of the species on the map (see Figure 6-10).

Figure 6-10. Cuban Flora and Fauna

○ Use Google News to set up a personalized news site about Cuba, its government, new leader, etc. Set up a Google News Alert to keep up to date on happenings in Cuba, the U.S. reaction to Cuba's change of leadership, and any action at Guantanamo Bay.

○ Summarize the news stories in Google Notebook.

○ Check for bias in the news stories and note comments in Google Notebook.

Economist:

○ Read at least five (5) news articles and press releases, publications and blogs about U.S. policy towards Cuba (www.usaengage.org/index.php?option=com_issues&view=issue&id =12&Itemid=55).

○ Review the embargo timeline to see how different U.S. leaders have dealt with Cuba. See www.historyofcuba.com/history/ and Figure 6-11.

○ Use Google Docs to create a spreadsheet of events based on the timeline.

Political expert:

○ Look at the video about Raul Castro and determine how you will convince the Cuban people not to be discontented living under the restrictions of no travel and a salary of approximately $15 a month. Write your thoughts in Google Notebook (www.cnn.com/ video/#/video/world/2008/02/26/neill.cuba.raul.inheritance.cnn).

○ On Google News review different points of view from world leaders about Castro stepping down as Cuba's leader and changes to expect (see Figure 6-12).

○ Create a spreadsheet using Google Docs that lists different points of view.

Figure 6-11. Cuban Embargo Timeline

<u>historyofcuba.com</u>
written & compiled by J.A. Sierra

ECONOMIC EMBARGO TIMELINE

"For the thing we should never do in dealing with revolutionary countries, in which the world abounds, is to push them behind an iron curtain raised by ourselves. On the contrary, even when they have been seduced and subverted and are drawn across the line, the right thing to do is to keep the way open for their return."
Walter Lippmann, July 1959

1960

March 17. President Eisenhower approves a covert action plan against Cuba that includes the use of a "powerful propaganda campaign" designed to overthrow Castro. The plan includes: a) the termination of sugar purchases b) the end of oil deliveries c) continuation of the arms embargo in effect since mid-1958 d) the organization of a paramilitary force of Cuban exiles to invade the island.

October 19. U.S. imposes a partial economic embargo on Cuba that excludes food and medicine.

1961

September 4. The *Foreign Assistance Act* of 1961 passes in the U.S. Congress. It prohibits aid to Cuba and authorizes the President to create a "total embargo upon all trade" with Cuba.

Figure 6-12. Google Cuban News

<u>cuba and raul »</u>   <u>edit</u> ☒

Your "cuba and raul" section has been created.   <u>undo</u> | <u>close</u>

<u>Cuba: What Comes Next?</u>
AS/COA Online - **2 hours ago**
There has been speculation that **Cuba** might move toward a model similar to the liberalized Eastern European markets or China's economy.
<u>EU envoy seeks new ties with **Raul Castro's Cuba**</u> Reuters
<u>All eyes on **Raul** Castro</u> Chicago Tribune
<u>BusinessWeek</u> - <u>Berkeley Beacon (subscription)</u> - <u>AHN</u>
<u>all 52 news articles »</u>

Canada.com

<u>President Bush Rejects Idea of Talks with Cuba's President Raul Castro</u>
Voice of America - **Feb 28, 2008**
He described **Raul** Castro as "nothing more than an extension" of what Fidel Castro did, which, as Mr. Bush put it, was to ruin an island and imprison people because of their beliefs.

Voice of America

<u>CUBA: BUSH, RAUL CASTRO "TYRANT", WILL NOT TALK WITH HIM</u>
Agenzia Giornalistica Italia - **Feb 28, 2008**
28 - George W. Bush has called the new president of **Cuba**, **Raul** Castro, a "tyrant" and has excluded the idea of starting bilateral talks with **Cuba**. Talking with **Raul**, who succeeded his brother Fidel this week, would mean "embracing a tyrant" said the US ...

- ○ Read about the politics and history of the prison camp located at Guantanamo Bay.
- ○ Use Google Notebook to compile notes and links to Web sites on the politics of Cuba.

In their groups: Together group members will collaborate and create their presentations for the special committee and formulate specific conclusions.

- • Students should discuss the information that they gathered according to their subject. All group members should have a basic understanding of all topics.

- Using Google Docs, "experts" share information they have collected about their area of expertise. Group members will edit, ask questions for clarification, visit Web sites via the links, and identify the five (5) most important facts from each expert to include in the group presentation.
- Once experts have shared their information with their group, each team must come to a conclusion regarding the future leadership of Cuba. This conclusion will be included in the group report. They will consider the following questions:
  - What do the Cuban people want?
  - Will the future leadership be similar to the dictatorship of Fidel Castro?
  - Will Cuba want a democracy like the United States?
  - Will it be the responsibility of one person or of many?
  - Will they have elections to decide the next leader?
  - How will all of this affect the economy?
  - Is there a historical trend that they need to follow or break?
- Using Google Docs, students will create a report in the form of a book, PowerPoint presentation or Web site that includes the following:
  - a tour of the island using the photos and placemarkers on the map that was created with Google Earth;
  - an individual report from each expert in the group;
  - a final recommendation for the future of Cuba;
  - a list of resources; and
  - visuals to represent their findings.

Activities to Use as Follow-Up to the Unit

It is important for students to reflect on what they have learned. As a follow-up students will do the following:

- Reflect on any changes to their opinions on Cuba and its situation, taking its politics, history, public opinion, and economy into consideration. Some questions to pose might be: Have their opinions changed at all since the beginning of this project? If so, how? If not, what opinions have been reenforced because of their research?
- Complete a one-page reflection paper during class.
- After writing the individual reflection papers, voice their opinions about Cuba, its current situation, and its future.
- Create a podcast and put it on the school Web site with each "expert" writing and presenting his or her information via the podcast.

Step 5: Evaluate What Was Learned

Evaluation is an important part of any unit. Because Google Docs is being used in the lesson, the teacher or library media specialist can evaluate student work as it progresses. Evaluation will include the following listed in the Evaluation Rubric (see Figure 6-13).

Summary

Social studies is a particularly good curriculum area in which to use Web 2.0 tools. A variety of Google Tools was incorporated into this unit to aid students in research, presentation, note-taking, mapmaking, collaboration, and compiling data. Using these tools provides hands-on activities to enhance student learning and make it more fun. However, the main emphasis of the learning is on the content not the availability of the technology. Educators creating lessons using Google Tools should consider:

Figure 6-13. Evaluation Rubric			
Group Presentation	Excellent	Good	Needs Work
Cuban Map Using Google Maps and Google Earth	Map is included and contains at least 5 place markers and 4 photos 5 points	Map is included and contains at least 3 place markers and 2 photos 3 points	Map is included with no place markers or photos 1 point
Final Presentation in Google Docs	Logical, well thought out, grammatically correct 30 points	Presentation is hard to understand or does not make sense; some grammatical errors 27 points	Little time has been spent on making the presentation; many grammatical errors 19 points
Research	Topic has been researched extensively; used a number of different resources 10 points	Topic has been somewhat researched; used some different resources 7 points	Topic has been researched very little; possible misinformation because few resources included 4 points
Organization	Content is easy to read and well organized 10 points	Some parts are hard to read or understand 7 points	Difficult to read and understand 4 points
Creativity	Presentation is extremely creative, neat and easy to read 5 points	Presentation is creative but something is missing 3 points	Presentation isn't creative or is sloppily done with errors 1 point
List of Resources	Group has cited all resources used and supplied URLs for all Web sites 5 points	Group has cited all resources but incompletely and supplied a few URLs 3 points	No list of resources is included 0 points
Visuals	Group has included one additional, appropriate visual 5 points	Group has included one additional visual that does not fit with the rest of the project 3 points	No visual is included 0 points

- the type of content for the lesson first and foremost;
- the abilities and prior experience of the learners;
- students' knowledge of the technology being considered;
- the relevance of Internet resources and Web 2.0 tools as related to the content; and
- evaluation of content learning, collaboration, and technology use.

The number of Google Tools used in the unit illustrates how versatile the tools are. Integrating one, two, or more tools into the curriculum will provide opportunities for students to learn history and geography—past, present, and future (see Table 6-2).

Teacher Exercises: Now You Try It . . .
You have already experimented with Google Tools. Now it is time to think about using the tools in your lessons as aids to student learning. The idea is to start simple.

Table 6-2. General Google Tool URLs

URL	Description
www.eastchester.k12.ny.us/schools/hs/teachers/fermann/documents/GEforESmanual.pdf	Google Earth manual for teachers
www.google.com/googlenotebook/tour1.html	Tutorial shows how to use Google Notebook
www.jakesonline.org/earth/placemarks.pdf	Tutorial on how to set up place marks
http://64.233.179.110/educators/learning_materials/Earth_Getting_Started_Guide.pdf	Getting started on Google Earth
www.google.com/intl/en_us/help/maps/tour/	Tour on how to use Google Maps
www.google.com/googlenotebook/faq.html	Frequently Asked Questions about Google Notebook
www.google.com/google-d-s-/tour1.html	Tour of Google Docs
http://news.google.com	Google News sites
www.google.com/alerts?hl=en&t=1	Create a Google Alert
www.google.com/a/help/intl/en/admins/tour.html	Tours and demos illustrate how to get started and live Webinars provide experts to answer questions

1. Based on the examples where educators used Google Tools in the classroom or library, identify one tool that you think would be useful in a lesson.
2. Go to Google Tools for Educators (www.google.com/educators/tools.html), click the tool you have selected, and read the material on the tool. Follow all of the links so you have a good overview of what the tool can do and how to use it. *Note:* if a download is required, download it now.
3. Check the classroom activities for your grade level and subject area for the selected tool (www.google.com/educators/activities.html).
4. Create one activity that is appropriate for a unit you are teaching that incorporates your selected tool.
   a. Share it with a colleague.
   b. Try it with your class or small group.
5. Reflect in your notebook (preferably your Google Notebook!) how the activity went, what you would do differently, how students reacted.

> ➤ Use the additional exercises at Bev's Web site at www.neal-schuman.com/webclassroom to practice what you have learned about Google Tools and how you can use them in different subject areas.

CONCLUSION

Google Tools have provided an incentive for educators to use technology in everyday classroom activities. Our goal is to equip young people for the twenty-first century who will be effective learners, collaborators, and creators. And this goal can be accomplished using Google Tools:

- Twenty-first-century learners continue to learn throughout their lives because they have learned "how" to learn. They are independent and intrinsic learners and focus on self-improvement.
- Twenty-first-century collaborators are effective communicators, socially and culturally aware, flexible, and take responsibility for their role at their job, in the community, and the world. They appreciate and internalize the essential interdependence of being part of society.
- Twenty-first-century creators synthesize and analyze and are innovative and creative contributors to society. They are goal-oriented and demonstrate ethical responsibility.

Using Google Tools and other Web 2.0 technology to enhance instruction, educators are teaching students how to be learners, collaborators and creators for the twenty-first century.

REFERENCES AND FURTHER READING

California State Department of Education. 1988. *History–Social Sciences Framework for California Public Schools, Kindergarten Through Grade Twelve*. Sacramento: California State Department of Education.

Dodge, Bernie. 2001. *WebQuest Taskonomy* [Online]. Available: http://webquest.sdsu.edu/taskonomy.html (accessed March 22, 2008).

CHAPTER 7

Enhancing English Language Learning with Web 2.0 Tools

PART 1: IDEAS AND INSIGHTS

Envision non-native English-speaking students being journalists in the target language fulfilling an authentic task of interviewing a native speaker. Imagine students using their cell phones to record a message in the target language that will be published on a blog or incorporated into a class podcast. Visualize students listening to authentic language on their own time, extending the learning time beyond the classroom. Picture a class project where students create a culturally authentic electronic recipe book and share it with the world. These are just some tasks that second-language learners can accomplish with Web 2.0 tools.

Perhaps some reading this book might wonder why we are including English Language Learning (ELL) in a book on Web 2.0 tools in the curriculum. The increase in numbers of non-native English speakers is growing at a rapid rate. Most teachers and librarians throughout the country have had contact in school with students whose first language is not English. For example, data from the National Clearinghouse for English Language Acquisition and Language Instruction Educational Programs (NCELA, 2002) indicate that there are at least five million students identified as Limited-English Proficient (LEP). Approximately 80 percent are Spanish-language speakers. Other languages include Vietnamese, Korean, Chinese, Russian, Hmong, Arabic, and more. Seventy-seven percent of those students identified are from low-income families.

These skyrocketing numbers of Limited-English Proficient students underscore the importance of ensuring that student academic success becomes a reality and that teachers provide their students with every opportunity to excel. Moreover, the No Child Left Behind (NCLB) Act of 2001 (NCLB, 2002) clearly sets as a goal for LEP students to meet the same challenging state academic achievement standards and state academic content standards expected of all students. The law also states that every student should be technologically literate by the eighth grade, regardless of student background or family socioeconomic status.

Thus, educators are faced with a real challenge. They must teach these students how to comprehend, speak, read, and write in English, use technology effectively, and adhere to culturally mandated goals. These tasks can be overwhelming for both educators and students. It is no wonder that the dropout rate among this student group is so high.

Some of the technologies that we have discussed already in this book provide new ways to engage English-language learners or anyone learning a new language to improve in the four skills—listening, speaking, reading, and writing. Understanding a bit about how students learn a second language will illustrate why.

Objectives of This Chapter

This chapter is designed to be used by educators who teach students whose first language is not English. Web 2.0 tools are ideal for these students because they provide opportunities for them to use authentic language to create meaningful projects that require them to listen well, speak effectively, read and think critically, and write clearly. By the end of the chapter, educators will be able to:

- understand how Web 2.0 tools can enhance the ESL curriculum;
- use VoiceThread, a Web 2.0 tool, to further LEP students' ability to listen, speak, read, and write—the four skills necessary to communicate in English;
- integrate VoiceThread and/or other Web 2.0 tools such as blogs, podcasts, and wikis into their lessons; and
- create lessons that include cultural content as students enhance their English language abilities.

Part 1 discusses theories that need to be considered to teach LEP students. It also discusses the reasons Web 2.0 tools can enhance the curriculum. Part 2 shows educators how to get started with one specific Web 2.0 tool—VoiceThread, and Part 3 illustrates a unit plan incorporating VoiceThread as an integral part of the unit. Examples using VoiceThread and exercises reinforcing what was discussed are also part of this chapter.

> ➤ Check Bev's Web site at www.neal-schuman.com/webclassroom to see how educators are using VoiceThread in other subject areas and grade levels.

Glossary

authentic language: Language that is appropriate and authentic to children's lives.

avatar: Person's persona in the virtual world.

communicative competence: The learner's ability to understand and communicate in L2 (the target language).

comprehensible input: Information that is understandable to LEP students.

ELL students: English-language learning students.

LEP students: Limited English proficient students, those whose first language is not English.

target language: The language being learned.

Thread mode: A form of discussion where a community holds a conversation.

VoiceThread: Allows group conversations to be collected and shared in one place from anywhere in the world.

Introduction

If you want to learn English or any other language for that matter, you need input, meaningful, interesting, and at your level. Today, language-learning experts emphasize input over output, listening and reading over grammar study. Before you can use the language, you must get used to the language. You don't need to be in a hurry to speak English, and you don't need to speak it all the time to improve.

Stephen Krashen (1992), professor at the University of Southern California and well-known for his study of language acquisition, states that real language acquisition develops slowly, and speaking skills emerge significantly later than listening skills, even when conditions are perfect. The best methods are, therefore, those that supply "comprehensible input" in low anxiety situations, containing messages that students really want to hear. These methods do not force early production in the second language, but allow students to produce when they are ready, recognizing that improvement comes from supplying communicative and comprehensible input, and not from forcing and correcting production. Even if you are an intermediate learner, extensive reading and listening will increase your familiarity with the language, enrich your vocabulary, and develop your confidence.

Learning language with Web 2.0 tools is effective because it is fun. The Internet avoids the tension and boredom of the classroom and increases students' motivation. For example, bloggers may post messages in their own language or in English. English becomes the medium of communication among people of different cultural backgrounds. Blogging isn't an assignment, but a genuine, enjoyable, and meaningful activity. A contagious enthusiasm will keep learning happening because it is not like studying, it is more like making new friends and discovering new cultures through language.

Here's what several classroom teachers and a student had to say about using Web 2.0 tools with second-language learners:

> "In our middle schools, students are given 20 vocabulary words to learn, and they were learning 40 percent. With the use of iPods and podcasts, learning has increased to 95 percent." (El Paso teacher)

> "I have high expectations when students are working with technology because they are self-directed, engaged, empowered, and are using high-order thinking skills." (El Paso teacher)

> "I love, love, love VoiceThread! I use it at home, but I can't use it in my school. It's blocked! Is there any way you can help?" (Student response to VoiceThread)

To understand why these statements are important, it is necessary to understand how children learn a second language.

Attaining Competence in a Second Language

When teaching LEP students, educators must keep several principles in mind (Stevick, 1980):

1. For most learners, acquisition of a second language will only take place as learners are exposed to and engaged in contextually rich, meaningful communication.
2. Most learners are not successful when they learn grammar rules and then try to use those rules in communication.
3. Communicative competence is achieved by subconsciously acquiring the language through active participation in real communication, such as conversation that is interesting to learners.
4. Language is most effectively acquired when it is used as a vehicle for doing something else—then learners are directly involved in accomplishing something via the language and thus have a personal interest in the outcome of what they are using the language to do.
5. Teachers need to create opportunities for students to be exposed to, and engage in, real communication.

As educators, then, how can you help your students gain competence in the second language that they need to succeed in school, in their jobs, and ultimately in their lives? Here are a few suggestions that we will illustrate later in this chapter in the unit plan:

1. Provide a meaningful context for the introduction of new items in order to engage students' interest. Web 2.0 tools can provide an interesting context for students through a multimedia presentation of information and by acting as a vehicle for communication.
2. Allow students to feel that their experiences are valid, important, and relevant to the learning of English. The unit plan in this chapter incorporates concepts that most students know about and feel are important.

3. Encourage students to use English for social reasons. Have students work in groups and talk with one another as part of completing a task to provide a vehicle for real communication for a specific purpose.
4. Provide opportunities to practice the four skills—speaking, listening, reading, and writing—while encouraging vocabulary building and grammatical competence.
5. Show respect for students' native cultures by illustrating the importance of contributions by members of their ethnic groups. At the same time, continue to familiarize students with the culture in which they are living.
6. Teach to the needs of different learning styles. It is especially important with non-native speakers, who are struggling with language and cultural differences, to learn in the style that best suits them.

Using a variety of resources can help promote interest in learning for English language learners and provide a change of pace in the language classroom. The Internet, especially with the introduction of Web 2.0 tools for communication and collaboration, provides a tool outside the ESL classroom for students to practice English skills. What better way to promote reading and writing competence in authentic situations than by communicating with a class in another part of the world. And, with blogs (Chapter 2), podcasts (Chapter 3), and wikis (Chapter 4), educators now have the tools, easy to use, to reinforce all four language skills.

Using these technological tools within their inquiry-based curriculum provides visualizations and animations that allow students to become active researchers and knowledge-generating participants able to better comprehend many abstract concepts. Presentations are made using technology to communicate the understanding of their new learning. The use of technology eases the LEP students' process of conceptualizing. Daily technology use in relevant applications gives them practical knowledge and twenty-first-century skills reflective of real-life applications, while enhancing their use of language acquisition skills.

Why Use Web 2.0 Tools with ELL Students?

ELL students benefit in a number of ways when they use Web 2.0 tools as integral parts of their lessons. Here are just a few:

- Web 2.0 tools engage them in learning by motivating them to listen, speak, read, and write.
- Tasks using Web 2.0 tools reinforce their new culture and that from which they came.
- Students can expand their opportunities with technology because many will not have access to computers or these Internet tools at home.
- By expressing what they learned, ELL students show others what they are capable of doing.
- ELL students see the importance of technology and apply it to the real world.
- Web 2.0 tools provide a venue to promote meaningful content for LEP students.

When students are engaged in meaningful activities, they are constructing their own knowledge, with the teacher as the facilitator of the process. The Web 2.0 tool that is described in this chapter is VoiceThread, which is ideal for ELL students who need authentic language and the ability to use comprehensible input.

What Is VoiceThread?

A VoiceThread (see Figure 7-1) is an online media album that can hold essentially any type of media (images, documents, and videos) and allows people to make comments in four different ways—using voice (with a microphone or telephone), text, an audio file, or video (with a Webcam)—

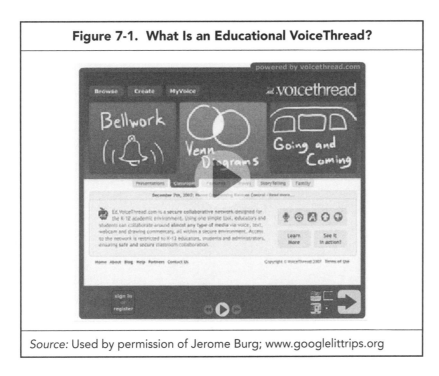

Figure 7-1. What Is an Educational VoiceThread?

Source: Used by permission of Jerome Burg; www.googlelittrips.org

and share those comments with anyone they wish. A VoiceThread allows group conversations to be collected and shared in one place, from anywhere in the world. Educational VoiceThreads contain enhanced security and identity features.

Examples of VoiceThreads in the Classroom

The Internet provides a number of examples of ESL classrooms using blogs, podcasts, and wikis integrated into lessons that emphasize language learning. Since we have already discussed some of these Web 2.0 tools, I thought it would be important to illustrate VoiceThread, a new tool that is equally as good at producing a venue for practicing listening, speaking, reading, and writing so important to second-language learners.

Example 1: Brazilian Project

In March 2008, a teacher in Brazil (see Figure 7-2) had his class of secondary school students create a VoiceThread to describe their country as part of an intercultural project. Students selected what they believed to be the five most important cities in Brazil, chose pictures that best represented them, and wrote scripts about them. They then recorded their descriptions in order to introduce Brazil to students who were not familiar with their country. One of their partner schools was a high school in Sacramento, California.

Almost three dozen students at Luther Burbank High School in California communicated via the Internet with 200 other students across the globe who, like them, were learning English as a second language. The "sister" class in California had responded to the project by posting pictures of cable cars in San Francisco. A class in Romania had posted Romanian architecture and yet another class showed videos of street tours in Budapest, Hungary, complete with music in the background. Then, students posted written and recorded messages commenting on one another's posts.

Larry Ferlazzo, who teaches history and English to non-native students in California, said the project has had many benefits for his students, chief among them being the practice they got in all aspects of language (see Figure 7-3). They read other students' written posts and listened to voicethreads. They wrote their own posts and recorded their own threads, which forced them to

Figure 7-2. Brazilian VoiceThread Project

Source: Used by permission of Ronaldo Mangueira Lima Jr., EFL teacher, Brazil; http://voicethread4 education.wikispaces.com/EFL+%26+ESL.

work on pronunciation and vocabulary. The project also exposed his students to technology. Since many had grown up in countries where technology was not a part of their daily lives, this process was new and exciting.

Figure 7-3. California Class VoiceThread

Teacher Larry Ferlazzo helps Long Lor, center, post a response with Tong Xiong, right, and Leepoeng Her, left. (Randy Pench / rpench@sacbee.com)

Source: Used by permission of Larry Ferrazo; http://voicethread4education.wikispaces.com/EFL%26+ESL.

According to Ferlazzo, "It's an authentic audience. It's one thing to make a product that's read by a teacher. It's a whole different picture when you're communicating to hundreds of other students around the world that really want to know what the United States is like. Another asset is that students also become teachers, representatives and ambassadors of their countries" (http://voicethread4education.wikispaces.com/EFL+%26+ESL).

What did teachers and students have to say about this project?

> "I like the chance to learn in a less traditional setting. Instead of sitting in a classroom listening to a teacher, we're interacting with one another and with students halfway across the world." (Bao Thao, 17)

> "I get to type and speak." "That's very good for English learners." (Maria Prieto, Mexico)

Example 2: Jose, the Bear, Travels to Egypt

In Example 2, students at the San Jose Episcopal Day School took a virtual trip to Egypt with Jose, their bear mascot. This extensive, in-depth presentation covered everything about Egypt from its history, including the pyramids and Sphinx, to the Cairo capitol and the Nile River to the markets, camel and donkey riding. Students created their own avatars (their personas in the virtual world), which are shown along with each photo that they describe in the audio VoiceThread recordings. Take a look at some of these VoiceThreads at http://voicethread.com/#q.b7626 (see Figure 7-4).

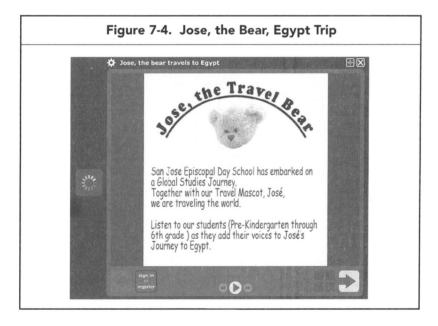

Figure 7-4. Jose, the Bear, Egypt Trip

Example 3: Uses of VoiceThread in a Primary Language Class

A blog post at http://primarymfl.ning.com/profiles/blog/show?id=738935%3ABlogPost%3A8621 provides a number of ways that VoiceThread was used with primary school students at different levels of language usage. Some activities included labeling parts of photos in the second language, for example, labeling parts of the body of a soccer player or describing and differentiating between cartoon-like animals or comparing and contrasting the clothing of two children. Using the VoiceThread doodle tool, students pointed to the parts of the body or article of clothing and recorded the name, described the animal, or explained what the children were doing in a picture. The level of language skill determined how much discussion children recorded.

Another activity required more language skills. Students looked at a map and used the doodle tool to locate a specific location while they recorded the directions in their own words (see Figure 7-5).

They also recorded weather forecasts for cities located on a weather map and even on a blank map they circled cities with the doodle tool and recorded the weather in those cities. Other activities included: having students draw pictures and tell what was happening in the picture; or developing a dialogue between a group or pair of students. As part of these activities, the VoiceThreads a class made were shared with parents or other classes in different parts of the world. Of course, the ability to add comments to the VoiceThreads provided that interactive collaboration important in language learning.

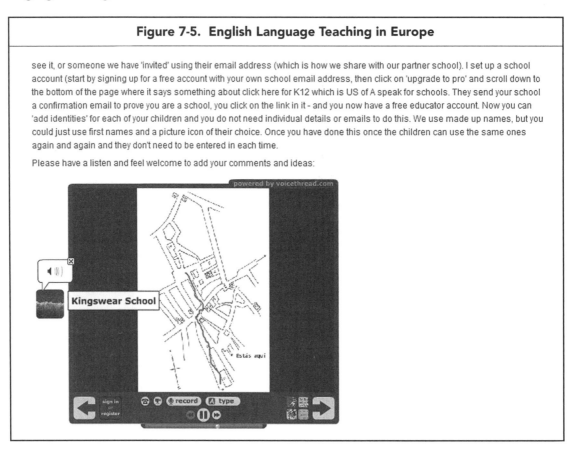

Figure 7-5. English Language Teaching in Europe

see it, or someone we have 'invited' using their email address (which is how we share with our partner school). I set up a school account (start by signing up for a free account with your own school email address, then click on 'upgrade to pro' and scroll down to the bottom of the page where it says something about click here for K12 which is US of A speak for schools. They send your school a confirmation email to prove you are a school, you click on the link in it - and you now have a free educator account. Now you can 'add identities' for each of your children and you do not need individual details or emails to do this. We use made up names, but you could just use first names and a picture icon of their choice. Once you have done this once the children can use the same ones again and again and they don't need to be entered in each time.

Please have a listen and feel welcome to add your comments and ideas:

How did these students get started using VoiceThread? In Part 2, we'll discuss how educators can begin using this new tool for the benefit of LEP students.

PART 2: GETTING STARTED

VoiceThread has many features that make it a useful tool for the K–12 classroom, especially second-language learners. A number of them are listed here.

VoiceThread Features

As an educator, you can use any number of VoiceThread features. Tutorials are also available to illustrate each one at http://voicethread.com/#c28.

- VoiceThreads can be embedded in blogs, Web sites, or MySpace profiles.
- Presentations can include images (e.g., .jpg, .gif, .bmp), documents (.docs), PowerPoint (.ppt), PDF documents (.pdf), Excel spreadsheets (.xls), and videos. You can also import pictures from Flickr (www.flickr.com) or Facebook (www.facebook.com) if you have accounts.

- Collaboration can be private, sharing only with a selected few, or public, allowing a broad range of participants. One account can have many identities so a teacher or librarian can set up identities for a class of students using one account (see Figure 7-6).

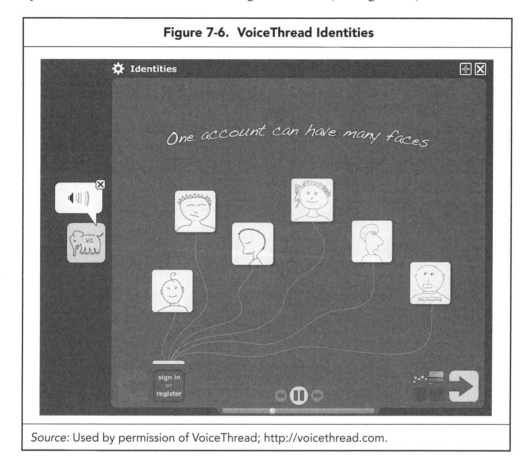

Figure 7-6. VoiceThread Identities

Source: Used by permission of VoiceThread; http://voicethread.com.

- You can comment on each slide using audio or text.
- The creation process is handled entirely within one window without the need to refresh or go to other pages.
- A photo navigation button lets you zoom out to show all the photos in the set. Once you're viewing a photo, you can simply click it to zoom in.
- You can doodle on your images to highlight something you really want to emphasize. You can also doodle on a video that may be part of your presentation.
- Multiple identities are available for one account, and identities can be monitored when messages are left because a VoiceThread attaches an identity to the comment.
- Security settings allow you to determine who can view or participate in the VoiceThread. A notice from the originators of VoiceThread addresses concerns about communication and protection issues for students. The key to safety on Ed.VoiceThread is not restraints, but accountability. When educators invite commentary from someone outside of Ed.VoiceThread, they are responsible for the commentary added to their VoiceThread. So it is important to realize that joining Ed.VoiceThread (http://ed.voicethread.com/) does not isolate your class; rather educators can invite anyone individually. They just can't invite the whole world at one time (see Figure 7-7).

> ➤ *See Bev's Web site at www.neal-schuman.com/ webclassroom for examples of video projects also ideal for second-language learners.*

Figure 7-7. VoiceThread Security

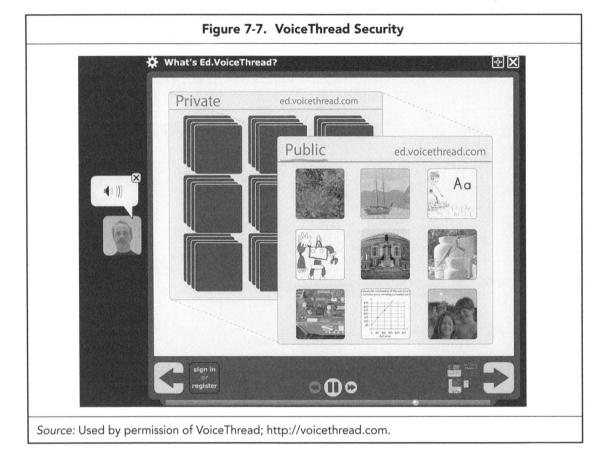

Source: Used by permission of VoiceThread; http://voicethread.com.

Signing Up

You may be saying to yourself, this sounds like a good tool, especially for my ESL classes. How can I sign up? Several easy steps will have your class up and running quickly. It is that easy:

- *Step 1:* Since students will be communicating with others outside the classroom, the first step is to notify parents of the projects you plan to conduct and get their approval. Explain how the project works and what their children will be doing. Note that you will need to decide whether you plan to communicate solely within the class or school or to classes in other parts of the world. Mention that you can make the VoiceThead private and moderate comments or turn comments off. Tell parents that they will have an opportunity to see and hear their child's work. You will also need to decide whether you would like parents (and others) to comment. Make sure to talk to your administrator, too.
- *Step 2:* Join the VoiceThread site (http://voicethread.com/) and set up an account. If you're a K–12 educator, you can apply for a free educator account by signing in and clicking the Go Pro! Button; then click the link that says "K–12 classroom educators" (see Figure 7-8). Educational VoiceThread is another inexpensive option (http://ed.voicethread.com/about/).
- *Step 3:* Assemble what you need. In the latest version of VoiceThread, you don't even need equipment. If you don't have a microphone, you can use your telephone. After you log-in and go to the media you want to comment on, you can have VoiceThread call you on your phone where you can follow the prompts and leave comments. Download FlashPlayer 7+ free on the Adobe site if you don't have it.
- *Step 4:* Practice using VoiceThread. There are many things you can do with VoiceThread. For example, you can embed the VoiceThread on your blog or Web page just by (1) clicking the

Figure 7-8. VoiceThread Registration

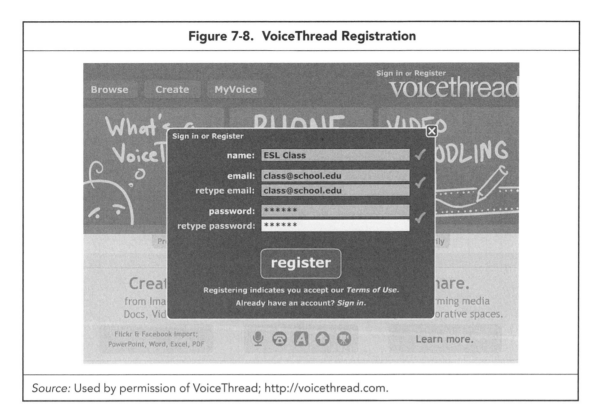

Source: Used by permission of VoiceThread; http://voicethread.com.

embed button on the VoiceThread create page, (2) selecting the size of the image, and (3) clicking the "copy this" button. Then go to the blog page and enter your VoiceThread there.

Teacher Exercises: Now You Try It . . .

Now that you know what a VoiceThread is and some of the features that are available to you, it is time to try using some of the features yourself.

1. At http://voicethread.com, click the Browse button and you will see a number of VoiceThreads. Click the one that says: "So what is a VoiceThread?" and go through the entire presentation trying the different features while you are listening and watching it. This will give you some ideas when it is time to create your own VoiceThread.
2. Sign up for a free VoiceThread account by clicking the Register link at the top of the page. Review the following page for instructions: http://voicethread.com/image/ voicethreads_ in_the_classroom.pdf.

> ➤ *To get started with video projects, check Bev's Web site at www.neal-schuman .com/webclassroom.*

3. Click the browse button at the top of the screen to view several of the VoiceThreads. Click each one you want to view. Add your comments to at least three (3) VoiceThreads.
4. In your Web 2.0 notebook, reflect on the tool so that you can create your own VoiceThread at the end of this chapter.

PART 3: PRACTICAL APPLICATIONS

A curriculum supported through a multisensory approach of text, graphics, speech, and sounds is best suited for language learners. The project for this unit aims mainly at encouraging language learning and intercultural dialogue among students in two classes whose first language is not the same. For elementary ESL students, using technology to engage in actual activity may lead to improved language skills by increasing their vocabulary, their ability to share their own and their peers' feelings, and hence feel accepted in a new environment. This might mean that an ESL class in the United States represented by multiple languages collaborates with a class learning English in Mexico or another country.

Cross-Curricular Unit Plan for ESL Students

This unit introduces a new Web 2.0 tool—VoiceThread. VoiceThread is a space for creating digital stories and documentaries, practicing language skills, exploring geography and culture, solving math problems, collaborating with other students, or simply finding and honing student voices. Figure 7-9 shows Pedro's comment on his class's use of a VoiceThread to communicate with classes in other countries.

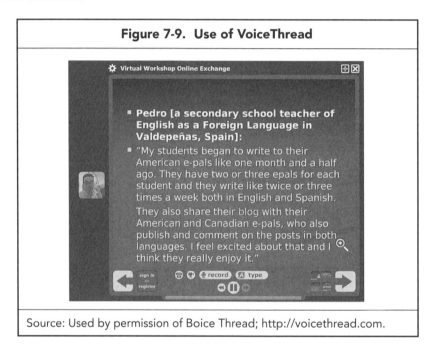

Figure 7-9. Use of VoiceThread

Source: Used by permission of Boice Thread; http://voicethread.com.

The unit is a collaborative project between students at a school in one country and those of similar age in another country both of which are learning English as a second language. At each school, groups of four students will focus their attention on one aspect of life in the country in which they live, specifically in their local area (e.g., United States, Mexico). Each group will gather pictures, for example, of the town where they live, clothing styles, entertainment, their school, weather in their region, geography of the area, food, music, folk art or other aspects of life in the local culture. They will then create a VoiceThread to present this information to their partner class.

Step 1: Apply Framework Standards—What Should Be Taught?

When students are engaged in activities like online collaboration with classrooms around the world or e-mail exchange and information searching, they are constructing their own knowledge, with the teacher as the facilitator of the process. This unit supports the California framework standard of providing a challenging curriculum for all students in several ways. Students will:

- use English to communicate in social settings;
- use English to interact in the classroom;
- use appropriate language variety, register, and genre according to audience, purpose, and setting; and

- become acquainted with Web 2.0 technology, specifically a VoiceThread, and how it can be used to improve language skills.

Performance-based assessment will be used to measure whether students can use the technology, with rubrics for evaluating listening, speaking, reading, and writing skill improvement. As a result of engaging in the activities in this unit and working together both in classroom groups and with their partner class, students will become information literate as stated in Information Power (American Association of School Librarians and Association for Educational Communications and Technology, 1988) and increase their knowledge of technology tools necessary in the twenty-first century as emphasized in the NETS standards (see Chapter 2).

Step 2: Identify General Goals and Specific Objectives

This unit is designed to engage students in learning that provides them with authentic opportunities to communicate and problem solve, as well as reinforce a positive identity. The activities promote meaningful content for LEP students because they relate to their preexisting knowledge and experiences. Thus, they will develop deep understanding of the concepts and ideas. By the end of this unit on local culture, students will have a deeper knowledge and understanding of their own local culture and the culture of their partner class.

Goals

Students will:

- use English to achieve academically in all content areas;
- use English in socially and culturally appropriate ways;
- use English to participate in social interactions; and
- expand their opportunities for using English with a specific purpose for a specific audience.

Objectives

This unit will provide authentic opportunities for students to collaborate and solve problems. Activities will provide challenging learning opportunities and reinforce a positive identity. More specifically as part of each goal, students will:

- collaborate with one another in a group to create a VoiceThread about their local culture;
- interact with students in another part of the world;
- express what they learned and show others what they are capable of doing;
- practice their public speaking and presentation skills; and
- practice their writing in English by providing comments to others' writing.

Step 3: Gather Materials

Interviews and observations are the two main forms of fieldwork for this project. Before interviewing someone, it is good to know what you hope to hear and learn. Are you looking for facts, stories, detailed steps in making or doing something, or reflections? Make a list of topics or questions, similar ideas grouped together, arranged in an order where one topic easily leads to another.

In addition, students working on a local culture project often conduct background research in libraries or on the Internet to help them better understand their fieldwork. Every photo, every piece of writing—historical or contemporary—is a document that might help them answer questions about local culture. Students will find most of the materials for this unit by interviewing friends, family, and citizens, collecting objects that represent local culture and photographing sites and other artifacts of the area. They may use the Internet to find historical information about the locale, weather, festivals, and more. They will also need to become familiar with how a VoiceThread works as discussed in Part 2 of this chapter.

Step 4: Create Sample Activities

The importance of this unit is to create an authentic audience and a chance to use L2 (the language they are learning) while at the same time assimilating the culture of their country. In the early grades, young learners draw upon immediate personal experiences as a basis for exploring geographic concepts and skills. They also express interest in things distant and unfamiliar. The activities that follow can be used to improve pronunciation, vocabulary, cultural awareness, as well as speaking, listening, reading, and writing skills.

Activities to Introduce the Project

These initial tasks require students to work in groups, thus necessitating that they practice their language skills. They also draw upon their prior knowledge about the local culture. To initiate the project, students will do the following:

- Answer these questions: What do they already know about their local culture? What do they want to understand more completely?
- Listen to several VoiceThreads so they see how other classes have used the technology. This will also give groups ideas for creating their own presentations (see Table 7-1 for samples to view).

Table 7-1. Sample VoiceThreads	
URL	**Description**
http://voicethread.com/view.php?b=579	Share their favorite poems to create an audio poem book.
http://greatbookstories.pbwiki.com/	Narrate five pictures to share why they love a specific book, and why other people should read it.
http://voicethread.com/view.php?b=971	Social Studies and geography applications.
http://voicethread.com/view.php?b=5777	Book review.
http://voicethread.com/#u3968	VoiceThread examples in ESL.

- Decide in their groups upon an avatar (representations of themselves to use while they are online) for each student. This is a fun activity to get students working together in their groups.
  - To explain the concept of avatar, each student describes something that others in the group will not know about him/her, for instance, "Ice skating is my favorite sport" or "I have a pet snake" or "I like Italian food the most."
  - After sharing, the group determines whether this fact was something a stranger could know and whether classmates would know this fact. This is a way to explain the concept to students before having them create their avatars.
- Create their avatars. Students can draw pictures of themselves based on the fact they shared. For example, the girl with the pet snake could use a picture of a snake as her avatar. They can also build their own picture at www.buildyourwildself.com/. They will use these avatars in the VoiceThread they create later.
  - If building their own pictures, first create pictures of themselves as they currently are.
  - Next, build a picture of their wilder side using different animal parts (see Figure 7-10).
  - Review the avatars in their groups.
- Select a facet (e.g., clothing, holidays, weather) about the country that they want to share with another class and have each group review their idea with the rest of the class to ensure each group is working on a different idea.

Figure 7-10. Wildside Avatar

Activities to Be Used During the Unit

Students must complete two separate tasks during the unit. First, they must gather information about the aspect of their country that they have chosen to talk about in the VoiceThread. Second, they must write a short script and record at least one or two facts about their topic. In their groups, students will do the following:

- Brainstorm and cluster ideas for their topics. Encourage second-language learners to use words and pictures, rather than phrases and sentences in their graphic organizers. See Figure 7-11 for a sample cluster.
- Take pictures of their topics (e.g., an important building in their hometown, kids in everyday clothing, snow in the winter or tulips in the summer).
- Get a notebook they will use only for their exploration of local culture. Use this notebook to organize their study by making lists, answering questions, keeping track of their thinking as they read and record some of the images they have of their local culture. Note that they could also use Google Notebook for this part of the project (see Chapter 6).
- Research the topics by interviewing citizens, other students, teachers, librarians, and parents. Write questions they might ask those they plan to interview as they are working on grammar in class. This allows practice in formulating questions. Review the questions in Figure 7-12.
- Model the task using clothing as the example topic:
  ○ Clothes are both practical and symbolic. Clothes are used for diverse practical needs and as symbols of cultural identity. This activity introduces the variety of clothing used by different groups and for different occasions.
  ○ Students will create a list of the different kinds of clothing found in their homes. What categories of clothing do they see (e.g., clothes for school, housework, yardwork)?

Figure 7-11. Topical Graphic Organizer

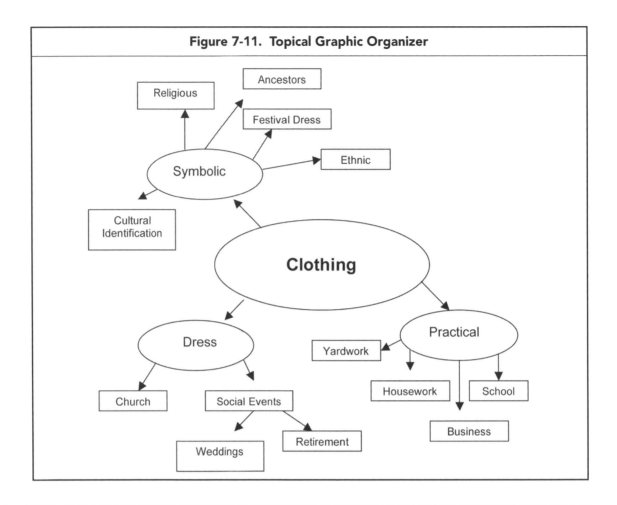

Figure 7-12. Interview Questions

Here are some sample questions to get you started on your interviews. Tailor the questions to those persons you plan to interview.

Tip: Your most important response is to ask follow-up questions that come from listening to what's just been said. If the person you are interviewing has just told you she loves gardening, your next question most likely responds to that statement. You might ask any of the following questions: "What do you most enjoy when you are gardening?" "Tell me about your garden." "What do you grow in your garden?"

Family
1. What is your family heritage? What country did your family come from?
2. Where were your parents born? Where were you born?
3. Do you have any brothers or sisters? How many?
4. Describe your house.

Food
1. What is your favorite food?
2. What is the strangest food you have ever eaten?
3. What new type of food would you like to try?

School
1. What do you like best about school?
2. What is your favorite sport to play and watch?
3. What do you do with your free time?

Clothing
1. Do you have a favorite type of clothes?
2. Do you think males and females dress the same in America?

Favorites
1. What is your favorite movie?
2. What is your favorite type of music?
3. What is your favorite holiday?

- ○ Students should think about the following while doing research:
  - – Do they have any fancy clothes? When and where do they wear them?
  - – What is something they wear that they think almost nobody else in the class wears?
  - – What groups—occupational, recreational, ethnic, religious—do they or other members of their family belong to that involve special clothes?
  - – Bring in objects of clothing from as many different categories as possible.
  - – Examine ethnic, regional, and religious traditions: What clothes do they wear that are most similar to the clothes worn by their ancestors? What clothes do they wear that are most unique—that people of other backgrounds probably don't wear? What clothes do they wear that make them feel very special?
- • Write individual scripts incorporating at least two (2) facts that deal directly with the group topic; then read it aloud to a partner in the group.
- • Work together to select pictures and scripts for each group recording.
- • Record the scripts individually using VoiceThread technology. The VoiceThreads will provide information on their local culture to their partner class.
- • Record or type at least three (3) comments on pages of the partner class VoiceThreads.
- • Create a VoiceThread in response to their partner school's recording. Have each group ask two or three questions that they still want to know about the local culture of the partner school. Some questions might include: What are their favorite traditions? What do people do on the weekend in their country? What is the weather like? Use Figure 7-13 to write their comments.

Figure 7-13. Comments on VoiceThread Presentations

Title: _____

Use this handout to write out comments that you plan to add to this VoiceThread presentation. This will help your recording, and you can also check for errors if you are giving a text response. There are three types of comments you might want to make. Here is some language to get you started.

1. *Adding a new image:* Focus the thinking of other viewers by asking a question such as:
   What do you notice about this picture (give name) that describes . . . ?
   _____
   _____

2. *Adding a first or different comment:* To add the first or totally different comment, respond to the person who put up the comment first; then ask questions to encourage other viewers to respond:
   In this image I noticed _____
   _____ .
   This was interesting to me because _____
   _____ . I wonder if _____
   _____ .

3. *Agreeing or disagreeing with comments:* First, quote the comment you are responding to and then respond civilly:
   X said _____ .
   I (agree, disagree) with (him, her) because _____
   _____ . I think that _____
   _____ and I'm wondering if _____

Activities to Be Used as Follow-Up to the Unit

As extension activities, have groups of students try some of the following:

- Reflect on the information from the partner school's VoiceThread and write paragraphs showing how the cultures are similar and different.
- Create VoiceThread 2: Look more closely at the culture they already know best, their families. Families are the most important cultural group—it is where they learn the most important social skills, spend the most time, and know people best. More elements of cultural behavior can be observed in families than in any other group.
  - Quickly sketch how they envision their families. It is usually better to make many quick sketches than to spend a long time putting in details. Select and redraw any sketches they intend to use in their VoiceThread.
  - Bring a photo or object keepsake from home that has a story connected with it.
  - Create a short script and prepare VoiceThread 2 based on the following questions:
    - What stories do their sketches tell?
    - What photos would they select to represent their families?
- After recording VoiceThread 2, students will reflect on the VoiceThreads created by answering the following questions:
  - What did they learn about their classmates' families by looking at these photos or objects? Give one example.
  - Did several students bring in similar photos? What patterns or themes did they notice?
  - Which photo that they brought in best represents their family? Why?
  - What weren't they able to tell about their families from the photos they brought in?
  - What photo did they wish they had?

Note: Either of these VoiceThreads could be embedded into a class blog or wiki.

Step 5: Evaluate What Was Learned

Evaluation can take several forms—by teacher, by group, and by oneself in a self-evaluation. The sample rubric in Figure 7-14 contains at least one sample question to assess group work, final product, presentation and use of VoiceThread technology.

Other types of rubrics you might want to create include peer rubrics to get student opinion on the workings of the groups and individual rubrics based on how students worked separately on pieces of the project. In addition, a self-evaluation rubric would help students assess their own work on the project. These types of rubrics are available in other chapters of this book and can be adapted to use with this technology.

Summary

VoiceThread technology can encourage language learners to take steps to speak out in the target language, communicate with their peers, increase their knowledge of a new culture, and demonstrate the real-world skills they have achieved. VoiceThread and the other Web 2.0 tools discussed in previous chapters can make an important difference to these struggling learners.

Teacher Exercises: Now You Try It . . .

You are now ready to try creating your own VoiceThread so that you become familiar enough with the technology to use it with your students. Note that although this chapter addresses needs of LEP students, this technology can be used with any students at any grade level.

Figure 7-14. Evaluation Rubric			
This rubric contains characteristics of content, working together, technology, and presentation skills. Each of these characteristics could be split into a separate rubric, if desired.			
Characteristics	**Superior (5 points)**	**Developed (3 points)**	**Limited (1 point)**
Planning	Extensive preparation of tasks for VoiceThread	Adequate preparation of tasks but lacking total organization	Preparation of tasks missing or weak
Collaboration	Collaboration demonstrates cohesive shared leadership of tasks, decisions, contributions, group management, roles and responsibilities for project goals being met successfully; appreciation and respect for abilities of others actively communicated	Collaboration generally performed as individuals completing tasks, assuming roles and contributing as assigned; appreciation and respect for abilities of others adequate	Collaboration weak or not evident; group has difficulty adjusting, communicating, and taking self-responsibility to effectively meet project goals; appreciation and respect for abilities of others apathetic
Content	Rich imaginary and innovative task(s) create a consistent and engaging learning experience of high interest for others	Adequate and appropriate tasks to sustain a learning experience	Task(s) may be fun and motivating but do not sustain a learning experience for others
Delivery	Exhibited poise, confidence, and personal style during delivery	Exhibited relaxed delivery. Fluent with some details	Exhibited nervous delivery. Lacking fluency, details or originality
Voice Quality	Quality of volume/diction/fluency/flow is high	Quality of volume/diction/fluency/flow is acceptable	Quality of volume/diction/fluency/flow is not acceptable
Images	Images highly engaging for content/audience	Images appropriate to content/audience	Images detract or are inappropriate for content/audience
In your own words describe the VoiceThread and its attributes.			

1. Search the Web or use some of the URLs listed in Table 7-2 to become familiar with VoiceThreads that teachers and students have created together in different subject areas and at different grade levels. In your Web 2.0 notebook describe at least five (5) ideas that you might use for creating VoiceThreads with your class.

   ➤ *Additional exercises related to VoiceThreads can be found at Bev's Web site at www.neal-schuman.com/webclassroom.*

2. Look at the tutorials listed on the VoiceThread site at http://voicethread.com/#c28 (e.g., how to set up a microphone, embedding a VoiceThread, using the doodle tool, and more).

3. Create a short two- to five-minute VoiceThread on a topic of interest to you, one that can be presented to other educators and the administration in your school.

CONCLUSION

Technology as a tool to enrich learning experiences can serve as an excellent instructional tool for language learners of all ages in any language instruction program. Combining second-language acquisition principles with content instruction and using Web 2.0 tools for collaboration and teaching

Table 7-2. General VoiceThread URLs	
URL	Description
http://news.bbc.co.uk/2/hi/in_pictures/7155727.stm	Pictures in the news for a current events unit. RSS subscription available.
http://voicethread.com/#u3968	VoiceThread of pictures in the news.
http://esleflstudents.edublogs.org/	ESL Edublogs.org with projects created by ESL students worldwide.
http://educators.pbwiki.com/VoiceThread+-+Group+ conversations	100 ways to use VoiceThread in education.
www.classroom20.com/	Classroom 2.0 for educators forum. RSS subscription available.
http://voicethread.com/ui/image/classroom.pdf	Printable guide for teachers on using VoiceThreads.
www.eslpod.com/	Podcasts with second language learners.

reading, writing, speaking, and listening provides educators with a way to motivate LEP students to improve their language skills. Activities incorporating Web 2.0 tools that were discussed in this chapter promote learning for non-native English speakers because they:

- provide opportunities for students to use academic language in meaningful ways;
- illustrate the use of visuals to increase comprehension;
- provide opportunities for students to work together in completing academic tasks;
- promote interactive discussions among students and teacher;
- maintain cognitive challenges; and
- connect the lesson to students' own experiences.

We cannot afford to neglect the needs of this population in the twenty-first century.

REFERENCES AND FURTHER READING

American Association of School Librarians and Association for Educational Communications and Technology. 1988. *Information Power: Guidelines for School Library Media Programs.* Chicago: American Association of School Librarians, and Washington, DC: Association for Educational Communications and Technology.

Capps, Randy, Michael Fix, and Jeffrey S. Passel. 2002. "The Dispersal of Immigrants in the 1990s." *Immigrant Families and Workers*, Brief No. 2. Washington, DC: The Urban Institute.

English Language Learners and The U.S. Census—1990–2000. Available: www.ncela.gwu.edu/policy/states/allcensus90s.pdf (accessed October 1, 2008).

Ferlazzo, Larry. Available: http://voicethread4education.wikispaces.com/EFL+%26+ESL> (blog accessed April 22, 2008).

Krashen, Stephen D. 1992. *Fundamentals of Language Education.* Torrance, CA: Laredo.

National Clearinghouse for English Language Acquisition and Language Instruction Educational Programs. 2002, Available: www.ncela.gwu.edu/ (accessed October 1, 2008).

No Child Left Behind. 2002. *Public Law print of PL 107-110, the No Child Left Behind Act of 2001*, signed into law on January 8, 2002. Available: www.ed.gov/policy/elsec/leg/esea02/index.html (accessed October 1, 2008).

Stevick, Earl W. 1980. *Teaching Languages: A Way and Ways.* Rowley, MA: Newbury House.

CHAPTER 8

Social Bookmarking and Putting It All Together

PART 1: IDEAS AND INSIGHTS

Before Web 2.0, when you discovered a really good Web site, you bookmarked it in your Favorites so that you could quickly visit it again in the future. This worked well for the most part. However, a couple of problems arose with this method of bookmarking. When you bookmarked a site on one computer, it was only available on that specific computer. If you changed computers, you lost your bookmarks. Another problem with this method of bookmarking was that you couldn't easily share your bookmarks with other people, and other people couldn't share theirs with you.

Then social bookmarking appeared on the scene. In 2003, Joshua Schacter created the unusually spelled del.icio.us (www.del.icio.us.com) social bookmarking Web site. Using this innovation you could now organize all of your favorite Web sites in one convenient, online location and easily share them with others. All you had to do was set up an account with a Web-based bookmarking site, and then add new Web sites to this account as needed. Your bookmarks remained stored online, so they were accessible and could be edited on any computer. Today, there continues to be a growing number of bookmarking sites, several of which we will explore in this chapter.

One teacher who has begun using social bookmarking has this to say: "My preference is a social bookmarking tool called Diigo (www.diigo.com). With Diigo, you can highlight, add sticky notes and make your comments private or public."

Part 1 of this chapter examines a Web 2.0 tool—social bookmarking—what it is and why we may want to use it in education. Examples illustrate how educators are using the tool both as a productivity tool and with students as part of the curriculum. Part 2 gets educators started by discussing several social bookmarking sites and providing instructions on how to use one site called Diigo. Part 3 is the culmination to the book in that the unit plan combines a number of Web 2.0 tools as they can be used together in the classroom in a cross-curricular unit about Earth Day.

Objectives of This Chapter

This chapter introduces teachers to a new Web 2.0 tool—social bookmarking—at both the elementary and secondary levels and puts together what they have learned throughout the book into a unit plan that incorporates several Web 2.0 tools. After reading the chapter and completing the exercises, educators will be able to:

- create social bookmarks for their own and their students' needs;
- explain the basics of social bookmarking;
- get started using social bookmarks; and
- create a unit incorporating several Web 2.0 tools, including social bookmarking.

Glossary

Del.cio.us: A social bookmarking Web service for storing, sharing, and discovering Web bookmarks.

Diigo: A social bookmarking Web site that allows signed users to bookmark and tag Web pages.

Flickr: A photo sharing Web site and Web services suite and an online community platform.

instant messaging: A form of real-time communication between two or more people based on typed text. The text is conveyed via computers connected over a network such as the Internet.

Ma.gnolia: A social bookmarking Web service.

MySpace: An international site that offers e-mail, a forum, communities, videos, and Weblog space.

Social bookmarking: A method for Internet users to store, organize, search, and manage bookmarks of Web pages on the Internet.

tag: A keyword or term associated with or assigned to a piece of information (e.g., a picture, article, or video clip), thus describing the item and enabling keyword-based classification of information.

tag cloud: A visual depiction of user-generated tags.

tagging: The process of assigning meaning to an object via tags.

What Is Social Bookmarking?

According to Wikipedia (2008), social bookmarking is a method for Internet users to store, organize, search, and manage bookmarks of Web pages on the Internet. The bookmarks are usually public, but can be saved privately, or shared only with specified people or groups. Most educators organize their bookmarks using tags that allow them to categorize bookmarks by grade level, subject, or lesson topic. Social bookmarking can be useful as a way to access a consolidated set of bookmarks from various computers, organize large numbers of bookmarks, and share bookmarks with contacts. Librarians have found social bookmarking an easy way to provide lists of informative links to patrons. One disadvantage, however, is that there is no uniform way to tag the bookmarks. Social bookmarking complements blogs, social networks, and RSS news aggregators.

Why Use Social Bookmarking?

There are a number of advantages to educators and students alike who use social bookmarking. Some of the benefits include:

- Keeping track of all source materials and commentary for a research project
- Using a shared account or tag to collect and organize bookmarks that are relevant and useful for a group project
- Accessing bookmarks from anywhere—at home, in class, in a library, or on a friend's computer
- Sharing bookmarks publicly so classmates, teachers, or librarians can view them for reference and collaboration or mark them private—only viewable by those invited
- Finding other people who have interesting bookmarks and adding those links to their own collection
- Annotating bookmarks
- Searching resources by popularity so they can find the most popular bookmarks on any subject
- Sending bookmarks to a blog or setting up an RSS feed for a specific tag
- Encouraging critical thinking in that students must read the information in an article, on a blog or Web site before they can create tags for it
- Seeing the number of times a site has been bookmarked to determine the relative value of a site
- Showing friends interesting links, or sending a helpful bookmark to another teacher or student, or even creating a list of resources for students that you can put on a course Web site

Classroom Social Bookmarking Examples

It is always a good idea to look at how other educators are using a particular Web 2.0 tool. Here are several examples of social bookmarking in the K–12 curriculum.

Example 1: Fifth Grade Class Bookmarks

Figure 8-1 shows the bookmarks of the fifth grade class at Mamaroneck Avenue School in Mamaroneck, New York, and how they keep track of their bookmarks (www.mamkschools.org/ mas/class/grade4/brune/2004/contact_us.htm). They have categorized the site by subject area such as Reading and Writing, Social Studies, Math, and Science. Within each category are bookmarks to interesting sites; for example, in the poetry category a "Meet the Authors" site (www.readingrockets .org/podcasts/authors) contains video and audio podcasts from different authors.

Figure 8-1. Fifth Grade Class Bookmarks

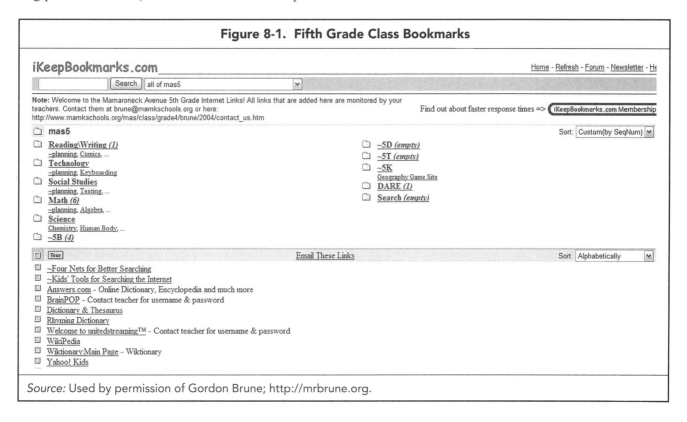

Source: Used by permission of Gordon Brune; http://mrbrune.org.

Example 2: Recording Radio Scripts

One seventh grade language arts teacher describes several activities where he can use social book-marking with his class. His first suggestion is to use the annotating feature of bookmarks to give an assignment. For example, the class assignment is to record radio scripts of the old classic radio shows. He highlighted the old advertisements that are a part of the scripts, and when students mouse over the highlighted text, a hidden message displays describing the new assignment—to write an ad for a virtue or trait they think is important. Now students have a writing assignment to accompany the recording of the radio play. Other possibilities include asking questions about a site, carrying on conversations about the text or the validity of the information. Notes can be private or public, organized on a blog or Web page. See Figure 8-2 at www.diigo.com/user/Grundy?tab=9.

Example 3: Reviewing for Quizzes

A five-minute video created by one teacher illustrates how he used Diigo and blogs to help students review for tests in his AP (advanced placement) literature class. During class each student acts as a

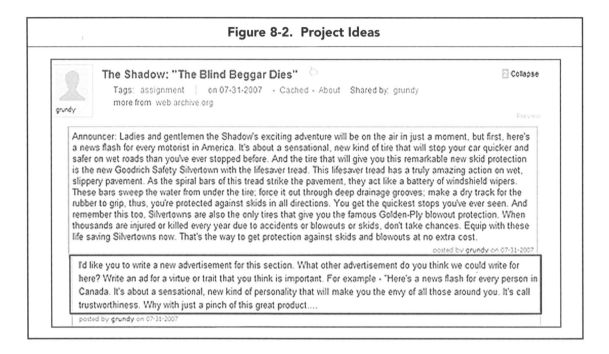

Figure 8-2. Project Ideas

scribe and summarizes in their blog notes the day's lesson, including key ideas, discussions and terms. The idea, of course, is then to put all the notes together so that the entire class benefits from each student's work. The notes also indicate what students learned from the lesson the teacher taught. The teacher then set up a Diigo class group and highlighted portions of the notes that he wanted to include in a quiz. All students can see the highlighted areas in the Diigo group to help them review for the test. In addition, the teacher placed sticky notes on highlighted portions of the notes to add additional information or connections between posts that he wanted to make.

Teachers and librarians can also set up their own bookmarking sites. Librarians might set up a page for each class or for topics within the class structure. Classroom teachers can tag their categories according to subject areas or topics within those areas. For example, Figure 8-3 shows a set of bookmarks that illustrates tagging in the science curriculum. For more about tagging, see Chapter 2.

PART 2: GETTING STARTED

Educators use a number of bookmarking sites for their own purposes and classroom activities. Two we will mention are Del.icio.us and Diigo. Each has features that are important to education. We'll review them now.

Social Bookmarking Sites

Del.icio.us (http://del.icio.us.com), one of the first social bookmarking sites, is still the most popular. It enables users to save search results, annotate and categorize them, and share saved results with other users. Users are asked to add descriptive one-word tags to each bookmark to help them remember and organize them. For example, a user might label a page about earthquakes with the tags "earthquake" and "science." By tagging pages, users can classify them and organize them into groups, making it easier to navigate the list of links. Del.icio.us also lets users search their list by keywords and organize the list chronologically by the date when links were added. The social part of bookmarking is that Del.icio.us lets users see others' collections of links so that they can subscribe to them using RSS feeds (see Chapter 2) and be notified when new links are available. Users can

---

Figure 8-3. Reviewing for Quizzes

Screencast: Using Diigo on Student Scribe Blogs as Test Reveiw "Sheets"

Here's one more tutorial, 4 minutes, on using Diigo on Scribe blogs as test review sheets, with students as members of a Diigo Group. I just trained my students today in AP Lit, set them up on the class Diigo Group, and "shared" my highlights and annotations of the class scribe posts (it only works on permalinks, not on main blog pages) with the kisAP07 group. They use that as "test reviw."

Here it is:

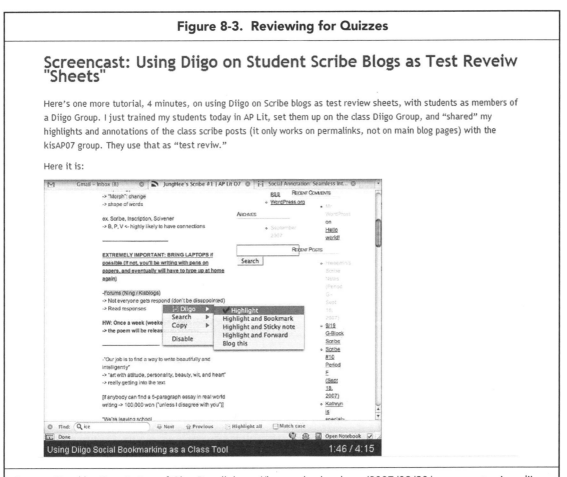

Source: Used by Permission of Clay Burell; http://beyond-school.org/2007/09/20/screencast-using-diigo-on-student-scribe-blogs-as-test-reveiw-sheets/.

---

also subscribe to tagged pages, such as "education" or "Macbeth," and be alerted when items are added to them. In addition, each link contains a list of every user who has bookmarked it. Users on Del.icio.us now become an online community, joined by their desire to share links to Web pages they like and find useful (see Figure 8-4).

Diigo (www.diigo.com), one of the newer social bookmarking tools on the market, calls itself a personal research tool, a collaborative research platform, a social content site, and a knowledge-sharing community. To meet these objectives, it has come out with numerous advanced features, in addition to the ones mentioned above. For example, one interesting feature is the ability to highlight and attach sticky notes or write brief descriptions to a page you bookmark. There are also many ways to share your bookmarks: post them to your blog, send multiple annotated pages by e-mail, or save them to other Web sites such as Facebook or del.icio.us simultaneously. You can also set up groups, ideal for collaborative learning in the classroom, and discuss group annotated Web pages. Groups can be public, private or semi-private. You can find bookmarks by popularity and the most recent bookmarks by site, user or tags (see Figure 8-5).

Other social bookmarking sites include Furl (www.furl.net) and Ma.gnolia (http://ma.gnolia.com/).

Creating Social Bookmarks

Social bookmarking is easy to use whether you are using del.cio.us or Diigo. Just follow these four steps to get started.

Figure 8-4. Del.icio.us Bookmarks

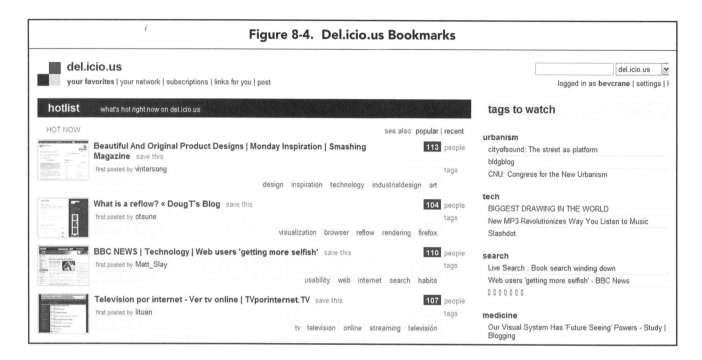

Figure 8-5. Diigo

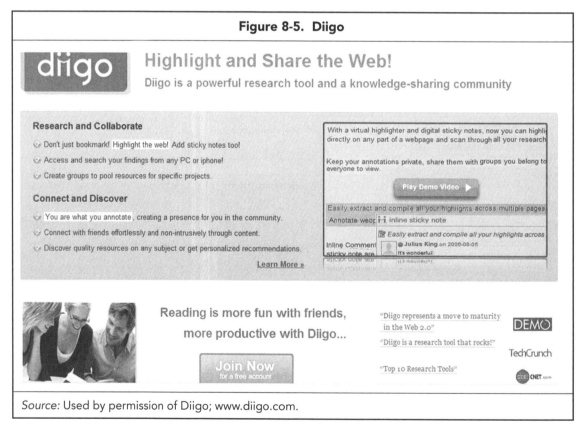

Source: Used by permission of Diigo; www.diigo.com.

Step 1: Sign Up for a Free Account

To create social bookmarks, register at a social bookmarking site: Go to Del.icio.us, Diigo or another social bookmarking site and complete the registration form. Click Register. If you receive a confirmation e-mail, click the link to confirm your registration to activate your account. See Figure 8-6 for an example from Diigo.

Figure 8-6. Sign Up Page

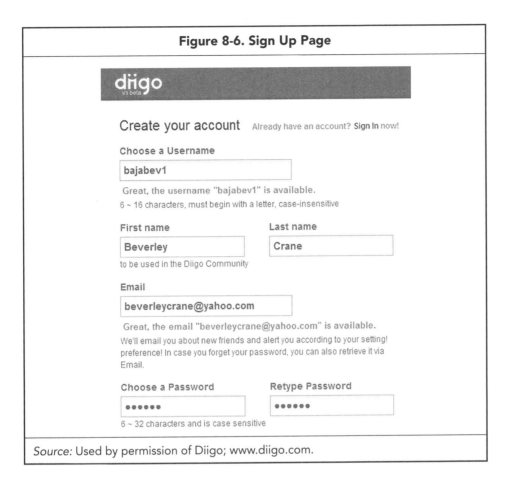

Source: Used by permission of Diigo; www.diigo.com.

Del.icio.us, Diigo and most similar tools install buttons on a browser (e.g., Internet Explorer, Firefox) toolbar. Click "Install Extension Now" to add those buttons to your browser. You probably also will have to close and then reopen your browser. Your browser menu bar now should have two new buttons on it as shown in Figure 8-7.

Figure 8-7. Toolbar

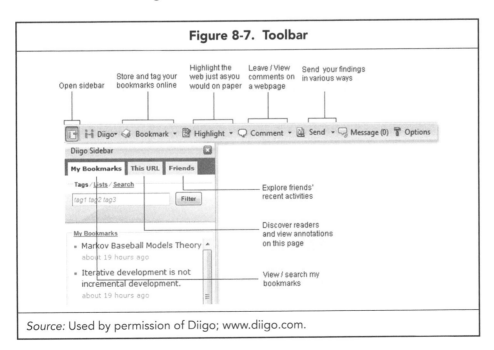

Source: Used by permission of Diigo; www.diigo.com.

You have the option on Diigo, for example, of setting up an avatar (your online identity) by uploading an image to represent yourself online. You can also create a private site to which only those you invite can visit or add bookmarks.

Step 2: Log In to Your Account to Become Familiar with the Site

On Diigo, for example, the first thing you see is your Dashboard, which contains all of your incoming messages, friend requests, group invites, and more. It also includes your bookmarks with any annotations you might have created: tags, groups, and lists. You can create groups so that you can work together with your class on a project or set up an international discussion group.

Step 3: Bookmark a Site

When you find a site you want to bookmark, click the Tag button on your toolbar. A pane similar to that shown in Figure 8-8 will display. The title and URL are already entered for you. The keyword box is blank so you can type keywords you would use if this was a site you wanted to find. You can enter more than one tag; for example, an English teacher who found a site on Hamlet might enter keywords: Hamlet, Shakespeare, English 12, and teaching. When you have added all tags, click Save. Note that you can see exactly how many users have saved that site as well. On Del.icio.us if you click the blue/black/white checkerboard icon, you will go to your saved bookmarks.

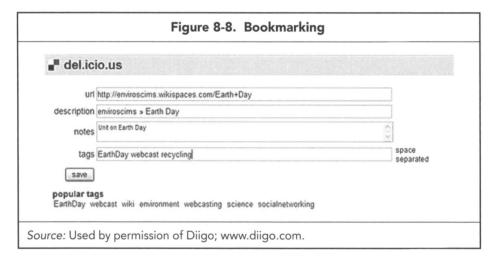

Figure 8-8. Bookmarking

Source: Used by permission of Diigo; www.diigo.com.

Step 4: Organize Your Bookmarks

When you have enough sites bookmarked, you may need to change the organization so they are easier to find. On the right side of your page of bookmarks, you see "view as cloud"; this enables you to sort your sites by the tags themselves (see Figure 8-9). If you click a specific tag, a list of sites you have saved with that keyword will appear. Some of the words are bigger or smaller than others. In a tag cloud, keywords are arranged alphabetically, and the size of the words indicates how often they've been used as keywords.

Students today are used to visualizing a research topic in the form of a Web or cluster as they brainstorm a topic; therefore, social bookmarking is a concept they are used to. Because some bookmarking services allow all users to have access to all sites, students may find bookmarks that are inappropriate for their age. You can set up a private bookmarking system so that only users you designate will have access to your sites and are allowed to combine their tags and sites with yours. That allows your students to experiment with social bookmarks in a

> ➤ *Learn how to use other social bookmarking tools at Bev's Web site at www.neal-schuman.com/webclassroom.*

Figure 8-9. Tag Cloud

Hot Tags

blog, design, web2.0, fashion, html, web, linux, windows, software, opensource, internet, news, book, google, security, collaboration, search, tools, wiki, links, music, graphics, ajax, education, howto, java, online, programming, tutorial, tutorials, travel, health, game, mp3, social, flickr, network, politics, community, article, javascript, tech, writing, magazine, research, calendar, photo, review, media, video, mobile, microsoft, audio, tv, storage, CSS, website, flash, download, hosting, science, mail, books, computer, annotation, photography, technology, wordpress, php, entertainment, mac, services, food, quickd, forum, learning, webdesign, shopping, networking, photos, library, maps, e-learning, resources, humor, productivity, blogging, sports, podcast, culture, techcrunch, youtube, recipes, guide, ipod, hardware, election, diet, lifehacker, inspiration

more»

Source: Used by permission of Diigo; www.diigo.com.

safe environment. Try using them for research or science fair projects, so the information students find can be shared collectively.

Teacher Exercises: Now You Try It . . .

You have completed Parts 1 and 2 of this chapter describing what social bookmarking is all about, providing examples of its educational use in the classroom and for professional use by teachers and librarians. You have also viewed two popular social bookmarking tools where the process for using them is outlined.

Now it is time to try social bookmarking for yourselves. The following exercises will get you started by having you open your own free account and start setting up your own bookmarks. Of course, you should also be thinking about how you will use this Web 2.0 tool with your students in a classroom lesson.

1. Start out by viewing the YouTube video on social bookmarking at www.youtube.com/watch?v=x66lV7GOcNU.
2. Sign up for either del.icio.us, diigo or another social bookmarking site that you have heard about.
3. Go to http://del.icio.us/tag/ and explore some of the most popular tags on del.icio.us. For example, click Education and then click one of the related tags in the right sidebar to see the tags.
4. Select an upcoming topic that you want your students to research. Review a number of Web sites on the topic and bookmark at least five (5) sites. Add one or more tags to each bookmark.

   ➤ *Try additional exercises that will improve your understanding of social bookmarking at Bev's Web site at www.neal-schuman.com/webclassroom.*
5. Add your students to your private group so they can view your bookmarks.

You now have your social bookmarking account ready so that you can incorporate this technology as well as others discussed in earlier chapters into this final unit plan.

PART 3: PRACTICAL APPLICATIONS

With the price of gasoline and heating fuel at an all-time high, everyone is talking about "going green." Thus, incorporating environmental education into the science curriculum has taken on greater importance. However, learning about the environment really has a cross-curricular impact. For example, instilling civic responsibilities is a goal promoted in most social studies curricula, and some see the roots of environmental problems as stemming from the basic values upon which society has been built. Since global change is only as good as its smallest players, it is important to instill an environmental ethic into our students at an early age.

Cross-Curricular Unit Plan on the Environment

Scientifically speaking, we want students to identify a real problem, hypothesize, collect data, formulate a procedure and come up with workable results. Thus, this unit is written around the topic of Earth Day, celebrated each year in April. The topic provides students with opportunities to select real problems (e.g., recycling, water pollution, trash, and many more), collect data on why the problem is important to solve, and decide how they are going to come up with positive solutions.

The unit will incorporate different Web 2.0 tools that have been discussed throughout this book. Students will also work in groups, collaborating and making decisions to attain positive results.

This unit provides a model to help you construct your own science lessons using Web 2.0 tools and different instructional strategies. Based on state framework standards, unit activities allow students to apply skills in scientific problem solving as they work on their projects, identify real-world problems through field experiences, and contribute toward solving problems that plague our world. The culmination of the unit will be the Earth Day Fair in which all groups in the class will participate for the entire school and parents.

Step 1: Apply Framework Standards—What Should Be Taught?

Frameworks today encourage learner-centered classrooms, resulting in learning that is more active and less authority dependent. Educational strategies that enhance student learning include cooperative learning, peer projects, and active collaborative endeavors that are alternatives to teacher-centered lectures. Technology standards both mandate active learning and assist it. According to science national standards, inquiry into authentic questions generated from student experiences is the central strategy for teaching science.

For this unit, then, educators should:

- structure the time available so that students are able to engage in extended investigations;
- create a setting for student work that is flexible and supportive of science inquiry;
- work collaboratively with others to enhance the understanding of science and foster the practice of many of the skills, attitudes, and values that characterize science;
- make the available science tools, materials, media, and technological resources accessible;
- work across the curriculum with other teachers to enhance the entire curriculum, including the science program; and
- promote opportunities to discuss ethical issues as they arise in the presentation of science.

Step 2: Identify General Goals and Specific Objectives

Use the goals and objectives that follow as a basis for the content and skills covered in this unit.

Goals

Goals for learning about the environment in general as it is promoted on Earth Day specifically should include the following:

- Presenting science in connection with its applications in technology and its implications for society
- Teaching science by developing concepts using the students' own experiences and interests through appropriate activities, such as hands-on activities, field trips, use of technology
- Promoting higher order thinking skills by forming a relationship among the other frameworks, such as mathematics, English/language arts, and history/social sciences

Objectives

By the end of the unit, students will be able to:

- define problems (e.g., pollution, waste) that negatively affect the environment;
- identify major causes of environmental problems;
- identify personal methods to "go green" to help save the environment (e.g., conserving water, recycling, waste management, reducing pollution, and more);
- work cooperatively in groups on an Earth Day project;
- communicate with other classes worldwide; and
- incorporate Web 2.0 tools to enhance their project.

Step 3: Gather Materials

In this unit each group will have some similar tasks and others that will be unique to their own Earth Day project (see Table 8-1). Thus, materials used may be somewhat different. All students will use the Internet and other sources for research on the problem they are trying to alleviate. These include research articles, blogs, wikis, videos, discussions with other students worldwide, and more.

Step 4: Create Sample Activities

Procedures for the unit focus on show, tell, try, and do. First, students will see that they can make a difference in protecting the environment. Second, they will see that working together with students in their own classes and other students worldwide enhances learning; and third, they will understand how Web 2.0 tools help them communicate their message about environmental problems and enable them to research and collaborate more easily to produce a product that accomplishes results. The activities that follow include cross-curricular areas to encompass science, social studies, language arts, technology, and art.

Activities to Introduce the Unit

A discussion of Earth Day and its historical beginnings will focus for students the importance of "going green." The activities require that students work together in groups throughout the unit. In teams of four, students will:

- Brainstorm at least five (5) different projects that their team could undertake to try to make a difference for Earth Day. At this point students do not evaluate ideas, rather they jot down as many as possible.
- Select a project and start to collect resources to use in the project. They will create a social bookmarking page and bookmark at least five (5) Web pages each on their topic from a variety of sources such as blogs, videos, and informational Web pages. See Table 8-2 for some sample URLs to visit.
- Evaluate each of their ideas on criteria presented in Table 8-3.
- Watch the YouTube video before the next activity to see different ways the planet's resources are being destroyed.
- Create a wiki so that each group has a page that the group can use to collect its resources and data.

Table 8-1. URLs for the Earth Day Unit	
URL	**Description**
www.greeniq.com/resources/100-ways-to-green-your-life-today/	100 ways to go green
www.npr.org/templates/story/story.php?storyId=89787388	Beach cleanup article
www.oceanconservancy.org/site/PageServer?pagename=vol_activities	Ocean conservancy
http://video.nationalgeographic.com/video/player/environment/ environmental-threats-environment/water-pollution/coastal-cleanup.html	Videos for water cleanup, pollution, global warming and more
http://spreadsheets.google.com/pub?key=pjhtZL6VSrXyIvsofEzr5Pw	Google Docs spreadsheet of litter collected
www.imbee.com/group/natgeokids	Join the National Geographic Kids group
http://kids.nationalgeographic.com/ngkids_mypage/mypage_login.jsp;jsessionid=E459E8D0BA4F477B075259F29A8B91FA	Kids' Web Pages on National Geographic
www.npr.org/rss/rss.php?id=1025	NPR environmental feeds
www.youtube.com/watch?v=hpl5-deexps www.youtube.com/watch?v=-utd0HRifOw	Recycling rap song on YouTube video
http://ecologue.com/ShowTopic/recycling-and-reducing-waste	Recycling and reducing waste
www.fightglobalwarming.com/page.cfm?tagID=136	The science of global warming
http://ww2.earthday.net/	Earth Day Web site
www.epa.gov/recyclecity/activity.htm#Information	A number of videos about kids recycling
www.epa.gov/osw/conserve/onthego/program/index.htm	Set up a recycling program
www.globalwarmingkids.net/	Global warming for kids
http://globalwarmingkids.net/streaming_videos/index.html	Videos about aspects of global warming

Table 8-2. General Social Bookmarking URLs	
URL	**Description**
http://k12wiki.wikispaces.com/Social+Networking+Acceptable+Use	Wiki to create acceptable use policy for social bookmarking
http://personal.strath.ac.uk/d.d.muir/Delicious1_2.pdf	Del.icio.us user guide
http://socialnetworksined.wikispaces.com	List of educational social networks
http://weblogg-ed.com/2005/08/02/	Tags vs. Trusted Sources-the downside of social bookmarking
http://blog.diigo.com/2008/03/23/tip-of-the-day-diigo-bookmarking-101/	Diigo bookmarking 101
www.kn.pacbell.com/wired/fil/pages/listweb20s.html	Web 2.0 tools
http://k12wiki.wikispaces.com/Social+Networking+ Acceptable+Use	Wiki to create acceptable use policy for social bookmarking

Table 8-3. Project Ideas					
Project Ideas	Impact on local community	How achievable or realistic is the idea?	How "global" is the topic?	How fun and interesting is the idea?	Totals
1					
2					
3					
4					
5					

Activities to Use During the Unit

Each group should now have selected an "Earth Day issue" such as recycling, littering, water conservation, and more. Sample activities are provided for each project. The activities include at least one or more Web 2.0 tools discussed in this book as an integral part of the project.

Activities for Each Group to Complete

Groups work on their projects by collecting data from various sources, synthesizing the data into a product (e.g., podcast, wiki, video) and presenting the product in a combined effort for the school at an Earth Day Fair. All groups will complete the following:

- Look at some of the YouTube videos listed in Table 8-2 to get some ideas about possible solutions for their Earth Day projects. Add the ideas to their wiki pages.
- Set up a site on the National Geographic Kids page to showcase the activities the group is completing during the unit.
- Keep up to date by bookmarking RSS feeds on the environment from National Public Radio (NPR) and other sites.
- Use their social bookmarking site to create at least five (5) or more bookmarks on the group topic.

Sample Topics for Earth Day Projects

- *Conserve water* (http://ecologue.com/ShowTopic/water-conservation). Team 1 will:
  - view at least three (3) videos illustrating how to save water;
  - read at least one (1) article by each team member;
  - brainstorm from information on the bookmarked sites a list of ways they think they can (1) conserve water as an individual; (2) make a difference in the community;
  - create a podcast with each team member participating in writing a part of the script and recording the podcast. The content explains what other students and parents can do to conserve water. Place the podcast on their school blog for other students and parents to see. Play it at the Earth Day Fair; and
  - create visuals that represent ideas for conserving water to add to the podcast.
- *Create grocery bags* (http://earthdaybags.org/). This project is an international project that has been underway for several years (see Figure 8-10). Team 2 will:
  - review the project starter kit and the four steps to get started at www.earthdaybags.org/gsprojstartkit.htm and bookmark the site. Look at the two PowerPoint presentations to see some sample grocery bag artwork and text used by other students (www.earthdaybags.org/powerpoint.htm);

Figure 8-10. Grocery Bag Project

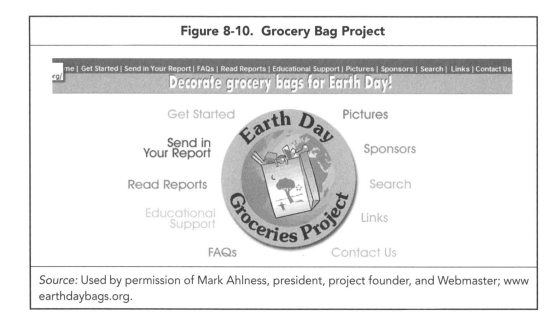

Source: Used by permission of Mark Ahlness, president, project founder, and Webmaster; www earthdaybags.org.

- post comments to their classroom wiki concerning the creation of the bags, delivering them to the store, and their feelings about the project;
- contact another school participating in the project and have each class create a VoiceThread that includes their wiki comments. Add comments to the partner class VoiceThread; and
- write a report on the work done by the team. Include pictures, if desired.
- *Recycle.* Recycling saves large amounts of energy. Recycling one glass jar saves enough energy to light a 100-watt light bulb for four hours. Recycling one soda can saves as much energy as if the can were half full of gasoline. Team 3 will:
  - go to www.epa.gov/recyclecity/activity.htm#Things and select at least three (3) activities to do in Recycle City;
  - read at least one (1) article each on recycling;
  - identify key questions and answers about recycling and post them on their wiki. Team members should add and modify the information on the wiki as they continue their research;
  - listen to the video "Recycling Propaganda–the other side of recycling" to gain information on both sides of the issue;
  - set up a task list of ways they have implemented recycling in their homes; http://ecologue .com/question_detail.aspx?qid=20080502140017AAtFkx1&category_name=Environment &keywords=recycling+OR++recycled&source=hom; www.epa.gov/earthday/home.htm #recycle;
  - present a persuasive, well-organized podcast promoting the establishment of a school recycling program. (1) review the basics of recycling at www.epa.gov/osw/conserve/onthego/ info/index.htm; (2) view recycling YouTube videos at www.youtube.com/watch?v=jPfU QDzJjKU&feature=related;
  - create a VoiceThread where the group creates and sings a recycling rap song they created; and
  - present the podcast and VoiceThread at the Earth Day Fair. Also at the Fair, explain how they used their wiki for research purposes.
- *Aid in reducing global warming.* Team 4 will:
  - watch the Gore video on global warming titled *An Inconvenient Truth*;
  - check some of the videos on global warming at YouTube (www.youtube.com/watch?v = n2Yl3bvs-Oo);

- divide their wiki into three parts: their research, their contributions, and their suggestions for others. All group members should contribute and ask other groups to also add their ideas;
- create a global warming wheel card (see Figure 8-11) (www.epa.gov/climatechange/emissions/wheelcard.html);

Figure 8-11. Global Warming Wheel Card

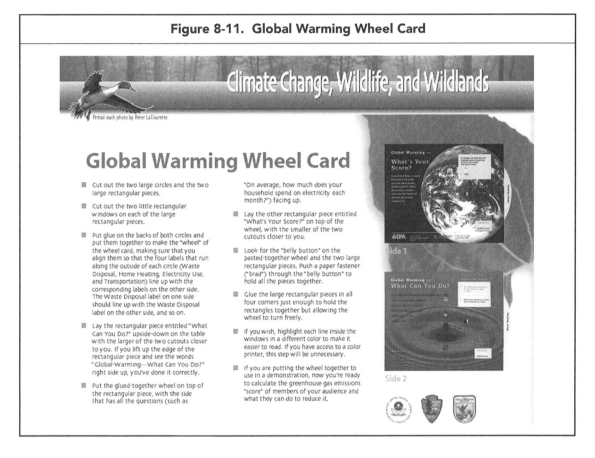

- create a podcast that has three parts: Part 1 identifies the problem and its causes; Part 2 describes ways the group has tried to do their share to reduce global warming; and Part 3 suggests how others can help; and
- present the podcast at the Earth Day Fair.
- *Decrease water pollution.* Team 5 will:
  - review videos on water pollution to see what other school-age children are doing to combat water pollution (www.youtube.com/results?search_query=water+pollution+&search_type=);
  - use Google Docs to create a spreadsheet of all litter collected in their group project along the beach, lake, sea, pond, waterway, etc. (see Figure 8-12);
  - view videos on coastal clean-up on beaches, by lakes and seas;
  - use Google Maps to identify areas regionally close by where water pollution might be a problem; and
  - present their report, including the spreadsheet, maps, and photos at the Earth Day Fair.

> ➤ *See additional suggested topics where you can combine different Web 2.0 tools into lessons at Bev's Web site at www.neal-schuman.com/webclassroom.*

Activities to Use as Follow-Up to the Unit

As extension activities resulting from the work by each group on its unit project, the class can do the following:

Figure 8-12. Ocean Conservancy Beach Debris Data

Ocean Conservancy Beach Debris Data

Itemized - Land v. Underwater	Itemized by Country	Itemized by State

Pounds-Miles by Country

	Land	Underwater	Total
Shoreline & Recreational Activities			
Bags	584706	3121	587827
Balloons	60770	162	60932
Beverage Bottles (plastic) 2 liter or less	491320	3327	494647
Beverage Bottles (glass)	345804	3339	349143
Beverage Cans	303475	4817	308292
Caps/Lids	653194	2894	656088
Clothing/Shoes	113767	835	114602
Cups, plates, etc	373563	2731	376294
Food Wrappers	690309	3303	693612
Pull Tabs	77430	304	77734
Six-Pack Holders	31040	104	31144
Shotgun Shells	23602	71	23673
Straws/Stirrers	323160	1520	324680
Toys	58497	418	58915
Total	4130637	26946	4157583

- Join the National Geographic Kids group and, as an ongoing project, create their own blog with photos, items from their projects, or videos so classmates and parents can see what the class is doing to "go green."
- Answer questions such as these: What are some ways that they might reduce the amount of garbage in their homes? Students present speeches to community groups, city council, county commissioners.
- Attend public meetings on other public problems and evaluate the effectiveness of the presentations.
- Write letters to the editors of local papers advocating that recycling and the other projects that groups undertook be included as community projects.
- Discuss how recycling and "resource recovery" can work together as part of a solid waste management plan.
- Create their own podcast on waste:
  - Trace their waste: Use Google Maps to identify their own locale. Stake out an area where they will search for litter and collect the litter to make a difference. Answer questions like: What options for recycling are available in their neighborhood or city?

Step 5: Evaluate What Was Learned

Evaluation is an important part of any lesson. A rubric is a device that serves two purposes. First, it evaluates students on the success of their final project, which has as its goal to alleviate a problem whether it is global warming, conserving water, removing litter, or others. It also helps the teacher evaluate the plan that the students undertook to reach the conclusion to the unit.

Process

The following questions will help evaluate the process students used to create the final product:

1. *Focusing on the problem.* Did students clearly define the topic so that they investigated relatively specific problems within a larger area of study—for example, Earth Day projects in the scheme of "going green"?

2. *Level of resources.* Did students use resource materials and/or equipment that is more advanced, technical, or complex than materials ordinarily used by students at their own age or grade level?

3. *Diversity of resources.* Which of the following sources, in addition to books, did students use: the Internet—Web sites, blogs, wikis, VoiceThreads, RSS, social bookmarking, videos and others?

4. *Action orientation.* Were investigations clearly directed toward some kinds of actions that helped make a difference for the environment?

Product

The following questions will help evaluate the products students created:

1. *Knowledge.* Do the products reflect advanced familiarity with the subject matter for students at this age?

2. *Quality.* Do the products reflect a level of quality beyond what is normally expected of students at this age and grade?

3. *Attitude.* Do the products reflect care, attention to detail, and overall pride in their achievements?

4. *Commitment.* Do the products reflect a commitment of time, effort, and energy on the part of the students?

5. *Originality.* Are the products original ideas and did students make original contributions for children of their age or grade level?

Two rubrics—a self-evaluation rubric (see Figure 8-13) and an evaluation checklist (see Figure 8-14)—will help in the evaluation process.

Summary

This culminating unit plan illustrates how numerous Web 2.0 tools can be incorporated into content area curricula to make a difference in student learning. Technology is not learned in isolation but

Figure 8-13. Self-Evaluation Rubric				
Student Group _____ Evaluator(s): _____ Peer _____ Teacher _____ Self				
	Proficient	**Developing**	**Emerging**	**Total**
Researches and gathers information	Collects a great deal of the information-all related to the topic	Collects some basic information—most related to the topic	Collects very little information—some related to the topic	
On Task	Always does assigned work—without having to be reminded	Usually does assigned work—rarely needs reminding	Rarely does assigned work—often needs reminding	
Listens to teammates	Listens and asks questions, offers ideas, never argues with teammates	Listens but sometimes talks too much; rarely argues	Usually does most of the talking— rarely allows others to speak; sometimes argues	
Group Work on Final Project	Students worked effectively as a group to organize, plan, and create a product	Students worked well as a group to organize, plan, and create a product		

Figure 8-14. Evaluation Checklist

Directions: Fill in the checklist below to assess students' final projects. These can be returned to students.

Process

1. Topic clearly defined? _____

2. Level of resource materials and/or equipment used?
_____

3. Resources used? More than 3? Internet? _____
_____

4. Actions resulting from the research? _____
_____

5. Specified audience? _____

Product

1. Shows advanced familiarity with the subject matter for students' ages? _____
_____

2. Reflects a superior level of quality? _____

3. Reflects care, attention to detail, and overall pride? _____
_____

4. Shows a commitment of time, effort and energy? _____

Technology

1. Identified the process they went through and any problems they encountered in using Web 2.0 tools? _____

Other Comments:
_____
_____

---

rather as a means to promote enthusiasm and motivation for learning. The Web 2.0 tools discussed in this book provide a starting point for educators to grasp technology and use it for what they know best—promoting learning for all ages, all grade levels, and all students, no matter what their level of learning.

Teacher Exercises: Now You Try It . . .

These are the culminating exercises for the book. You have learned much about Web 2.0 tools and how to use them in the classroom to enhance student learning in each chapter. Reflect back to Chapter 1 and review your Web 2.0 notebook:

1. Review your Web 2.0 notebook and prioritize the Web 2.0 tools that you have learned about. Identify and write about each tool that you:
   ○ plan to try first in a lesson;
   ○ think is the most useful for your students and why; and
   ○ think meets standards and objectives for your students.

2. Review your curriculum for the next month and brainstorm places where you can incorporate one or more Web 2.0 tools.
   ○ Select the tool in your Web 2.0 notebook that you plan to include in your next lesson: write objectives and activities that include the tool that will enhance the lesson.
   ○ Set up a rubric for the lesson that assesses content knowledge, students' abilities using the tool, and group work, if used.
3. In the next month use at least two (2) Web 2.0 tools that will help you as a teacher improve the learning of your students.
4. If possible, attend a conference where Web 2.0 tools are being demonstrated and illustrated in the classroom.
5. In your Google Notebook, continue to write about Web 2.0, find examples of tools' use in the classroom, comment on blogs, and add to wikis.

As a result of your continued participation with Web 2.0 tools, you should be comfortable enough to expand use of these tools in your classroom and communicate with other educators who are doing the same. You might even take the leadership role in your school to encourage other teachers to try these new technologies.

CONCLUSION

The best Web 2.0 teachers are a part of the Web themselves. They have an RSS reader and subscribe to blogs in their subject areas. They comment on blogs and stay abreast of real time innovations in their fields. They are connected to other educators in their subject area and often share their own best practices with others. They consider new technologies and are not prone to make spontaneous statements without considering the facts. They model what they teach.

Engaged teachers have the following characteristics:

- They are connected.
- They are open-minded.
- They are vigilant.
- They hold students and themselves accountable.
- They have character.
- They are passionate about their topic.

Remarks like the following from K–12 educators encourage other teachers and librarians to engage and join the Web 2.0 community:

> "When it comes to technology in education, you can create it, you can design it, you can produce it, you can legislate it, you can order it, restructure it, give it standards, and write outcomes for it. But the bottom line is that if it is going to happen, teachers have to make it happen." (Jacqueline Goodloe, Washington, DC, teacher; http://aztea.wikispaces.com/Favorite+Web+2.0+Quotes)

> "It is important to remember that educational software, like textbooks, is only one tool in the learning process. Neither can be a substitute for well-trained teachers, leadership, and parental involvement." (Keith Krueger, CEO, Consortium for School Networking; http://aztea.wikispaces.com/Favorite+Web+2.0+Quotes)

> "As we provide our students with models of how to use their digital containers for learning, the role of the teacher will be more crucial than ever. The fact remains: These tools can be a major distraction from learning or they can be a major catalyst to it. It will be the

courageous educator who works with students to explore the power of these tools and in turn empowers students to be lifelong learners and active shapers of a world we cannot yet imagine." (Alan November, educational technology leader, author, consultant, and speaker; www.techlearning.com/showArticle.php?articleID=196604487).

"The most dangerous experiment we can conduct with our children is to keep schooling the same at a time when every other aspect of our society is dramatically changing." (Chris Dede, written statement to the PCST panel, 1997; http://aztea.wikispaces.com/Favorite+ Web+2.0+Quotes).

Throughout this book, we have examined how Web 2.0 tools can be used in the core subjects— language arts, science, social studies, and with students whose first language is not English. More and more classrooms are integrating the Read Write Web into the curriculum.

➤ *Bev's Web site at www.neal-schuman.com/webclassroom will continue to update URLs in this book. Check the site often for the latest educational URLs.*

Students have embraced Web 2.0 tools—blogs, YouTube, wikis, social bookmarking—in their personal lives. It is now time that educators incorporated these tools into their lessons, thus enabling students to see that education and new technology go hand in hand toward enhancing learning.

REFERENCES AND FURTHER READING

Hammond, Tony Timo Hannay, Ben Lund, and Joanna Scott. 2005. "Social Bookmarking Tools: A General Review." *D-Lib Magazine* 11, no. 4 (April). Available: www.dlib.org/dlib/april05/Hammond/04hammond .html (accessed October 1, 2008).

National Science Educational Standards. *National Committee on Science Education Standards and Assessment, National Research Council.* 2008. Washington, DC: National Academy Press. Available: http://books.nap.edu/catalog.php?record_id=4962 (accessed October 2, 2008).

"Seven Things You Should Know about Social Bookmarking," EDUCAUSE Learning Initiative. (May 2005). Available: www.educause.edu/ir/library/pdf/ELI7001.pdf (accessed October 2, 2008).

Warlick, David. 2004. *Redefining Literacy for the 21st Century.* Worthington, OH: Linworth.

Wikipedia. Social Bookmarking. Available: http://en.wikipedia.org/wiki/Social_bookmarking (accessed October 2, 2008).

List of URLS by Chapter

CHAPTER 1

http://en.wikipedia.org/wiki/Creative_Commons_licenses—Creative Commons licenses

http://docs.google.com/View?docid=dfqjmd6d_24dfbht8d4—Acceptable Use Policies with personal responsibility

www.doe.virginia.gov/VDOE/Technology/AUP/home.shtml—AUP from Department of Education in Virginia

http://del.icio.us/techsavvygirl/acceptable_use?setbundleview=show—Several examples of AUPs

http://k12wiki.wikispaces.com/Social+Networking+Acceptable+Use—AUP for social networking

www.edutopia.org/mary-scroggs-elementary-school—Video about Mary Scroggs Elementary School learning with technology

www.21centuryconnections.com/node/1—Article about twentieth-first-century learning—Intro to digital vid

http://blogsearch.google.com/—Google Blog Search

http://images.google.com/—Google Image Search

www.del.icio.us.com—A social bookmarking site

www.technorati.com—An Internet search engine for searching blogs

www.youtube.com—A video-sharing Web site where users can upload, view, and share video clips.

CHAPTER 2

http://weblogs.hcrhs.k12.nj.us/beesbook—Secondary English blog on the novel *The Secret Life of Bees*

http://weblogs.hcrhs.k12.nj.us/beesparents—Parents blog on *The Secret Life of Bees*

http://dl1.yukoncollege.yk.ca/takpilotblog/—Ms. Howard's class writing blog, Yukon, Takhini Elementary

http://jtubbs.21publish.com/—Mr. Tubb's Sixth Grade Homework and student blogs

http://bobsprankle.com/writingblog/—Mr. S and Mr. I student poetry blogs

http://landmark-project.com—Blogmeister, the Landmark project, blogging service

www.classblogmeister.com/—Home page for Blogmeister

http://edublogs.org—Home page for Edublogs, an educational blogging service

www.blogger.com—Blogging service used by educators

www.teachersfirst.com/content/blog/tools3.cfm—Compares blogging services' features

www.bloglines.com—Another popular blogging service

www.google.com/reader—Blogging service provided by Google

http://allrss.com/rssreaders.html—List of feed readers from RSS Compendium

www.budtheteacher.com/wiki/index.php?title=Blogging_Rules—Blogging guide created by a Colorado teacher for his students

http://classblogmeister.com/bloggers_contract.doc—Blogging pledge created by Blogmeister blogging service as a sample

www.teachersfirst.com/content/blog/Sample%20Blogger%20Agreement.doc—Sample blogger agreement that you may edit to fit your circumstances

http://patterson.edublogs.org/all-about-blogs/—Sample blog guidelines

http://cnets.iste.org/students/s_stands.html—ISTE Nets Technology Standards

www.npr.org/templates/story/story.php?storyId=14556298—Finding less controversial stem cell information

www.npr.org/takingissue/takingissue_stemcells.html—Arguing the ethics of stem cell research, an NPR site with pros and cons on the issue

www.npr.org/templates/story/story.php?storyId=5252449—Key moments in the stem cell debate

www.npr.org/templates/story/story.php?storyId=9533577—Q&A about the science behind the stem cell debate-exploding the myths

http://usliberals.about.com/od/stemcellresearch/Stem_Cell_Research_Basics_Issues_Advocacy_Positions.htm—Pros and cons of embryonic stem cell research

www.whitehouse.gov/news/releases/2001/ 08/20010809-2.html—Bush speech on stem cell research issue

www.npr.org/templates/story/story.php?storyId=11279411—Political point of view on stem cell research (Bush side)

www.npr.org/templates/story/story.php?storyId=9533577—Q&A about the science behind the stem cell debate-exploding the myths

www.npr.org/templates/story/story.php?storyId=11279411—Political point of view on stem cell research (Bush side)

www.npr.org/templates/story/story.php?storyId=5252449—Key moments in the stem cell debate

www.npr.org/templates/story/story.php?storyId=9533577—Q&A about the science behind the stem cell debate-exploding the myths

http://archives.cnn.com/2001/HEALTH/07/17/stem.cell.hearing/—Political con side of embryonic research

www.biotechnologyonline.gov.au/human/sctypes.cfm—Types of stem cells

www.biotechnologyonline.gov.au/human/usessc.cfm—Potential uses of stem cells

www.biotechnologyonline.gov.au/human/ethicssc.cfm—Ethics of stem cell research; Australian student worksheet

www.bmj.com/cgi/content/full/—Regulation of the collection and use of fetal stem cells

http://millersenglish10.blogspot.com/—English teacher blog

www.bmj.com/cgi/content/full/ 332/7546/866?ijkey=B56vvkOcFrIPcPz&keytype=ref—Regulation of the collection and use of fetal stem cells

www.copyblogger.com/embrace-brevity/—Tips for writing blogs

www.geocities.com/vance_stevens/papers/evonline2002/week5.htm—Lots of blog examples

http://learnerblogs.org/—Free blogging service

http://librarygoddess.blogspot.com—A high school librarian who reviews books written for, or appropriate for, teens.

http://ewleditorials.blogspot.com/—Students write editorials on classic novels

www.weeklyreader.com/readandwriting/—Official blog of Read and Write Magazine Online

http://opencontent.org//docs/begin_blog.html—Beginner's Guide to Blogs http://mywebspace.quinnipiac.edu/PHastings/what.html—Blogging across the curriculum

www.alistapart.com/stories/writebetter/—Rules for writing good blog posts

CHAPTER 3

www.landmark-project.com—Landmark for Schools Project

http://nausetschools.org/podcasts.htm—Site for podcast information for teachers

www.firstmonday.org/issues/issue10_9/crofts/index.html—Stats about podcasts

http://ezinearticles.com/?2007-Was-A-Very-Good-Year-For-Podcasting&id=1061321—Report on podcast stats

http://en.wikipedia.org/—Wikipedia Encyclopedia Main Page

www.intelligenic.com/where/where.pdf—Where in the World Project (podcast)

www.mrcoley.com/coleycast/index.htm—ColeyKid podcasts

www.sdlax.net/longfellow/sc/ck/index.htm—Coulee Kids' podcasts

www.conversationsnetwork.org/levelator/—Site for the Levelator to level out discrepancies in volume

http://audacity.sourceforge.net—Audacity, a free software editing tool

www.apple.com/ilife/garageband—GarageBand, a software editing tool free with the Mac

www.voicethread.com—VoiceThread, another editor (Chapter 7)

www.soundzabound.com—Soundzabound, a free music download site

www.musicbakery.com—The Music Bakery, free music download

http://freesound.iua.upf.edu/index.php—The FreeSound Project, a collaborative database of licensed sounds with a Creative Commons license

www.feedburner.com—Equipment for uploading podcasts for distribution

www.itunes.com—PC or Mac is a digital media player application for playing and organizing digital music and video files

http://lcweb2.loc.gov/learn/lessons/psources/types.html—Primary sources Web site

www.pbs.org/independentlens/newamericans/foreducators_lesson_plan_09.html #HistoryAssignment—Sample PBS interview

www.sloganizer.net/en/—Sloganizer to help pick a title for podcast

www.thepcmanwebsite.com/free_slogan_creator.php—Web Site's Free Slogan Creator, to help create the podcast title

http://memory.loc.gov/learn/features/immig/interv/toc.php—Interviews with immigrants

www.pbs.org/wnet/americannovel/video/ANamericandream.html—Interviews with immigrants

http://library.thinkquest.org/20619/Past.html—Interviews with immigrants\

http://library.thinkquest.org/20619/Timeline.htm—Interviews with immigrants

http://library.thinkquest.org/20619/Present.html—Interviews with immigrants

CHAPTER 4

www.wetpaintcentral.com/pageSearch?contains=Privacy+ &+Terms+of+Use&t=anon—Wetpaint privacy policy

http://flatclassroomproject.wikispaces.com/Lesson+Plans—The World is Flat Project

http://flatclassroomproject.wikispaces.com/space/showimage/Flat_Classroom_LL_August07 .pdf—The World is Flat Project

http://villagewiki.pbwiki.com/—Example of elementary school wikis

http://terrythetennisball.wikispaces.com/—Digital storytelling wiki example http://studyingsocietiesatjhk.pbwiki.com/—Social studies elementary wiki topics

www.wikispaces.com/help+teachers—Wikispaces, a site for hosting wikis

www.wetpaint.com/category/education/?zone=module_e3—Wetpaint, a site for hosting wikis

http://pbwiki.com/education.wiki—PB Wiki, a site for hosting wikis

www.wikipedia.org/—Wikipedia, an encyclopedia that anyone can edit

http://edutechation.wordpress.com/2007/08/03/which-wiki-to-use/—Educator comments on wikis

www.ncte.org/about/over/standards/110846.htm—Standards created by The National Council of Teachers of English (NCTE)

http://coollessons.wikispaces.com/Administrator_Academy_Read-Write-Web—Group of lessons incorporating wikis

www.thesolutionsite.com/lesson/1603/gatsbycharacters.ppt—Introduction to the characters in *The Great Gatsby*, PowerPoint created by Pamela Fuller of Capital High School

www.geocities.com/BourbonStreet/3844/index.html#nick—Beginner's Guide to Gatsby

www.huffenglish.com/gatsby/index.html—*The Great Gatsby* Web page

http://en.wikipedia.org/wiki/The_Great_Gatsby—Wikipedia entry

http://www.webquest.org/questgarden/lessons/25768-060531185118/task.htm—WebQuest lesson using a wiki to compare life in Gatsby's time to life today

www.kn.pacbell.com/wired/fil/pages/webtheroarch.html—The Roaring 20s WebQuest

www.fcps.k12.va.us/westspringfieldhs/academic/english/1project/99gg/topics.htm—List of character synopses written by students on Sarah Chauncey's library wiki

www.wikispaces.com/site/tour#introduction—Tutorial showing how to use Wikispaces

www.wikispaces.com/site/for/teachers100K—Sign up for Wikispaces for free

http://edutechation.wordpress.com/2007/08/03/which-wiki-to-use/—Blog showing comparisons between wikispaces and pbwiki

http://www.wikispaces.com/site/tour#introduction—Introduction to wikispaces, including how to get started

www.newmediaworkshops.com/tripleAlecture/editwiki/editwiki.html—Tutorial on how to use PBWiki

www.readwritethink.org/lessons/lesson_view.asp?id=979—NCTE Read, Write and Think lessons

www.schoollibraryjournal.com/article/CA6277799.html—*Library Journal* Wiki article

www.wikihow.com/wikiHow:Tour—Wiki How to Tour

www.wikihow.com/wikiHow:Tour/Understand-the-Writer%27s-Guide—Wiki Guide

http://coollessons.wikispaces.com/Administrator_Academy_Read-Write-Web—Cool lessons for wikis at all grade levels and subject areas

http://cte.jhu.edu/techacademy/web/2000/kajder/wqeval.html—Scoring rubric on American Dreams

www.grandviewlibrary.org/ThirdGradeWikis.aspx—Sarah Chauncey's library wiki

CHAPTER 5

www.dtc.scott.k12.ky.us/technology/digitalstorytelling/studentstories.html—Digital stories by students in Scott County

http://sfett.com/html_movie/Ican4/the_power_of_one.html—Many examples of digital stories

http://walledlake.k12.mi.us/aal/digstorytelling/Examples.htm—Examples of digital stories from Walled Lake

http://villagewiki.pbwiki.com/Digital+Stories—Digital stories from Village Elementary School

http://dsi.kqed.org/index.php—KQED digital stories from contests
http://creativecommons.org—Creative Commons, a new form of copyright
www.flickr.com—Photo-sharing Web site
http://walledlake.k12.mi.us/aal/digstorytelling/Directions.pdf—Step-by-step instructions for
    using Movie Maker 2 to digitize photos, import pictures, and add voiceover
www.energyquest.ca.gov/story/index.html—Background on energy sources
www.mpsomaha.org/willow/radio/index.html—Podcast on energy from Willow Radio
www.planetpals.com/partnerenergy.html—Planetpals provide energy facts
www.pbs.org/now/ media_player/player.html?id=413ss&caps=low—PBS video on energy
    conservation at home
www1.eere.energy.gov/kids/roofus/—Roofus' house and energy used
http://home.howstuffworks.com/how-to-conserve-energy-at-home3.htm—Articles describing
    ideas for conserving energy
www.energyhog.org/pdf/ScavengerHunt.pdf—Energy Hog Scavenger Hunt
www.sciencemuseum.org.uk/exhibitions/energy/site/EIZgames.asp—Energy Ninjas
www.schooltube.com—School Tube enables digital stories to be published to the world
www.techlearning.com/shared/printableArticle.php?articleID=60300276—Telling Tales with
    Technology
www.umass.edu/wmwp/DigitalStorytelling/How%20to%20Create%20a%20digital%20story
    .htm—Storytelling Info
www.umass.edu/wmwp/DigitalStorytelling/Steps%20to%20Creating%20a%20Digital%20Story
    %20in%20MovieMaker.doc—Steps for using MovieMaker to create a digital story
www.umass.edu/wmwp/DigitalStorytelling/Lesson%20Plans%20for%20Digital%20Storytelling
    .htm—Lesson plans
www.picosearch.com/cgi-bin/ts.pl—Storytelling search engine
www.folktale.net/openers.html—Folktale openings
www.folktale.net/endings.html—Folktale endings
www.timsheppard.co.uk/story/storylinks.html—Story links of all kinds
www.timsheppard.co.uk/story/tellinglinks.html#Articles:%20story%20in%20education—Great
    site with excellent links to all aspects of storytelling
http://pblmm.k12.ca.us/PBLGuide/MMrubric.htm—Multimedia rubric
http://falcon.jmu.edu/~ramseyil/storyhandbook.htm—Handbook for storytellers
www.storycenter.org/cookbook.pdf—Center for Digital Storytelling
www.mcli.dist.maricopa.edu/learnshops/digital/examples.php—Examples of digital stories
www.dtc.scott.k12.ky.us/technology/ digitalstorytelling/studentstories.html—K–12 Digital stories
    in the Scott County Schools
http://cinedelagente.com/html/muves.htm—Digital story examples from all over the world
www.digitales.us—DigiTales
www.jasonohler.com—Jason Ohler.com
http://techszewski.blogs.com—Techszewski
http://tech-head.com/dstory.htm—Tech Head stories
www.techteachers.com/digstory/gradclass/rubrics.htm—Everything you wanted to know about
    digital stories and media
http://jdorman.wikispaces.com/digitalstorytelling—Everything you wanted to know about digital
    stories and media
http://teacher.scholastic.com/products/instructor/thinkgreen.htm—"Green" scavenger hunt
www.pbs.org/now/shows/413/index.html—Energy savings

www.pbs.org/now/media_player/player.html?id=413ss&caps=low—Energy slide show
www1.eere.energy.gov/kids/roofus/—Roofus, the dog's energy-efficient home
www.epa.gov/greenkit/student.htm—Sustainable energy for students/teachers
www.eirc.org/website/Programs-+and+-Services/Green-Apple-Program/Green-Classroom.html—
    Green classroom with lots of K–12 projects on energy
www.planetpals.com/partnerenergy.html—Energy saving ideas
www.planetpals.com/recyclefacts.html —Recycle center
www.planetpals.com/precycle.html—Precycle center
www.cnn.com/EVENTS/1996/earth_day/facts.html—Facts about energy
www.eere.energy.gov/—U.S. DOE Energy Efficiency and Renewable Energy
www.energyquest.ca.gov/story/index.html—Energy story
www1.eere.energy.gov/education/report_resources. html—Student resource section of the Dept.
    of Energy Web site
http://geocities.com/researchguide/energy.html#general—All about different types of energy, a
    comprehensive site with links

CHAPTER 6

www.c4lpt.co.uk/recommended/willrichardson.html—Will Richardson Web site
www.google.com/educators/tools.html—Google Web site for Educators
www.google.com/educators/p_pagecreator.html—Page Creator
www.google.com/educators/p_booksearch.html—Book Search to search books
www.google.com/educators/p_picasa.html—Picasa, to edit and share pictures
www.google.com/educators/community.html—Google Educators' discussion group
www.google.com/educators/p_docs.html—Google Docs
www.google.com/educators/p_news.html—Google News
www.google.com/educators/p_groups.html—Google Groups
http://groups.google.com/group/google-for-educators?lnk=gschg—Google discussion group for
    educators
www.google.com/educators/p_notebook.html—Google Notebook
www.google.com/educators/p_earth.html—Google Earth
www.google.com/educators/p_maps.html—Google Maps
http://sites.google.com/—Google Sites
www.google.com/reader/view/#overview-page—Google Reader
www.google.com/intl/en/googlereader/tour.html—Google Reader tour
www.activehistory.co.uk/Miscellaneous/free_stuff/google_earth/drake/index.htm—More
    information about the Sir Francis Drake site
www.googlelittrips.com—Google LitTrips
http://groups.google.com—Google Groups
http://bbs.keyhole.com/ubb/download.php?Number=151193—Google Earth at Antarctica
http://earth.google.com/—Download site for Google Earth
http://earth.google.com/tour/index.html—Virtual tour for Google Earth
www.blogger.com/start?utm_source=en-cpp-edu&utm_campaign=en&utm_medium=cpp—
    Blogger site to set up a blog
www.google.com/intl/en/googlereader/tour.html—Tour the Google Reader site
www.google.com/a/help/intl/en/edu/index.html—Google Apps page
www.google.com/a/your-domain.com—Administrative control panel for Google Apps

www.historyofcuba.com/history/funfacts/embargo.htm—History facts about Cuba

www.usaengage.org/index.php?option=com_issues&view=issue&id=12&Itemid=55—News articles about policies toward Cuba

www.cnn.com/video/#/video/world/2008/02/26/neill.cuba.raul.inheritance.cnn—CNN video about Raul Castro

www.google.com/educators/activities.html—Google Tools for Educators activities

www.historyofcuba.com/history/baypigs/pigs2.htm—Invasion at Bay of Pigs

www.cia.gov/library/publications/the-world-factbook—CIA Fact Book

www.pbs.org/newshour/bb/latin_america/cuba/life.html—Life in Cuba

www.usaengage.org/index.php?option=com_issues&view=issue&id=12&Itemid=5—Business organization supporting policy changes toward Cuba

www.forbes.com/home/business/2008/02/19/cuba-castro-retirement-cx_0220oxford.html—Will Cuba change under Raul?

www.slate.com/id/2185087/—Will any changes occur with the passing of the baton?

www.reuters.com/article/worldNews/idUSN0738669420080207—How do the young Cubans feel about the change?—What do they wish for? What do Cuban bloggers say about the change?

www.reuters.com/article/worldNews/idUSN2017089720080220—Reuters: Cuban students openly challenge government

www.reuters.com/article/worldNews/idUSN1926216920080219—Raul raises hopes for economic change in Cuba

www.nytimes.com/2008/03/01/world/americas/01cuba.html?em&ex=1204520400&en=83c44165cfcdf9e7&ei=5087%0A—Human rights violations in Cuba under Fidel Castro. Has anything changed since Raul Castro has taken office?

http://edition.cnn.com/TRANSCRIPTS/0205/12/sm.11.html—Carter goes to Cuba (2002)

www.usatoday.com/news/opinion/columnists/wickham/ 2002-05-21-wickham.htm—History, race must be factored into Cuban equation

http://edition.cnn.com/TRANSCRIPTS/0104/15/sm.12.html—Article on Bay of Pigs

www.guardian.co.uk/world/1959/jan/11/cuba—Cuba article from news archive from 1959

www.eastchester.k12.ny.us/schools/hs/teachers/fermann/documents/GEforESmanual.pdf—Google Earth manual for teachers

www.google.com/googlenotebook/tour1.html—Tutorial shows how to use Google Notebook

www.jakesonline.org/earth/placemarks.pdf—Tutorial on how to set up place marks

http://64.233.179.110/educators/learning_materials/Earth_Getting_Started_Guide.pdf—Getting Started on Google Earth

www.google.com/intl/en_us/help/maps/tour/—Tour on how to use Google Maps

www.google.com/googlenotebook/faq.html—Frequently Asked Questions about Google Notebook

www.google.com/google-d-s-/tour1.html—Tour of Google Docs

http://news.google.com—Google News sites

www.google.com/alerts?hl=en&t=1—Create a Google Alert

www.google.com/a/help/intl/en/admins/tour.html—Tours and demos illustrate how to get started and live Webinars provide experts to answer questions.

CHAPTER 7

http://voicethread4education.wikispaces.com/EFL+%26+ESL—ESL class working on VoiceThreads

http://voicethread.com/#q.b7626—Jose, the bear, VoiceThread project
http://primarymfl.ning.com/profiles/blog/show?id=738935%3ABlogPost%3A8621—Primary
    VoiceThread examples
http://voicethread.com/#c28—VoiceThread tutorials
www.flickr.com—Flickr home page
www.facebook.com—Facebook home page
http://ed.voicethread.com/—Educational VoiceThread Web page
http://voicethread.com/—VoiceThread home page for signing up
http://ed.voicethread.com/about/—Information about Educational VoiceThread, including cost
www.buildyourwildself.com/—Site enables a student to build an avatar
http://voicethread.com/view.php?b=579—Share their favorite poems to create an audio poem book
http://greatbookstories.pbwiki.com/—Narrate five pictures to share why they love a specific
    book, and why other people should read it
http://voicethread.com/view.php?b=971—Social Studies and geography applications
http://voicethread.com/view.php?b=5777—Book review
http://voicethread.com/#u3968—VoiceThread examples in ESL
http://news.bbc.co.uk/2/hi/in_pictures/7155727.stm—Pictures in the news for a current events
    unit. RSS subscription available
http://voicethread.com/#u3968—VoiceThread of pictures in the news
http://educators.pbwiki.com/VoiceThread+-+Group+conversations—100 ways to use
    VoiceThread in education
www.classroom20.com/—Classroom 2.0 for educators Forum. RSS
http://voicethread.com/ui/image/classroom.pdf—Printable Guide for Teachers on using
    VoiceThreads.
www.eslpod.com/—Podcasts with second-language learners

CHAPTER 8

www.del.icio.us.com—Delicious.com a social bookmarking site
www.diigo.com—Social bookmarking site of interest to educators
www.mamkschools.org/mas/class/grade4/brune/2004/contact_us.htm—List of a fifth grade
    classroom's bookmarks
www.readingrockets.org/podcasts/authors—"Meet the Authors" bookmarked site with podcasts
    and audio from the authors
www.furl.net—Social bookmarking site
http://ma.gnolia.com/—Social bookmarking site
www.youtube.com/watch?v=x66lV7GOcNU—Video on social bookmarking
http://del.icio.us/tag/—Shows some of the most popular tags on del.icio.us
http://ecologue.com/ShowTopic/water-conservation—Site related to water conservation
http://earthdaybags.org/—Earth Day grocery bag project
www.earthdaybags.org/gsprojstartkit.htm—Getting started with the grocery bag project
www.earthdaybags.org/powerpoint.htm—PowerPoint presentations on the grocery bag project
www.epa.gov/recyclecity/activity.htm#Things—EPA recycling ideas
http://ecologue.com/question_detail.aspx?qid=20080502140017AAtFkx1&category_name=
    Environment&keywords=recycling+OR++recycled&source=hom—Questions and answers on
    recycling
http://ecologue.com/ShowTopic/recycling-and-reducing-waste—Recycling and reducing waste

www.epa.gov/earthday/home.htm#recycle—Ways to recycle in the home

www.epa.gov/osw/conserve/onthego/info/index.htm—Basics of recycling

www.youtube.com/watch?v=jPfUQDzJjKU&feature=related—Recycling videos

www.youtube.com/watch?v=n2Yl3bvs-Oo—Videos on global warming on YouTube

www.epa.gov/climatechange/emissions/wheelcard.html—Global warming wheel card

www.youtube.com/results?search_query=water+pollution+&search_type=—Ideas to reduce water pollution

http://aztea.wikispaces.com/Favorite+Web+2.0+Quotes—Quote from teacher about Web 2.0

www.techlearning.com/showArticle.php?articleID=196604487—Quote by Alan November on Web 2.0 tools

www.greeniq.com/resources/100-ways-to-green-your-life-today/—100 ways to go green

www.npr.org/templates/story/story.php?storyId=89787388—Beach cleanup article

www.oceanconservancy.org/site/PageServer?pagename=vol_activities—Ocean Conservancy

http://video.nationalgeographic.com/video/player/environment/environmental-threats-environment/water-pollution/coastal-cleanup.html—Videos for water cleanup, pollution, global warming and more

http://spreadsheets.google.com/pub?key=pjhtZL6VSrXyIvsofEzr5Pw—Google Docs spreadsheet of litter collected

www.imbee.com/group/natgeokids—Join the National Geographic Kids group

http://kids.nationalgeographic.com/ngkids_mypage/mypage_login.jsp;jsessionid=E459E8D0BA4F477B075259F29A8B91FA—Kids' Web Pages on National Geographic

www.npr.org/rss/rss.php?id=1025—NPR environmental feeds

www.youtube.com/watch?v=hpl5-deexps—NPR environmental feeds; recycling rap song on YouTube video

http://ecologue.com/ShowTopic/recycling-and-reducing-waste—Recycling and reducing waste

www.fightglobalwarming.com/page.cfm?tagID=136—Science of global warming

http://ww2.earthday.net/—Earth Day Web site

www.epa.gov/recyclecity/activity.htm#Information—Number of videos about kids recycling

www.epa.gov/osw/conserve/onthego/program/index.htm—Set up a recycling program

www.globalwarmingkids.net/—Global warming for kids

http://globalwarmingkids.net/streaming_videos/index.html—Videos about aspects of global warming

http://k12wiki.wikispaces.com/Social+Networking+Acceptable+Use—Wiki to create acceptable use policy for social bookmarking

http://personal.strath.ac.uk/d.d.muir/Delicious1_2.pdf—Del.icio.us user guide

http://socialnetworksined.wikispaces.com—List of educational social networks

http://weblogg-ed.com/2005/08/02/—Tags vs. Trusted Sources-the downside of social bookmarking

http://blog.diigo.com/2008/03/23/tip-of-the-day-diigo-bookmarking-101/—Diigo bookmarking 101

www.kn.pacbell.com/wired/fil/pages/listweb20s.html—Web 2.0 tools

http://k12wiki.wikispaces.com/Social+Networking+Acceptable+Use—Wiki to create acceptable use policy for social bookmarking

Bev's Web Site and Blog

Using Web 2.0 Tools in the K–12 Classroom provides the basics to understand and get started using Web 2.0 tools in the library and content area classrooms. One way to keep a book current is to have it constantly updating. Bev's Web site (Figure B-1) allows *Using Web 2.0 Tools in the K–12 Classroom* to keep up with new teaching material, technology, and ideas. Look for the italicized boxed text in each chapter pointing out where to find these ideas on the Web site.

Here's what I'll put on my Web site at **www.neal-schuman.com/webclassroom**:

- **Models for Educators**—descriptions of educators using Web 2.0 tools in subject areas at different grade levels. Educators are now really starting to incorporate new technologies into their classroom lessons. I hope models will help those of you who have not yet tried these tools.

- **What's New**—new technologies and updates on Web 2.0 tools illustrated in *Using Web 2.0 Tools in the K–12 Classroom*. For example, I will look for innovative ideas, technologies that promote learning and are easy to use, ideas that motivate students and much more.

- **Now You Try It . . .**—additional exercises in different subject areas at elementary, middle, and secondary grade levels to challenge teachers and librarians not yet using Web 2.0 to take the plunge and incorporate technology into their lesson and unit plans.

- **Resources**—articles, books you don't want to miss, lesson plans, conferences, projects, sites to see, and more.

- **Special Topics**—provide more in-depth discussion of specific tools, for example, podcasts, which have become quite popular with educators and students alike.

- **Features from Teachers**—descriptions from teachers and librarians who have had special success with a project or lesson to motivate or teach students.

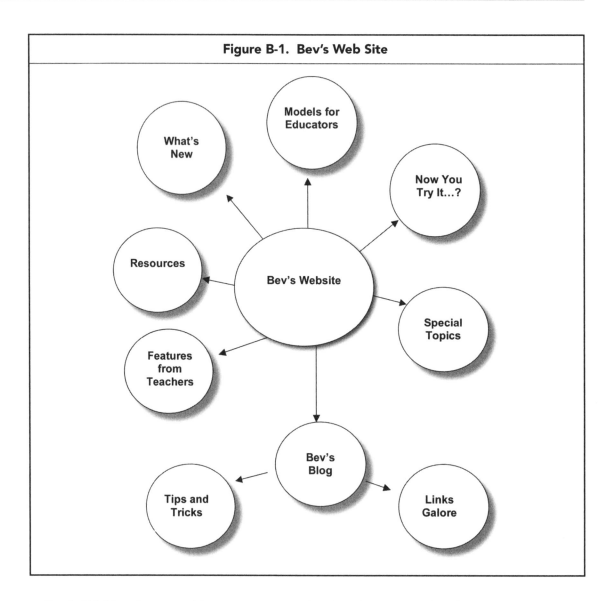

Figure B-1. Bev's Web Site

Bev's Edublog (bevcrane.blogspot.com)—Updated weekly, Bev's Educational Blog (Figure B-2) brings you:

- **Tips and Tricks**—I will tell you about ideas from other educators around the world. And, I want you to submit ideas, tell us about a brilliant lesson you taught with technology or kids' reactions when using a blog, or a Web site that other educators might find interesting.

- **Links Galore**—links to articles about teaching practices, classroom blogs, technology conferences, teacher publishing sites, projects.

I encourage you to add your ideas and examples of how you are using Web 2.0 in classrooms and libraries to the blog to make it useful to all K–12 educators worldwide.

Figure B-2. Bev's Educational Blog

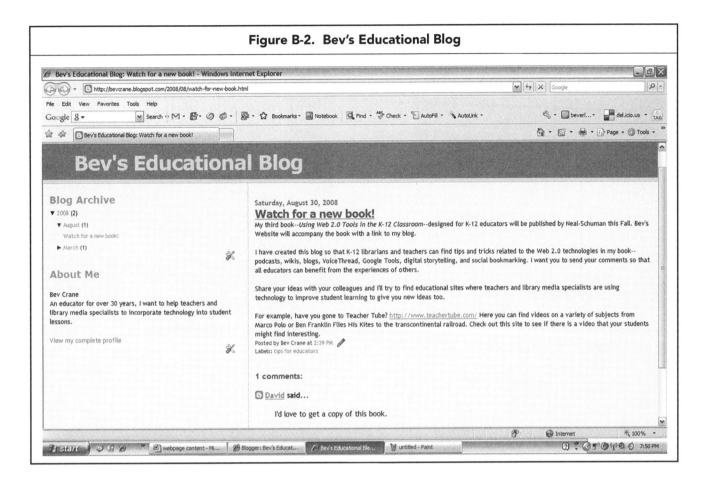

Index

About the Author

Beverley E. Crane received a BA in Spanish and English and an MEd in Bilingual Education and English as a Second Language from Penn State University. She obtained an EdD in Curriculum and Instruction, with emphases in Language Arts and Educational Technology from Oklahoma State University. She has taught English-language arts and ESL at the middle-, high-school, and college levels.

While working on a grant for a five-state area multicultural resource center, she conducted workshops for K–12 teachers on such topics as literacy, writing and the writing process, ESL, and integrating technology into the curriculum. In addition, for the last twelve years at The Dialog Corporation, she has created educational materials and conducted workshops for K–12 library media specialists and teachers on using online searching in the curriculum. She has presented yearly throughout the United States across curriculum areas at conferences, such as the American Association of School Librarians (AASL), the National Educational Computing Conference (NECC), Computer-Using Educators (CUE), American Educational Research Association (AERA), National Council for the Social Studies Conference (NCSS), California Media and Library Educators Association (CMLEA), among others on topics ranging from using online searching in the elementary and secondary curricula to computers and writing to integrating online searching into social studies to online research across the curriculum.

As director of the English Education Program at San Jose State University for five years, she worked closely with classroom teachers and administrators to provide guidelines for mentor teachers supervising English student teachers at SJSU.

Currently, she continues to write a guest column on using the Internet in the curriculum for the *Information Searcher*, edited by Pam Berger, and other educational articles on technology such as the Virginia Education Association magazine. She also creates training materials, including distance education online courses in searching techniques for Dialog and is editor of the Dialog customer e-newsletters. Her books *Teaching with the Internet: Strategies and Models for K–12 Curricula* and *Internet Workshops: 10 Ready-to-Go Workshops for K–12 Educators* were published by Neal-Schuman in 2000 and 2003, respectively. She lives in Santa Fe, New Mexico, with her husband and dog Carmen.

DATE DUE